DEMOCRACY IN THE COURTS

INTERNATIONAL AND COMPARATIVE CRIMINAL JUSTICE

Series Editors:

This series explores the new and rapidly developing field of international and comparative criminal justice and engages with its most important emerging themes and debates. It focuses on three interrelated aspects of scholarship which go to the root of understanding the nature and significance of international criminal justice in the broader context of globalization and global governance. These include: the theoretical and methodological problems posed by the development of international and comparative criminal justice; comparative contextual analysis; the reciprocal relationship between comparative and international criminal justice and contributions which endeavor to build understandings of global justice on foundations of comparative contextual analysis.

Other titles in the series:

The Disruption of International Organised Crime
An Analysis of Legal and Non-Legal Strategies
Angela Veng Mei Leong
ISBN 978 0 7546 7066 7

Restorative Justice
Ideals and Realities
Margarita Zernova
ISBN 978 0 7546 7032 2

The Criminal Law of Genocide
International, Comparative and Contextual Aspects
Edited by Ralph Henham and Paul Behrens
ISBN 978 0 7546 4898 7

The Crime of Destruction and the Law of Genocide
Caroline Fournet
ISBN 978 0 7546 7001 8

Democracy in the Courts
Lay Participation in European Criminal Justice Systems

MARIJKE MALSCH
Netherlands Institute for the Study of Crime and Law Enforcement (NSCR), The Netherlands

ASHGATE

Published by
Ashgate Publishing Limited
Wey Court East
Union Road
Farnham
Surrey GU9 7PT
England

Ashgate Publishing Company
Suite 420
101 Cherry Street
Burlington, VT 05401-4405
USA

www.ashgate.com

British Library Cataloguing in Publication Data
Malsch, M. (Marijke)
Democracy in the courts : lay participation in European criminal justice systems. - (International and comparative criminal justice)
1. Criminal procedure - Europe 2. Criminal courts - Europe
3. Lay prosecutors - Europe 4. Democracy - Europe
I. Title
345.4'05

Library of Congress Cataloging-in-Publication Data
Malsch, M. (Marijke)
Democracy in the courts : lay participation in European criminal justice systems / by Marijke Malsch.
p. cm. -- (International and comparative criminal justice)
Includes bibliographical references and index.
ISBN 978-0-7546-7405-4
1. Criminal courts--Europe. 2. Lay judges--Europe. 3. Juries--Europe. I. Title.

KJC9455.M35 2009
345.4'01--dc22

2008053603

ISBN 978-0-7546-7405-4

Mixed Sources
Product group from well-managed forests and other controlled sources
www.fsc.org Cert no. SA-COC-1565
© 1996 Forest Stewardship Council
FSC

Printed and bound in Great Britain by
MPG Books Ltd, Bodmin, Cornwall.

Contents

List of Figure and Tables

Figure

Tables

Preface

This book is concerned with both the systems of lay adjudication in European countries and with the way lay people are involved in the administration of justice in practice. The book furthermore seeks to unravel the various arguments in favour of and against lay participation in the adjudication of cases. The design of the various European systems of lay participation differs strikingly, ranging from tribunals that decide almost without any professional input to fully professional decision making. For some countries discussed in this book the subject is highly topical. In Belgium the abolition of the jury was proposed but rejected and in the Netherlands a debate has taken place about introducing lay participation. Both the government and the House of Representatives decided not to proceed with any proposal for introducing lay adjudication in the Dutch legal system. As such, the country remains a conspicuous exception in the Western part of Europe.

Various methods have been used to investigate lay participation. The national systems of a large number of European countries have been studied by use of the literature, internet and other sources. Providing an overview of how jurisdictions involve ordinary citizens is, however, not sufficient for understanding how these systems work and how the public and participants appraise them. For that it is necessary to talk to the lay adjudicators directly as well as to the professional judges who, in one way or another, have to work with them. The interviews that were conducted with lay and professional adjudicators form an important part of this book.

Participation in the trial of cases is an overwhelming experience. At the same time, an ordinary citizen doing so may learn a lot about how the system works. Professional judges for their part may enjoy collaboration with people from outside the formal judiciary. Others, however, may experience the involvement of lay adjudicators as a hindrance to the speedy trial of cases. This book pays due attention to the actual experiences of the lay decision makers and their professional counterparts in five European countries. Observations of court sessions conducted in these countries and interviews contributed to a better understanding of lay and professional decision making and how the two groups perceive each other.

It was difficult to obtain funding for the research in the Netherlands. At first the Council of the Judiciary seemed enthusiastic about the research. They suggested a number of issues related to lay participation that could also be studied in the framework of the project. The project description was adjusted and widened to meet the Council's request. There followed a long delay before the Council came back to the researchers. In the meantime articles appeared in Dutch newspapers and in scientific journals in which professional judges reflected on the negative sides of lay adjudication and their own fears regarding its introduction into the Dutch legal system. Finally, after negotiations lasting for more than a year, the Council ultimately declined, making it clear that it was not willing to pay for the research. However, the Council made available a compensatory grant which allowed the Netherlands Institute for the Study of Crime and Law Enforcement (NSCR) to nevertheless make a start with the project.

Fears of a comparable nature seemed to exist in Belgium, where the researchers were requested to emphasize in their report that the views presented were strictly their own. Naturally, we wish to comply with this request and hereby stress that the views and observations in this book are exclusively those of the researchers.

Although the three-year research on which this book is based thus had a slightly complicated and delayed start, the intention is to advance an informed debate about whether or not lay people should participate in trials. Until now, this discussion has unfortunately not always been as rational and as informed as one would wish. Extreme positions have been taken, for example in the Dutch context, which do not always seem to be justified by sufficient knowledge of the subject matter. It is surprising that both proponents and critics of lay participation could be found to hold such positions. Obviously, this is a highly emotional issue!

First of all, I want to express my gratitude to my former colleague Charissa Efstratiades, who contributed most valuably to the research, by cooperating in the setting up of the project and collecting information on the legal systems in the various European countries. An important portion of the observations and interviews was done in cooperation with her.

The supervisory committee that was instituted for this research consisted of Frits Bakker, president of the District Court of The Hague, and of professors Leny de Groot-van Leeuwen, Paul De Hert and Theo de Roos. The committee played an important role in appraising and monitoring the research and in coming up with suggestions for it. Fortunately, differing opinions existed within the supervisory committee with respect to suitability and desirability of lay participation and these differences were very helpful for the researchers in clarifying their own arguments. The same applies for the supervisory committee as was indicated previously: the views and opinions in this book are the researchers' alone and not those of the supervisory committee.

I owe special gratitude to many people who helped us find our way in the countries we visited, the trials we observed and the legal systems we investigated. All countries were very helpful in this respect. I specifically want to mention Barbara Flaxman, Cindy Barnett, Sally Dickinson, Martin Wasik, Lieve Gies, Jan Heuvelmans, Geert Vervaeke, Jan Snelders, Rachida Boumbarek, Tom Decaigny, Kira Kolby Christensen, Charlotte Meincke, Hanne Fog-Petersen, Nanna Blach, Anders Granhag, Dr Sojka, Dr Hornung, Dr Kilbinger, Stefani

Ross, René de Ruijter, Albert Klijn, Liene Malsch and my colleagues Peter van der Voort, Ariena van Poppel and Danielle Reynald.

Without the contribution of many judges, both lay and professional, who remain anonymous but who gave their time to cooperate in an interview, this research would have lacked the aspect which I find the most interesting: the views of those involved on how they experienced their contributions (and those of others) to the administration of justice.

Marijke Malsch

Chapter 1
Introduction

Lay participation in the administration of justice differs between countries. Some countries, like the United Kingdom and the United States, have always attached considerable value to the participation of 'ordinary people' in the legal system in the form of juries. Other systems, like that of France, have at a later point in time adopted the view that citizen participation in the legal system is a necessary requirement of democracy. Citizen participation in a legal system may vary over time *within* countries as well. Countries such as Russia and Spain have recently re-introduced the jury into their legal systems after previously having abolished it. Other countries, such as Belgium, are discussing modifying their jury system and in the Netherlands, where lay participation in the legal system is largely absent, a small number of politicians have advocated the introduction of lay judges in criminal cases.

This book examines lay participation in judicial systems. It presents the results of interviews conducted with professional and lay adjudicators in five European countries. These interviews focus on the lay persons' and the professional judges' experiences of lay involvement and their perspectives on how the legal system operates in this respect. Alternatives to lay participation, such as an increased transparency and greater accessibility to the trial of cases, are discussed as well. An attempt is made to establish how far the various legal systems comply with certain democratic values. In the opening chapters the concept of 'democracy' is elaborated on, and the question is asked in how far the concept is applicable in the legal domain. In the final chapter, a model for democracy in courts is presented as a result of the research done for this book.

Arguments in Favour of Lay Participation

Arguments in favour of and against citizen participation in a criminal justice system have been widely debated in many countries. Some arguments can cut both ways, in favour of and against lay participation. That is the case, for example, with the argument regarding 'emotions', which it is assumed can play a more substantial role with lay adjudicators (Malsch 2003). Emotions may stand in the way of an objective judgement about a case, but they might also be welcomed to prevent overly bureaucratic decision making by professionals. The same is true for the expense of lay participation. Some people stress the higher costs related to the principle of 'immediacy', which requires that all witnesses and experts should be heard in open court and legal issues should be explained to the lay participants; immediacy is enforced more strongly when lay adjudicators are involved than when cases are dealt with only by professionals (van Koppen and Penrod 2003; Malsch and Nijboer 2005). Others, however, are of the opintion that the remuneration of lay participants is substantially lower than the salaries of professional judges, leading to reduced expenses for the judicial system as a whole in the case of lay participation (Casper and Zeisel 1972; de Roos 2006). In this section the arguments most likely to be identified as being in favour of lay participation are discussed. The next section deals with arguments against lay participation.

What are the arguments for offering citizens the opportunity to take part in the adjudication of cases? The democratic argument is the strongest and the most often expressed reason for lay participation: citizens should be able to take part in the trial of cases as representatives of the population at large. Deciding cases should not be the task of only a small elite, and everyone should at least have a chance of being appointed a member of a jury or to be called to act as a lay judge (Machura 2001; Ivkovic 2003; De Hert 2004b). The type of democracy that is served by such involvement is called 'representative democracy'. In the United States, a strong advocate of this type of democracy, the view is generally held that defendants have the right to be tried by their peers (Devine et al. 2001). There, juries are considered to be a safeguard against the power of the state or against other biases of appointed judges or corrupt officials. It is held that juries inject democratic values into the legal process and function as a source of 'common sense'.[1] Such a view is more or less absent in the Netherlands (de Roos 2006). Countries thus appear to differ in their reaction to this argument. One of the aims of this book is to uncover and examine these different types of approach between countries.

There is another aspect in support of the democracy argument: that the discussion of justice and the trial of cases would be enhanced if citizens had the opportunity to participate in the trial of cases. The gap between the population and the judiciary would be diminished if ordinary citizens were able to participate and to reach informed opinions on how the legal system works. By telling their family and friends about their experiences in the administration of justice, knowledge about the system would be spread and a discussion within the wider society made possible. Individuals would become better equipped to form their own opinion on the legal system if they participated in it. Their opinions would, then, be more informed by the actualities of the trial of cases than if the administration of justice remained the prerogative of a small group (Warren 1992; Young 2000).

Another argument supporting participation of citizens in the legal system is that this would be an incentive for the professionals to keep the trial of cases

1 For a reflection on such values in jurisdictions that make use of juries, see Vidmar 2000.

comprehensible for lay people. Most lay adjudicators are not masters of legal language, so the professional judges, defence lawyers and prosecutors would be forced to use colloquial language to a greater degree than in a situation where the tribunal consists of professionals only. It may be hypothesized that the more lay people participate in the legal system, the more every-day language would be used (Enschedé 1982; Malsch and Nijboer 2005)

Directly related to the issue of comprehensibility are the aspects of orality and immediacy of the trial, referring to the degree in which process participants do or do not rely on written materials and the extent to which witnesses are heard in court. In legal systems where a jury or lay judges are involved, orality and immediacy of the trial are generally high. Lay participants are not expected to read the case file before the hearing of a case; they should be as unprejudiced and open-minded as possible (van Koppen and Penrod 2003). In an oral and immediate trial, the review of the evidence can be expected to be more direct and, therefore, to be more reliable than in a situation where all evidence is related in reports and handed over in written form to the decision makers (De Hert 2004b).

Participation by citizens would also enhance the system's legitimacy. Public confidence in the system would increase. Research from the social sciences, which indeed suggests that actual participation in a procedure may enhance acceptance of the outcome and respect for the authority that tries the case (Tyler 1990; Benesh 2006), is relevant to this point, and it serves as a background for the research presented in this book.[2]

Participation has certain effects on the citizens involved. They learn about the system, it educates them on the juridical aspects and they become knowledgeable about what kind of people commit particular types of crime, and how these crimes impact on the victims. It has been contended that in participating they develop a better understanding of the complexities involved in trying legal cases (Finkel 1995). By communicating with the professionals in the system, the distance between judges and lay people may be reduced.

Chapter 2 will elaborate on these arguments. In the chapters that follow, the book explores how these various arguments and aspects of democracy have found their place in the legal systems under review in this book.

Arguments against Lay Adjudication

There are also important arguments for *not* having lay people decide cases in a legal system. Lay people do not have legal knowledge, which implies that a lot of explanation of the legal aspects will be required. Because all witnesses have to be heard again in court, and all items of evidence have to be presented and

2 See Chapter 2.

explained, procedures take substantially longer. This requires time, and time is scarce nowadays in many legal systems (van Koppen and Penrod 2003).

It is contended that lay people would make more mistakes. They lack experience and familiarity with the routine, especially the members of a jury. They are generally less educated than the professional judges and thus there is a risk that they would not understand everything that is going on in court. Therefore the trial of cases would have to be simplified, at least to a certain degree. An elaborate doctrine on, for example, various types of guilt would not be appropriate in systems that make use of lay people. Such a complex doctrine could lead to misunderstandings or even miscarriages of justice, which cannot always be easily redressed. Such fears are regularly expressed with respect to systems that make use of a jury (van Langenhove 1989; Malsch 2003; Tubex and De Hert 2004). The drawbacks of the need for more explanation and the risk of mistakes appear to be common among the various jurisdictions discussed in this book, as the following chapters will make clear.

It is further argued that as a consequence of lack of familiarity with the routine in deciding cases, lay people would be more easily influenced by their emotions. Seeing a defendant who is accused of having killed his wife and daughter sitting just in front of you, hearing the details of the killings and seeing the pictures of the lifeless bodies in colour, may upset people who are not used to this. This is true for professional judges as well but, by and large, they become used to such aspects of serious crime. This type of horrific evidence produces a strong reaction particularly in those presented with it for the first time. During the trial lay people may be overwhelmed by their emotions, but they are not allowed to express them. Such emotions may lead to an overreaction in the opinions that they form of the case. Crimes that are highly upsetting may have such an impact that the decision makers want only the most serious penalty possible (Tubex and De Hert 2004). For this reason human rights organizations fear increased repressiveness if juries are introduced in a legal system; they expect the jury's opinion to be more extreme than that of panels including professionals (De Hert 2004a).

However, there are also indications that when lay people are involved in decision making their opinions change in such a way that they become more lenient. Learning about the defendant's background and motives may induce empathy in the decision maker, leading to a more balanced opinion on the case (Diamond 1990). In some cases the balance may even swing to the other side: lay people acquire so much empathy that they only want the lowest penalty or even an acquittal of an apparently culpable defendant (Kalven and Zeisel 1966). In such a situation cooperation with a professional judge might help to maintain balance in opinions.

Other effects of inexperience may also occur: attractive defendants, witnesses and victims may affect the opinions of lay adjudicators to a larger extent that those of professional judges who, thanks to their experience, have acquired some degree of immunity to appearances. It is feared that jurors would judge attractive defendants more leniently than unattractive defendants (Kalven and Zeisel 1966; Hastie et al. 1983; Wasserman 1985). Defence lawyers often make use of such an effect by suggesting that the defendant puts on certain clothes or behaves in certain ways. Naturally, such effects can be found in professional systems as well, but according to some these would be less prominent (Klik and van Koppen 2002).

In jury cases media coverage often plays an important role in shaping public opinion of a trial, as can be seen in the American criminal case of O.J. Simpson and the Belgian case of Dutroux. In contrast, cases involving lay judges, as can be found in Germany and in the Scandinavian countries, are hardly ever covered by the media. In these countries the media play a far less dominant role in the dissemination of information regarding criminal trials. The influence of media coverage, thus, differs between legal systems (Tubex and De Hert 2004).

This book pays due attention to the disadvantages outlined here. In all countries under review, these and other drawbacks have been mentioned, but the respondents attach differing degrees of value to them. Many of these disadvantages imply that democracy is hindered in one way or another, or that the quality of decision-making is reduced. The book assesses how far limitations on one aspect of democracy can be complemented by other aspects of democracy that are better served in that country.[3]

Research Relating to Participation

There is a vast body of research into *procedural justice* focused on perspectives of the individuals who take part in a procedure, such as plaintiffs, defendants, victims and witnesses (Thibaut and Walker 1975; Lind and Tyler 1988; Tyler and Lind 1992; Röhl and Machura 1997). Participants in a procedure who have been given the opportunity to express their own opinions and to present evidence to the decision maker are generally more satisfied about the outcome than people who have not been offered such opportunities (Röhl and Machura 1997). Being able to exert influence on procedures and on the outcome is therefore of relevance for acceptance of the decision (Malsch 2004). Similar effects may be expected when people can take part in the legal system itself by acting as a juror or as a lay judge. They may, in such a situation, not perceive themselves as outsiders. They are listened to and their opinion contributes to the decision that is made. Even when their own opinion on a case does not become the 'final' decision, they have had the opportunity to make a statement about what they think of the case (Bovens 2006). In legal systems where no lay participation exists, such opportunities are withheld from the general public and this may widen the gap between society and the judiciary. Research into

3 For a final overview of aspects of democracy in legal systems, see Chapter 11.

procedural justice serves as a general background to the research described in this book. The general thesis which the analysis in this book takes as its starting point is that commitment to and involvement in a system may increase satisfaction with the operation of that system. This thesis is further explored in Chapter 2.

What Types of Lay Adjudication Exist?

In earlier times the involvement of citizens in the trial of cases was the natural and self-evident situation. Every (male) citizen had the duty to act as a lay judge or to assist in the trial of cases in other ways when called to do so. Later, after the Middle Ages, the trying of cases increasingly became the task of delegates who gradually developed into professionals (van de Pol 1986; Malsch and Nijboer 2005). In most countries decision making by lay people has continued alongside or in combination with the trial of cases by professionals. The various forms of lay participation that exist nowadays in Europe bear a relation to the national histories of each country and the influences exerted by other jurisdictions. In this way Europe appears to be far more diversified than, for instance, the United States, where each individual state has a jury system that, as far as can be discerned from this side of the ocean, resembles that of the other states to a large degree (Vidmar 2000; Devine et al. 2001).

In Europe there are countries that have only juries and no lay judges in criminal law, there are countries that have only lay judges who decide cases together with a professional judge or judges and there are countries that have both. Luxembourg and the Netherlands, along with a number of the former communist countries, have none of these (Jackson and Kovalev 2006; de Roos 2006). Chapter 3 of this book presents an overview of the legal systems of a large number of mostly Western European countries. For each country we established what forms of lay participation are to be found in the trial of criminal cases, when the involvement of lay people was introduced in the system and the decision making power of each panel. An assessment was made of the proportion of criminal cases that were tried with the help of lay people. The variety of forms of lay participation is striking. This makes the question of how the arguments in favour of and against lay participation work out for each system a challenging one.

The Lay Person and the Professional

The definition of a lay person is clear. It is a man or woman who has no, or almost no, education, training and experience in a certain field. The term 'lay person' always refers to a specific situation: lay people are non-professionals in many fields, but most of the time not in all fields. They often possess expertise in at least a few areas. A schoolteacher is not a professional in medicine and a judge generally knows nothing about agriculture. It is less clear what the definition of a professional is (Malsch and Nijboer 1999). Naturally, professionals have followed certain education or training and have obtained specific qualifications. On top of that, they generally have experience in a certain field. It is often the case that this sort of experience turns into some sort of routine. Professionals usually specialize in a certain area. This throws up a number of questions: is a person who has the training but no experience in dealing with cases a professional, or does a professional need to have practical working experience? How much experience should someone have before we can label them a professional? Where does the boundary lie between lay people and professionals in this respect?[4]

Questions of this type are particularly pertinent to the subject of lay participation in a legal system. In case of the members of a jury, it is clear that we are dealing with lay people. For most of them it is the first time that they will have participated in a trial, and it will also be their last opportunity to do so (de Roos 2006). It is less common for members of a jury to repeat their participation as it is for the lay judges such as can be found in Germany and the Scandinavian countries.[5] This implies that members of a jury are unable to acquire certain sorts of experience. The situation is different for lay judges and even more different for the magistrates and Justices of the Peace who function in a number of English-speaking countries. They act as a judge for a given period (often four years) which can be, and most of the time is, extended, in some occasions even until their retirement. They acquire knowledge of legal matters and legal procedures. This longstanding involvement gives them the opportunity to develop experience, and sometimes even routine. In the five countries that have been investigated in more depth, the issue of the degree of professionalism of decision makers has been discussed with judges and lay participants.

Another element that may lead to experience and expertise, is cooperation with the professional judges. This occurs most visibly with lay judges who work closely with professional judges. Juries in some legal systems also make decisions about the sentence in cooperation with professional judges, but the decision about guilt is generally made without the professionals. The 'summing up' by the professional judge before the jury retires to make a decision about the defendant's guilt contributes to the jurors' legal knowledge. Cooperation with and the instruction by the judge may be seen as a sort of educational process for the lay participants, which it could be said makes them less of a lay person. Magistrates and Justices of the Peace generally sit without a professional judge, but in deciding cases over many years they become highly

4 These and similar issues are addressed in Chapter 4.

5 See Chapter 3 for an explanation of the legal systems in a large number of European countries.

trial of cases, how far professional judges interact with other circles in society, the adherence to democratic parts of a legal system and to what extent the lay participants were offered the opportunity to actually take part in the hearing of the case and the deliberations (Hoekstra and Malsch 2003).

When studying different legal systems, certain comparative problems have to be confronted. For example, particular concepts that are used in one jurisdiction may not have exactly the same meaning in another (Brants and Field 2000; Bruinsma and Nelken 2007). The concept of 'professional judge' refers to slightly different types of officials in one system as compared to another. Legal concepts such as 'force majeure' and 'self-defence' have a different meaning in various systems. Discussing these concepts without being aware of such differences may lead to flawed conclusions as to the comparative findings of the research. This book attempts to deal with these and other comparative problems by using a plethora of methodologies, as has been described. The book's focus is, moreover, mainly directed at experiences and perspectives of legal and non-legal decision makers. Such a focus can be expected to be more appropriate for making comparisons among jurisdictions than comparing distinct characteristics of legal systems themselves, because respondents can be questioned thoroughly about the impact of their experiences and the basis of their perspectives.

Nevertheless, respondents' expectations as to what it is like to act as a judge may hinder the ability to make such comparisons. These expectations, after all, are determined by the legal system of the country in which the respondent lives (Malsch and Nijboer 1999). For example, being accustomed to considerable lay participation in state institutions and other sectors of society may colour the views and expectations of respondents living there, when compared to respondents coming from countries where almost no lay participation is allowed. The latter may lack adequate concepts or a frame of reference for evaluating lay participation. Thus, the portrayal of the individual views and attitudes may differ between respondents as a consequence of what they know and expect from their own system, without it being clear whether such differences originate from real differences in views, or from cultural differences (Nelken 2000). These issues have been tackled by interviewing the respondents in-depth and by explicitly paying attention to the basis of the respondents' views, in combination with both a review of the literature on former empirical research and observations of real-life cases in each country.

The comparative analysis in this book focuses on three aspects of democracy: representation, participation and deliberation. Chapter 2 is devoted to a theoretical analysis of these aspects. For each country that is examined in this book, among the questions we attempt to answer are: how far the lay people who participate in the administration of justice can be considered representative of the population at large; how far and in what way they actually participate in the trial of cases; and to what extent they disseminate knowledge about the legal system. The role of the system itself and the media in the dissemination of information is also worthy of note and could potentially lead to an informed debate.

Outline of the Book

Chapter 2 of this volume examines the theoretical underpinning of arguments in favour of and against lay participation in the trial of cases. Theories from social sciences and theories of a legal nature are both discussed. Attention is paid to various aspects of democracy and to the issue of to what extent the operation of legal systems can be characterized as 'democratic'.

Chapter 3 gives an overview of types of lay participation in a large number of European countries. This overview provides insight into the question of whether there is a jury system or a system with lay judges in these countries, how the benches reach a decision, what types of question are answered by lay adjudicators, and whether they do so in cooperation with a professional judge or not. This overview illustrates the variety of shapes that lay involvement can assume in European countries. The chapter pays specific attention to five countries that are studied in more depth.

Chapter 4 explores the various aspects of professional and lay decision making. The chapter further categorizes the various types of tribunals and decision makers that were discussed in the previous chapter and particular attention is paid to two aspects: *education* and *experience*.

Chapter 5 presents the results of interviews that were conducted in the Netherlands. Of all criminal justice systems studied, this country has least lay involvement. In regular criminal cases, the participation of honorary judges[12] provides the only input of decision makers from outside the judiciary. The chapter discusses involvement of honorary judges.

Chapter 6 focuses on the involvement of *experts* in the trial of cases in the Netherlands. Three types of court are explored: the Agricultural Tenancies division of the District Court, the Execution of Sentences division of the Arnhem Court of Appeal and the Companies and Business Court in Amsterdam.

Chapters 7 to 10 present the results of literature research, interviews and observations conducted in Denmark, Germany, England and Wales, and Belgium. In all countries interviews were conducted with both professional and lay decision makers. The emphasis in these interviews is on several issues, including what input lay judges have, if and how they cooperate with professional judges, and how they experience being a judge themselves. As far as possible within the framework of the study, the relation between the involvement of lay people and the characteristics of the national legal culture is addressed.

12 *Rechters-plaatsvervanger.*

Chapter 11 elaborates on the findings of the previous chapters. Arguments in favour of and against lay participation that were outlined in the introductory chapters are revisited. The factors most often referred to and which play the most important role are considered. An attempt is made to answer the question of to what extent democratic elements are present in the various national legal systems under review, and if it is desirable that these elements are strengthened. As a result of the research conducted for this book, a model for democracy in the courts is presented and alternatives for lay participation are considered.

Chapter 2
Citizen Participation as a Form of Democracy

Introduction

Chapter 1 provided a preliminary overview of arguments in favour of and against lay participation in the administration of justice. Some of these arguments relate to democracy within courts. This chapter elaborates on a number of issues pertaining to democracy. It further discusses theories and findings of empirical research that are relevant for the question of whether or not, and if so in what form lay participation in a legal system would be desirable. Alternatives to lay participation in the legal system, such as improved dissemination of information and special attention to fair treatment aimed at increasing the public's commitment to the system on the part of individuals are also considered in this chapter. Actual participation in procedures, the relevance of how panels are composed, and the way they reach decisions are discussed too, with special attention to the risks of biased decision making.

Participation in Procedures

Modern societies need rules and authorities to enforce them. Procedures to decide conflicts are necessary for allowing life in society to proceed smoothly. Rules provide a legal basis for the existence of state institutions; in addition, they establish and limit the powers of state authorities as well as citizens' rights, responsibilities and obligations (Tyler and Lind 1992). In times of uncertainty and threat from, for example, terrorism or crime, people are prepared to transfer more, and more invasive powers to authorities than in quieter and more peaceful eras. In advanced legal systems the powers of state authorities are stipulated in constitutions and in national legislation. In principle, a legal basis is required for the use of force or for an invasion of personal freedoms by state institutions.

Citizens' satisfaction with the state is related to the procedures that are employed by state institutions, authorities and officials to decide issues in society and to resolve conflicts. Theories of and research into procedural justice have found indications that the types of procedures that are applied by authorities and the ways authorities treat citizens are more important in this respect than the outcomes of the decisions that are made. Citizens involved in a legal case attach relatively less value to a positive outcome when they perceive the procedure to have been fair. The way they are treated in a procedure is more relevant than the question of what benefits they receive (Tyler and Lind 1992). The term 'procedure' has a rather broad meaning in this type of research. With respect to the criminal justice system, it covers a wide variety of contacts between authorities and citizens. This may range from a police officer reprimanding a youngster for riding his bicycle on the sidewalk, through to information supplied to a victim by a prosecutor regarding an on-going case and the extent to which judges permit process participants to express their views in a trial to, last but not least, the way the actual hearing of a case in court is conducted.

In general, participants in a legal procedure value process control more highly than decision control. In other words, they attach more importance to being able to provide evidence to the decision maker, to expressing their opinions and arguments in court and to choosing their own lawyer than to having actual input in the decision (Thibaut and Walker 1975; Crombag and van Koppen 2002). Possibilities to actively participate in procedures are highly valued. Adversarial legal systems, such as can be found in most English-speaking countries, provide more opportunities for the parties to have input in the process and to adduce evidence themselves than the inquisitorial systems that generally exist on mainland Europe.. In the latter, the centre of gravity lies with the judge instead of with the parties (van Koppen and Penrod 2003). It has been found that indeed adversarial systems generate more satisfaction for participants than inquisitorial systems do (Thibaut and Walker 1975; Lind and Tyler 1988; Tyler 1990; Crombag and van Koppen 2002). The concept of *participation* therefore is of great relevance. Individuals who are involved in a legal case often attach great value to having their 'day in court': to be able to present a case to the decision maker and to communicate with him or her. Defendants in a criminal matter whose cases are dismissed before reaching a hearing in open court sometimes even feel dissatisfied because they did not have this opportunity (Röhl 1997). Victims may also want to participate in various ways in the criminal trial against the defendant (Wemmers 1996). Depending on their relation to the crime, witnesses may even want a certain amount of participation in a criminal procedure such as, for example, being able to express their views on a case or having an opportunity to make clear their wishes concerning the way the case is dealt with (van der Leij 2002).

In conclusion, opportunities for participation in individual cases are of great relevance to citizens involved in legal procedures. Participation can be expected to increase trust in the legal system and to enhance satisfaction with the system. What counts as participation at the level of the individual may also count at the level of the legal system, whether for a jury or a lay judge. Opportunities for participation in the actual trial of cases may increase general confidence in the administration of justice and lead to satisfaction with the operation of a legal system. It can be expected that in national legal systems that allow for lay participation in the administration of justice there will be more confidence in the system than in countries where no such involvement of lay people exists. Unfortunately, it is extremely complicated to measure the effect of lay participation on satisfaction and to compare countries in this respect, because these effects are to a large extent interwoven with other features and characteristics of legal systems.

The concept of *participation* is the central theme of this chapter and it is treated in various ways. First, we seek to determine what aspects form part of the concept of participation at the individual case level, and what are the possible alternatives. Next, various types of democracy and how these relate to participation by ordinary citizens in the criminal justice system are discussed. A final issue covered in this chapter is the way decisions in (legal) cases are made in practice. It has been contended that groups of people make better decisions than a single person. This would be an argument in favour of the jury or of a panel of decision makers. This chapter explores empirical research on the importance of the composition of panels in this respect.

Participation in Criminal Cases

A distinction has been made here between participation in *individual cases* and participation at the level of the *criminal justice system*, in the form of acting as a juror or as a lay judge. This section discusses the first of these forms. Participation in individual cases ranges from attending the hearing of a case to, at the other extreme, having some kind of input in the final decision in a case – the most far-reaching degree of involvement. Below a number of aspects are outlined that are related to this type of participation:

1. attending the hearing of cases;
2. being able to ask questions and to express wishes regarding the procedure;
3. choosing one's own lawyer;
4. expressing one's views on the case;
5. calling witnesses and experts to testify;
6. presenting other evidence to the decision maker;
7. being able to influence the course of the proceedings;
8. having input in the decision (for instance, in the case of mediation).

Most of the forms of participation mentioned are applicable to the people involved in procedures; only some of them apply to the public at large as well. Provision to attend cases is obviously one of the most important requirements with which contemporary legal systems should comply. Those directly involved, the public and the media should all be able to attend the hearing of cases. Modern legal systems that intend to be open and accessible should make it easy for citizens to attend court sessions, both as participants in the case itself as well as those who are merely interested members of the public (Malsch and Nijboer 2005; Malsch 2008). A similar line of thought can be extended to the other aspects of participation: time and opportunities should be offered to individuals involved to express their views and wishes, to allow the choice of a lawyer and the presentation of evidence to the decision maker. These aspects are only relevant to participants in procedures. Having direct input in the final *decision*, for example in mediation procedures, is the most far-reaching form of participation. Criminal cases tried in court generally do not allow for this type of participation.

To make these types of participation possible the legal system needs to be accessible and flexible and should be oriented towards the needs of those who wish to, or who have the right to participate. Most of the time it is the citizen who has to take the initiative for realizing participation possibilities as depicted here, however.

Alternatives to Participation

Legal systems that do not offer substantial opportunities for participation as detailed here may instead invest more energy in the provision of information to citizens or pay increased attention to fair treatment for people involved in cases. As a consequence although they are unable to have a direct input in the procedure or decision, they are nevertheless treated fairly and well informed on every aspect of the case which may increase their commitment to the legal system.

People have a desire to see justice done (Tyler 2003).[1] Individuals are willing to accept *outcomes* of cases if these are viewed as being fair. A similar effect of acceptance is found if the *procedures* that are applied are viewed as fair. Perceptions thus are central in forming the public's opinion on the operation of the criminal justice system. This is the case for both participants in a procedure and the general public. Research on the views of victims of crime who have suffered damage has shown that they entertain a desire to be kept informed on the proceedings of the case against the suspect. If they are adequately informed this increases their satisfaction with the legal system (Wemmers 1996). *Information provision* thus is an important complement to, or alternative to participation. Or, more broadly phrased, beyond the argument of participation, the element of information – what do citizens know of the system, how do they perceive the system, how well informed are they? – is of relevance too.

These general statements about the public's reasonable desire to be kept informed do not preclude there still being a certain need in society for the

1 *R v Sussex Justices; Ex parte McCarthy* [1924] 1 KB 256 at 259.

mystification and rituals that are used in court. The symbolic nature of many formalities that are customary in court may appeal to many. This is one of the reasons that in the legal domain special clothes, such as robes, are worn and the procedures that are followed involve actions with a highly symbolic nature that emphasize the authority of the judges and of the court. These aspects of 'theatre' may to a large extent determine the image that citizens form of the court system (Hol 2006) and they may lead to those involved attaching less explicit value to openness and receiving objective information. These mechanisms need consideration when advocating an increased processing of information to the public.

Furthermore, certain types of information can be expected to be mandatorily and definitively excluded from dissemination to the public. Among these feature information on the private lives of the professional participants involved, as well as information that regards other cases or other defendants. The argument put forward here is therefore certainly not for a disclosure of literally *all* information that is available.

A number of aspects of *information provision* are outlined below:

1. informing process participants, the general public and the media;
2. distribution of information on the adjudication of cases via press releases and other media;
3. explaining and justifying decisions that are made;
4. using jargon-free language, both in court and in written documents;
5. having a comprehensive website;
6. deciding cases in open court rather than by an invisible procedure.

These points may lead to a better understanding and knowledge of the criminal justice system, and may increase the citizens' personal commitment to the system. Most of these aspects of provision of information require an active attitude on the part of the legal system.

A second complement (or alternative) to participation is fair treatment of citizens. Fair treatment occupies a central place in the Theory of Procedural Justice (Lind and Tyler 1988; Tyler and Lind 1992). When participants are treated with respect and dignity by an impartial and independent decision maker this increases their feelings of satisfaction. They are then more prepared to accept the outcome, and are more ready to cooperate in following procedures. The reporting rate of crimes is also influenced by fair treatment: people are more inclined to inform the police and to assist in an investigation if they have been treated fairly on an earlier occasion (van der Leij 2002). Sherman (2002) suggests that suspects and offenders are greatly influenced by the way police and judges treat them. If a legal official takes the time to listen to both suspect and victim, and does not make use of unnecessary violence, this decreases the likelihood of recidivism. Respectful treatment of offenders in prison may induce or facilitate feelings of regret and shame regarding the crime that was committed, which may help to prevent further crime (Braithwaite 1989). Fair treatment can, thus, be expected to play an important role in increasing trust in the legal system and in encouraging future cooperation with the system

The concept of 'fair treatment' focuses specifically on the direct interaction between legal officials and citizens. The general public's opinion may also be affected when citizens perceive that others are treated disrespectfully or harshly. Unfair treatment of participants in a trial that becomes publicly known may lead to a significant decline in the public's confidence in the judicial system. When visitors to court buildings feel unwelcome, for example, when court employees wrongly suggest that the hearing of cases is not open to the public, such perceptions may influence the public's trust in the system. The concept of fair treatment thus has a wider scope than just the relation between the citizen and the legal officer (Tyler 2003; Sherman 2002; Malsch 2004).

Elements of *fair treatment* consist of:

1. respect;
2. friendliness;
3. communication;
4. offering time and attention to process participants;
5. an open and accessible attitude.

Fair treatment primarily requires an active attitude on the part of the legal system.

The three concepts that have been sketched here overlap to a certain degree. The question may be asked whether and to what extent participation can be replaced by the provision of information and fair treatment. Table 2.1 gives an overview of the three concepts: *participation*, *information processing* and *fair treatment*.

Table 2.1 Interaction between citizens and the criminal justice system

	Direction	Initiative
Participation	citizen ←→ system	citizen
Information	system → citizen	system
Fair treatment	system → citizen	system

As Table 2.1 illustrates, of the three concepts, *participation* embodies bidirectionality the most strongly. During participation, both citizen (either as a participant or as a member of the general public) and the system contribute to the interaction. The other two concepts, information provision and fair treatment, less obviously involve bidirectionality.

The bidirectionality of participation is clearly illustrated by the situation where a victim who wishes to express her feelings of grief during the trial of the criminal case is offered the opportunity to do so by the judge (victim impact statement). Or, a defendant wishes to engage new expert testimony and the court adjourns the trial to a later date to make this possible. Or, a family member wanting to attend the court session of the defendant, asks the court official for directions and is given courteous and practical assistance. Participation requires time and effort on the part of both the citizen and the legal system. The initiative for participation however generally lies with the citizen. Nevertheless, to be able to participate citizens should be informed by the system about their opportunities and rights in this respect, and the exercise of these opportunities and rights should be made possible by law enforcement officials.

The concept of *information processing* has a far more unidirectional nature. The direction of information processing is, in principle, from the system to the citizen. Only in specific situations can it be expected for a plaintiff or a defendant to provide information on their own initiative. The initiative for providing information should lie with the legal system itself. It should disseminate information on court decisions and on the operation of the legal system on its own initiative, without waiting for requests to do so. The legal system may even process information without anyone taking cognizance of it. That might be the case when brochures are offered that nobody reads, or when a court official announces loudly the beginning of the hearing of a case for which there is no public audience. Information provision is a highly important element of interaction between the system and the public. Should the court keep all information to itself the gap with citizens would widen and confidence in the legal system would seriously decrease (Malsch and Nijboer 2005). The unidirectionality of information processing may become problematic if legal systems tend to exclusively publicize positive information and try to disguise any miscarriages of justice that may have taken place (Roberts and Stalans 1997; Malsch and Nijboer 2005).

The concept of *fair treatment* is also primarily unidirectional in nature, and again it is the legal system that has to take the initiative. Citizens should not first have to ask for respectful treatment before the interaction begins; court officials and others working in the legal system should treat citizens correctly without being compelled to do so. An adequate and effective interaction between citizens and the criminal justice system can be expected to be strongly enhanced by correct treatment.

Various jurisdictions all over the world employ different ways of treating citizens, informing them and offering opportunities for participation. Legal systems may, to a certain degree, compensate for deficiencies in one aspect with more activity on another. It might be the case that the Dutch system, which compared to other jurisdictions offers only limited opportunities for citizen participation, pays relatively more attention to fair treatment and to information processing.

The concepts are not totally interchangeable, however. Each contemporary legal system should comply with the requirements of each concept, at least to a minimum degree. Systems in which participation is not possible at all, or that provide no information to outsiders at all, or that treat both participants and the public contemptuously should have no place among contemporary legal systems.

The most prominent form of citizens' participation at the level of a court system as a whole involves decision-making in cases in collaboration between lay persons and professional judges, in the situation of a jury trial or a trial with lay judges. Participation by citizens, both in individual cases and at the level of the court system, can be considered as a form of democracy. Various aspects of democracy are of relevance, and the following section elaborates on these.

Democracy

There is no consensus about exactly what democracy is and what it encompasses. It is an 'essentially contested concept' that is differently defined, depending on the authors by which, and the era in which it is used (RMO 2007). Nevertheless, a general consensus seems to exist with respect to certain characteristics of democracy. Democracy, in any definition, has to do with controlling the powers of the state, the question of how citizens can take part in the institutions of society, and how citizens with varying backgrounds live together. This implies that in any democratic country particular procedures for decision making have been developed in which citizens have been guaranteed a certain degree of equality and a certain degree of freedom (Schuyt 2006). Living together peacefully is guaranteed by the existence of certain state institutions, rights and procedures, such as an independent judiciary, freedom of expression and elections of representative bodies. Basic principles such as decision making by majority and the protection of minorities are inherent to democracy, as is equality of all citizens before the law and protection of human rights (Adams and Popelier 2004).

Participation by citizens in society and its institutions can be considered a constituting element of democracy. As such, it can be expected that there also is an association between lay involvement in a legal system and democracy (Hans 2003). It has been contended that such lay involvement would substantially increase democratic legitimacy of the legal system (De Hert 2004b). Further chapters of this book explore the degree to which opportunities to participate exist in various jurisdictions and what the perspectives on participation are for the citizens involved and for professional judges. In the last chapter an assessment is made of the extent to which the varying forms of participation contribute to democracy. The concept of democracy consists of various aspects that are discussed below (Adams and Popelier 2004; De Hert 2004b).

Representative Democracy

The first aspect of democracy treated here is *representation*: the lay person who takes part in a system represents the 'general population', or at least is expected to do so. The right to participate directly in adjudication of legal cases can be traced back to Ancient Greece where the principle that citizens should govern, judge and legislate was established under Athenian democracy. The rationale behind the involvement of ordinary citizens is that the trial of cases should not be the prerogative of a small elite. Each citizen should at least have the opportunity to be selected for participation in the trial of cases. During the Enlightenment certain philosophers and politicians, such as Montesquieu, Beccaria, Voltaire and others pursued this thought (Jackson and Kovalev 2006). All citizens of a country plainly cannot sit, deliberate and make decisions concerning every case that passes through the courts, however. Therefore, representatives have to be chosen. Where lay people are used for deciding cases, they are no more than a tiny proportion of the population as a whole (Jackson and Kovalev 2006).

As they are expected to act in name of the population at large, those who represent the population should, to a certain degree, resemble it. However, no selected group of individuals can accurately mirror all the standpoints and views present in the wider community (Smith and Wales 2000). The question therefore is in what respects the representative should resemble those who are represented. A perfect correlation is not possible, and therefore the aim is to find people who have certain descriptive characteristics in common with the general population. For example, it is argued that the representing body should match the general public in age, gender and race. A serious objection against the assumption underlying this type of representation is that it is not certain whether members of a certain group, for instance women or certain groups of minorities, share an essential identity. This assumption may be incorrect, and moreover the representatives may not have (or have only to a limited extent) the abilities to represent others. It is questionable whether all women in fact share an identity and would, as a consequence, be able to represent all women. The same is true for other groups in society. Moreover, representation of *all* relevant groups is difficult, and the question always remains which groups can be considered to be sufficiently 'relevant' to be represented, while other groups are not (Sloot 2004).

Notwithstanding these difficulties, most countries seem to adhere to the general principle that the judiciary, including members of a jury and lay judges, should at least to some extent reflect the various groups that live in a country (Pitkin 1967). If the judiciary, juries and lay judges are seen to reflect the composition of the population, it may be expected that this will substantially contribute to the legal system's legitimacy (Sloot 2004).

Representativeness of both the formal judiciary and of lay adjudicators has been, and still is, the subject of a lively debate in many countries. Discussions conducted in the Netherlands in the 1960s on the representativeness of the judiciary centred around the involvement of Catholics, and later, from the 1980s onward, of women and immigrants (Sloot 2004). At the beginning of the 1960s, the US Supreme Court was accused of not acknowledging the difficult position of blacks because it consisted of white men only (Sloot 2004). Other countries also show an awareness that representation is not perfect, for example because certain occupations are not represented in the formal judiciary or among juries and lay judges.

In the countries under review in this book there are various ways for candidates to excuse themselves from participation as a member of a jury or as a lay judge, and in many judicial systems the parties in a case have opportunities to challenge potential members of a jury which may lead to lessened representativeness (Cleiren and de Roos 2002; Thaman 1997/1998). Moreover, selection procedures work out in such a manner that only a limited segment of the population is reached for duty as a lay adjudicator. The degree to which the decision makers in legal systems reflect the general population is thus reduced by varying causes.

Representation has a certain symbolic relevance, and it is expected to improve communication with and participation by certain groups in society (Pitkin 1967; Sloot 2004). Opportunities for dialogue with members of different groups in society should be improved by their participation. By including them in certain institutions or in political parties, for example, the message is conveyed that relevant groups in society are not neglected. In how far these effects can also be extended into the legal domain is not totally clear, however. The difference between representation in, for example, the political domain and in the judiciary is that judges do not represent someone else, whereas politicians do. Judges are accountable for the administration of justice primarily by reference to the law and by the justification of their decisions. They do not represent a 'party', the general population, or an association with members. Moreover, in most countries judges are appointed for life, which implies that they cannot be discharged because of the verdicts they pronounce, which also is an indication of their lack of accountability to society. This lack of direct democratic accountability would form an extra argument for ensuring that the judiciary mirrors the composition of the population in a country. Sloot (2004) argues that the most important reason for representation is the need for a visibly impartial judiciary. In a situation where all relevant groups in society, and not only an elite, form part of the judiciary, impartiality can be expected to increase.

In legal systems that make use of a jury or of lay judges, a more extensive and comprehensive group of people participates in the adjudication of cases than in the case of an exclusively professional judiciary. The circles in society from which the members of a jury and the lay judges are drawn should therefore not only be representative of the better educated. As a result, these legal systems provide fuller representation than those systems where the trial of cases is the prerogative of a small elite. Later chapters outline the debates on representativeness that are being conducted in the various countries under review here.

In summary, representative democracy in the framework of a criminal justice system consists of:

- lay and professional decision makers coming from all walks of life; and
- a substantial proportion of all cases being tried with the help of lay decision makers.

Deliberative Democracy

A second aspect of democracy is *deliberation.* Democracy can be defined as an informed debate among equal, rational citizens (Habermas 1989 [1962]). Democratic deliberation helps encourage mutual recognition and respect. It is argued that the requirement to put forward reasons and to respond to challenges should eliminate irrational preferences. In case of deliberative democracy, legitimacy and trust in authorities should be enhanced by ongoing debate (Smith and Wales 2000).

Can a legal system create adequate conditions to promote an unconstrained, open and reasoned dialogue? Because discussing a case within a panel or a jury enables the participants to take account of differing views, better informed judgements by citizens are, in theory, possible as a result of lay participation. A further condition is that imbalances of power and resources in society are not replicated in the debate that is conducted when trying cases in a panel involving lay persons (Smith and Wales 2000). The literature and the empirical evidence presented in this book suggest that such constraints unfortunately do still exist, especially in the situation where lay persons make decisions in cooperation with professional judges. The latter exert a relatively stronger influence on the outcome of these decisions. Lay people do not always feel completely free to bring up any views they may have on a case.[2]

Cleiren and de Roos (2002) contend that jury systems do poorly as a platform for debate on cases, because members of a jury generally are only allowed to say 'yes' or 'no' to the questions they have to answer, and they are not allowed to give reasons for their decisions. As a consequence, discussion *within* panels is restricted. Nor would the public have real opportunities to discuss jury verdicts, because these do not reflect the full contents of the cases and the decisions made.

Insufficiency of court decisions as a basis for debate in society is not restricted to jury decisions, however. In many countries court decisions

2 In a later section of this chapter attention is given to other types of impediments to optimal debate and decision making in small groups.

are not accompanied by clear rationales. A comparison between written court decisions of a number of European countries showed that there are considerable differences in this respect (Malsch et al. 2005). The court decisions of all countries in this study (Germany, Belgium, France and the Netherlands) tended to lack any explicit justification of the decision to find an alleged crime proven: courts simply state that in view of the evidence presented, the defendant is found guilty of the crime. This method of implicitly justifying a decision, without explicitly presenting reasons for it, reduces the potential to review court decisions. Nor did the court decisions analysed contain systematic overviews of *all* available evidence, revealing their contents. German courts produce very long written verdicts that seemingly are very well-reasoned, whereas verdicts in France and the Netherlands are brief and consist primarily of formal language and standard phrasings (Malsch et al. 2005). But even the German court decisions, the most extensive of those under investigation, do not present overviews of all available evidence. Court decisions that are not well-reasoned are probably less comprehensible and, as a consequence, risk being not well understood by the public. Such court decisions cannot be expected to advance an informed debate (Malsch et al. 2005).

Attending court sessions and learning about the administration of justice via the media can also contribute to deliberative democracy. On this point, we have only information about the Dutch situation at our disposal. For various reasons the Dutch criminal justice system is not widely accessible to the general public (Malsch and Nijboer 2005). Few people visit the trials of criminal cases in the Netherlands out of general interest. Most visitors are related to the defendant in one way or another. A comparably small proportion of all Dutch cases are covered by the media (Malsch and Nijboer 2005). Settlements and other ways of resolving cases outside of open court have seen an enormous growth in recent years in the Netherlands. In an increasing number of cases, the prosecutor proposes an out of court deal to the suspect (Malsch and Nijboer 2005). Public deliberation about the operation of the judicial system can be expected to be hampered by such ways of handling cases outside open court. At the same time, provision of information to the outside world has improved in the Netherlands, and also in other countries, by the introduction of websites on which court decisions and other information are made available to the public on a large scale, thereby increasing the opportunities for an informed debate about the operation of the Dutch criminal justice system.

In conclusion, although deliberation is an important aspect of democracy, not all legal systems seem to promote discussion about decisions made and procedures followed in all respects. The failure to give reasons for decisions, the dissemination of information and accessibility of courts are all relevant in this respect. Deliberation about the operation of a legal system can be expected to be restricted if these elements do not operate well in practice.

In summary, deliberative democracy in the framework of a criminal justice system consists of:

- debate within panels on cases;
- dissemination of experience by lay adjudicators at the local level;
- reasons given for court decisions;
- media reporting, articles and books about the criminal justice system;
- lay adjudicators speaking publicly about their experiences
- debate within society on the criminal justice system.

Participative Democracy

The central theme of this chapter is *participation*. Participation is at the heart of democracy. It makes it possible for citizens to decide for themselves about issues that concern them, or that are relevant to the general public. Moreover, it makes possible a certain control over state powers. All (or the majority of) institutions in society should therefore allow for at least a minimum degree of citizen participation.

The participation of citizens as decision makers in criminal justice systems is not without criticism. One of the problems noted has been that jury members are only marginal participants in the trial: the jury is passive and cannot conduct research on their own (Cleiren and de Roos 2002; De Hert 2004b). Further, in most countries where juries are involved, only a very small percentage of all cases are tried by them. Even in these countries, most cases are tried by professional panels (Tubex and De Hert 2004). Nevertheless, the fact remains that the jury *is* a method of participation by citizens in a legal procedure.

Lay judges have more decisional powers than members of a jury: their task is to decide about both guilt and the sentence. A relatively larger number of cases are tried by lay judges, for example magistrates, than by a jury. That means that participation of citizens in a criminal justice system takes place on a larger scale in systems with lay judges than in systems with only juries. However, lay judges are open to criticism for the same reasons as the jurors: they are not highly active during the hearing of cases (de Roos 2006).

Research into public administration suggests that participation by citizens in local governance contributes to their personal development. Citizens increase their personal autonomy by taking part in the solution of complex problems in the field of local governance. Their abilities to form critical opinions are improved by participation in administration. Furthermore, they learn important democratic capacities, such as solving conflicts, articulating views, compromising differences, patience when finding solutions for problems and acknowledging cultural differences (Warren 1992). However, serious objections to this form of participation have also been voiced. It has been argued that citizens would not be greatly interested in playing such a role and they are not able to provide a useful input in the administration. Expertise is required for governance and ordinary citizens do not have that at their disposal (Dewey 1927; Held 1996). Participation by citizens consumes time and effort, while it is not clear what the advantages are. A further objection is that citizens who are involved in local administration over a long period tend to lose their fresh view on what is going on in their neighbourhood and, by and large, develop in the direction of the professional administrators (Wagenaar 2004). Over a long period the ability to look at problems primarily from the perspective of a *citizen* gets lost, precisely as a result of their participation.

Effects as described here for public administration can be expected in the legal domain as well. Both the citizens learning the ropes themselves, and the effect of adopting the characteristics of the professionals with whom they cooperate, are plausible. Lack of preparation to contribute to the common good also plays a role with lay adjudication. This book devotes substantial attention to such influences of participation on the citizens themselves and on their willingness to take part.

In summary, participative democracy in the framework of a criminal justice system consists of:

- taking part in the preparation of a trial (reading case files);
- asking questions during the hearing;
- taking part in the discussions during deliberations;
- having a role in decision making on guilt and on the sentence.

The three aspects depicted here, *representation*, *deliberation* and *participation*, represent different aspects of the concept of democracy. In this book – focused as it is primarily on citizen participation and its effects in the criminal justice systems of various countries – it is participatory democracy that receives the most attention. In the following chapters opportunities for participation in various jurisdictions are examined and attention is given to how they are realized in legal practice.

Group Decision Making

Cooperative decision making involving persons with varying backgrounds has been the subject of empirical research. Authors have maintained that under certain conditions a group of people is better suited to make decisions than persons acting alone (Sunstein 2003; Surowiecki 2004). Such conditions include that all information that is available is to be shared by the decision makers, and that all members of the group have the opportunity to have input in the decision. A group of people knows more than a single person and group members are, in principle at least, able to correct one another. This can be expected to contribute to improved decision making. Many studies that make use of an experimental design have been devoted to the question of whether large or small groups make better decisions. These studies address questions such as what composition of the group is most beneficial and which procedures can best be used. Not all studies will be discussed here; only those that are relevant for our subject, the involvement of lay persons in various types of tribunals, will be discussed.

Decision making by juries and by lay judges, by professional judges and by mixed panels are forms of group decision making. Groups benefit from members talking to and learning from each other. While large groups are often good for solving certain kinds of problems, these groups can also be unmanageable and inefficient. Small groups, on the other hand, have the advantage of being easy to run, but they risk having too little diversity of thought and aiming too much at reaching consensus (Surowiecki 2004). Diversity and independence are important because the best collective decisions would be the product of disagreement and contestation, not consensus and compromise. Making a group diverse makes it better at problem solving. Intelligence alone does not imply different perspectives on a problem; on the contrary (Surowiecki 2004, 30). Having only smart people together in a group results in the members resembling each other in what they know and what they can do. Groups that are too much alike stop taking in new information and learning from the information they receive. They become progressively less able to investigate alternatives. In such groups a certain pressure toward conformity can be expected (Sunstein 2003; Surowiecki 2004).

Apart from diversity, independence of group members is an important requirement for the quality of group decision making (Surowiecki 2004, 41). To a certain degree, human beings can be independent decision makers. They are not like ants, which coordinate their actions almost exclusively with those of other ants. Independence means a relative freedom from the influence of others. When decision makers are independent, one person's incorrect judgement is not reinforced by the same incorrect judgement on the part of other group members following the first person. For mistakes and misconceptions to be corrected, independent group members are needed. Moreover, independent individuals are more likely to introduce new information to the group. The most intelligent groups appear to be made up of people with diverse perspectives who are able to stay independent of each other (Surowiecki 2004, 41). The confrontation with dissenting views forces the majority to interrogate its own positions more seriously. Having even a single different opinion can make a group wiser. On this issue, a reference can be made to types of legal systems that allow for a wide contest and types of systems that do not. Thibaut and Walker (1975) found that in adversarial systems, which are based on contest and party-autonomy, more relevant facts about a case are revealed than in inquisitorial systems (Thibaut and Walker 1975; Crombag and van Koppen 2002).

With respect to differences between large and small groups, Elster argues, 'In a large assembly, it is not possible to pursue an argument in a coherent and systematic fashion. The debates tend to be dominated by a small number of skilled and charismatic speakers ... who count on rhetoric rather than argument' (Elster 1998a). Large groups thus have their own specific drawbacks. In comparison, in a small jury setting, 'one is more likely to observe the substance and not only the form of deliberation. The small size reduces the scope for demagogy and allows all speakers to be heard' (Smith and Wales 2000, 59) The direct interaction between members of a small group enables them to think not as isolated, anonymous individuals, but as citizens, working together via dialogue and consensus for the 'common good' of society.

But small group decision making can also go the other way round. Some small groups do not begin with an open mind, but start with a certain assumption about the facts that, in spite of their confidence with regard to the facts' accuracy, later may prove to be incorrect. Rather than begin with the evidence and end with a conclusion, such groups work in the opposite direction. Such groups tend to dismiss the need to gather more information. Their conviction about a certain state of the facts limits discussion and makes the group discount evidence of another state of affairs. 'Confirmation bias' is the term that is attached to the inclination of people to seek and interpret evidence in such a way that an existing conviction, expectation or hypothesis is strengthened (Kahneman et al. 1982). This way of thinking and of decision making is not restricted to lay people but is found in all groups in society (Crombag 2006). In some groups, dominant participants may suppress other perspectives on the facts.

Groups that work in isolation, without being checked from the outside, may be especially vulnerable to such negative tendencies. The same applies to individuals forming their opinions and coming to conclusions in isolation. Democracy cannot be expected to work well when individuals hold preferences and make judgements in isolation from one another (Sunstein 2003). A serious danger that small groups face is emphasizing consensus over dissent. The effect may be 'groupthink': members of the group become so identified with the group that the possibility of dissent seems practically unthinkable (Surowiecki 2004, 180). Debate and minority opinions are not tolerated in such a situation. Discussions may take the form of one person asking questions and another answering them in a predictable way.

'Group polarization' is another phenomenon that may occur in small groups: under certain circumstances, deliberation does not moderate but rather radicalizes a participant's point of view. Shifts can go in any direction. As a general rule, discussion tends to move both the group as a whole and the individuals within it toward more extreme positions than the ones they entered the discussion with. Such tendencies are stronger in small groups (Surowiecki 2004, 185).

Not only is the size of a group and the independence of its members relevant, but the order in which people speak can also play a role. This order has a profound effect on the course of a discussion. Earlier comments made during a group discussion are more influential than later remarks. They tend to provide a framework within which the discussion occurs. Once that framework is in place, it is difficult for a dissenter to come up with contradicting statements (Surowiecki 2004, 186). However, people who speak first are not always the people who know best. There is no guarantee that the best-informed speaker will also be the most influential. On juries, for instance, two-thirds of all forepersons are men and during deliberations men talk far more than women do. Status tends to influence the outcome of deliberations as well. Higher-status people talk more and more often than lower-status people. Again, a clear correlation with experience and expertise is not present (Hastie 1993; Surowiecki 2004; van Stokkom 2006).

Talkativeness has a major impact on the kinds of decisions small groups reach. Talkative people are listened to: the more someone talks, the more they are talked to by others in the group. Talkativeness does not imply that the person possesses more expertise than the more silent members of the group. Other tendencies correlate with talkativeness: people who imagine themselves as leaders will often overestimate their own knowledge and project an air of confidence and expertise that is unjustified (Hastie 1993; Surowiecki 2004, 188).

There are ways to counteract the negative tendencies outlined here, however. One of the constant findings from decades of small-group research is that group deliberations are more successful when they have a clear agenda and when leaders take an active role in making sure that everyone has an opportunity to speak (Surowiecki 2004). By ensuring that all relevant information is used while making a decision, deliberations and outcomes can be improved (Sunstein 2003).

The research findings presented here are relevant for the operation of both legal systems with and without lay participation in various respects. One-off groups that come together on only one occasion, such as juries, are less likely to fall prey to a number of the mechanisms described here. Juries generally represent a diversity of backgrounds and degrees of intelligence. They do not cooperate over a long period of time and thus the inclination to compromise each difference of opinion might be less strong than in a situation where people work together for years. However, one-off groups still run the risk of being subject to other negative, if not downright disastrous tendencies, such as group polarization and the adoption of extreme positions.

Decision making by just professional judges runs the risk of too much consensus and lack of different perspectives as described by Sunstein (2003): these panels show little diversity and they work together for longer periods, thereby strengthening tendencies to compromise. There is a risk that their decisions become based on routine, which may form an impediment to an in-depth investigation of cases. On the other hand, the possibility of decisions going very strongly in a particular direction that is not foreseen in advance is much smaller in the case of professional decision making. The effect of 'group polarization' leading to extreme viewpoints is more plausible in groups with lay people only, especially with juries. Groups that are composed only of lay people lack a mechanism for correction in case they have to take extremely complicated decisions. Adding a professional judge to such a group could constrain extreme decisions, but it can also lead to a situation where the lay people customarily adjust their opinions to those of the professional. The lay element in the decision might get lost in such a situation.

All groups, professional, non-professional and mixed, large and small, established and one-off, may suffer from psychological biases such as the confirmation bias, belief perseverance, cognitive dissonance and other biases affecting a correct judgement (Kahneman et al. 1982; van Koppen et al. 2002). It is important that decision makers, both in groups and acting individually, are aware of such biases and try to counteract them.

Conclusions

This chapter has presented a theoretical framework for evaluating lay participation in judicial systems. Because lay adjudication has not always been made possible, or is sometimes not considered as desirable, alternatives have been discussed as well, such as a wide dissemination of information about the operation of the judicial system and fairer treatment of the parties and the public within and by the system. Such alternatives are aimed at increasing knowledge of the system and they may be expected to enhance the commitment of both the participants and the public to the criminal justice system. Participation remains the most encompassing form of involvement of citizens in a judicial system, however, and it can be expected to serve as a condition for democracy in the courts.

This chapter has pictured various aspects of democracy. When participation has been made possible by a system, this does not automatically imply that democracy is increased. Citizens may sit in panels without delivering any contribution to the hearing of cases and decisions that are made. Nor does their participation necessarily lead to an increase in the discussions that are being conducted on the administration of justice. Further, those citizens taking part may not be sufficiently representative of a country's population. This book attempts to explore to what extent the opportunities that citizens receive to participate are actually used to improve the democratic quality of the various court systems, or whether they remain of only a symbolic nature. Furthermore, lay people may not be very eager to participate. Not all citizens have time and are sufficiently motivated to expend effort on taking part in the trial of cases. The past decades have even seen a considerable decline in willingness to contribute to the common good all over the world (Barber 1995; Putnam 2000).

A third perspective of this chapter has been the way group decision making takes place in practice and the empirical research that has been conducted on this issue. Biases in decision making have been discussed and findings of empirical research on this issue have been related to different types of panels that decide legal cases. In many of the following chapters attention is given to biases that are expected to be inherent to certain combinations of professional and lay decision making. In the five countries that have been investigated in more depth in this book, concerns appear to exist in this respect. Regarding all types of panels that can be found in the various jurisdictions in Europe, criticisms have been voiced with respect to problems that would be inherent to either predominantly professional decision making or predominantly lay decision making. The choice that each country makes for either professional or lay adjudication or a combination of them, however, has much to do with the legal culture and traditions in that jurisdiction. Changes in a legal system are thus not easily developed and implemented. This book therefore does not purport to suggest radical changes in any system under review (Blankenburg and Bruinsma 1994; Nelken 2007).

Taking as their point of departure that direct, actual participation in trials (on a micro level) or in the adjudication of cases (on the level of the system as a whole) provides the best guarantee for at least a certain degree of democracy in the courts, the following chapters reflect on the individual statements, experiences and perspectives of both professional and lay decision makers who have been interviewed.

Chapter 3
Lay Adjudication in European Countries

Most European countries have some form of lay participation in the trial of cases. This chapter examines the ways citizens take part in the adjudication of criminal cases in the following countries: Denmark, Germany, England and Wales, Belgium and the Netherlands. It explains how the selection of the lay participants is conducted, what their tasks are and what their involvement encompasses in practice during the process. Only criminal law is considered in this chapter, with the exception of the Netherlands, where other legal procedures allowing for direct input by citizens are discussed as well. Further sections of this chapter present a brief sketch of lay involvement in a number of other European countries, including some from the former Communist bloc.

Belgium

Belgium introduced its jury system under French influence and the ideas of the Enlightenment. Article 150 of the Belgian Constitution states that criminal cases, among others, must be decided by juries. It is the Belgian *Hof van Assisen* that tries cases with the help of a jury. This court does not sit permanently but is called together each time a court is needed to try a case that must be dealt with by a jury. Each of the 10 Belgian provinces has a *Hof van Assisen* and Brussels has two (one in Dutch, one in French). This court is composed of three professional judges and 12 jurors. The cases that are tried by the *Hof van Assisen* are crimes for which the maximum penalty is at least five years imprisonment. In principle, most crimes covered by this criterion can be 'correctionalized', which means that they can be tried by a court without a jury. In practice nowadays only the most serious crimes, such as murder, are tried by a jury court (de Roos 2006).

Tasks

The task of the jury is to decide on the defendant's guilt. The basis for this decision is a questionnaire. The jury is only allowed to answer 'yes' or 'no' to the questions. There are two types of question: first, those about the crimes with which the defendant is charged, such as whether the defendant is guilty of the alleged crime and what legal qualification would apply. The second type of question covers those that arise during the trial of the case, for example relating to mitigating or aggravating circumstances, or the presence of certain mental disorders. Jury members are allowed to ask questions during the court session, but not many of them make use of this power. As is the case for all juries, it is forbidden to give any sign of one's conclusions regarding the defendant's guilt or innocence during the court session. If a member of a jury does so in spite of this prohibition, he or she can be challenged and may have to be replaced.

Voting on the defendant's guilt takes place in secret without the professional judges attending. When the votes are equally divided between guilty and not-guilty, the defendant is acquitted. In case only a small majority (seven jurors) finds the defendant guilty, the three professional judges have to give their opinion as well. When two of them do not agree with those seven jurors, the defendant is acquitted.

In Belgium, as in France, *conviction intime* is the basis for the jury's judgement about the defendant's guilt. Each individual member of the jury has to be personally convinced as to the defendant's guilt or innocence. The Belgian Code of Criminal Procedure states that jurors are not allowed to give reasons for their judgement about whether the evidence is sufficient. They should consider the questions that have to be answered, and consult their conscience, in silence. There are no specific rules of evidence that should be followed for reaching a decision as to the defendant's guilt. Jury verdicts thus do not contain the reasons on which they are based. In contrast, decisions about the sentence include a rationale.

The jury and the professional judges cooperate in deciding about the sentence. This decision is made by majority vote. The youngest member of the jury gives his or her opinion first and the president is the last one to do so. A jury decision is not subject to appeal. In case of a factually incorrect decision, however, the case can be brought before a new jury. That is only possible in the event that the defendant is found guilty of the alleged crime. The highly unusual decision to do this is up to the professional judges. Furthermore, the case can be sent to a new *Hof van Assisen* if an appeal to the Court of Cassation has been granted. The Court of Cassation, however, can only deal with legal and procedural matters and does not reinvestigate the factual merits of the case.

Selection

Every four years candidates for jury duty are selected randomly by the provinces in Belgium. The list thus composed is sent to the president of the District Court in the capital of each province. The president is responsible for the definitive list that is drawn up. Special attention is paid to ensuring an equal representation of people with a certain level of education and those without. Jury members must meet certain requirements: they must be between 30 and 60 years of age, able to read and write and possess Belgian nationality. They must live in the province where the *Hof van Assisen* sits.

At least one month before a jury trial 30 or more candidates for jury duty are selected randomly (Snelders and Heuvelmans 2007). On the first day of the jury trial these people can ask to be excused. Acceptable reasons for excuse, presented by the candidates themselves, may include personal or family reasons, or reasons that have to do with one's job or other occupation. Prosecution and defence can both challenge six to 12 candidates without giving reasons for it (peremptory challenges).

Among the grounds for disqualification by the courts on its own initiative are those of not being of good moral standing, being a member of the Senate or the Parliament, being a judge or religious leader, or serving in the army.

Representativeness

Only a small number of cases are dealt with by a jury. It is estimated that only 0,01 per cent of all criminal cases in Belgium are tried by a *Hof van Assisen* (Traest 2001; Tubex 2004). Various types of people and professions only rarely appear on a jury. Among them are self-employed persons, businesspeople and mothers of large families. Most members of a jury have backgrounds as teachers or civil servants. As a consequence, the jury cannot be considered representative of all inhabitants of Belgium.

Members of a jury receive compensation for their work. Employers are obliged to pay the first five days of jury duty.

Debate

A Commission has been instituted to formulate recommendations on Belgium's future jury system.[1] It has proposed that the number of members of the jury should be reduced to eight and that they reach their decision about the defendant's guilt together with the professional president of the *Cour d'Assises*. At present, the jury deliberates and decides on this matter without the judges. The Commission is of the opinion that, unlike the current situation, a rationale should be given for the jury's decision by having the president of the court state the reasons for the decision in a written verdict. Members of the jury should give their consent to the final formulation. A full appeal is not deemed to be necessary by the Commission. However, according to the Commission, appeal to the Court of Cassation of Belgium should remain (de Roos 2006).

The background to this debate on the jury in Belgium is that the procedure in jury cases is considered to be lengthy, complex and old-fashioned. The quality of jury decisions cannot be guaranteed.[2]

---

1 *Intermediair rapport van de 'commissie-assisenprocedure', overhandigd aan Mevr. de minister van Justitie op 8 maart 2005.*

2 In Chapter 10, the interviews with professional judges and others will reflect on the debate that is taking place about various issues related to the operation of the jury in Belgium.

Denmark

The Danish Constitution of 1953, Article 65, introduced the phrase 'in criminal procedures, lay judges must take part'. For centuries lay people have participated in this country's criminal justice system. Denmark has both juries and lay judges. The jury system has existed since 1683, but fell into disuse around the year 1800. Lay assessors, however, were retained, but they were used extremely rarely (Garde 2001). In 1919 legislation came into force that stipulated that a jury must decide in extremely serious crimes. The system of lay judges existing today was introduced in 1936 (de Roos 2006; Tak and Fiselier 2004).

Juries decide in cases of very serious crimes, as well as in drug cases and political cases. About 100 such cases are dealt with by juries each year. Until recently juries sitting in the two Danish Courts of Appeal were composed of one professional judge and 12 jurors. As of 1 January 2008, this jury system changed. A new jury was introduced at the *Byret* (District Court), consisting of one professional judge and six jurors. At the two Courts of Appeal (*Landsret*) a jury composed of three professional judges and nine jurors handles cases on appeal.

A substantially larger number of cases is decided by lay judges in cooperation with professional judges. The composition of mixed courts at the *Byret* is two lay persons and one professional judge, who chairs the trial. A condition for cases to be brought before this court is that the defendant denies having committed the alleged crime and that the prosecutor does not request a more serious penalty than four years of imprisonment. If the defendant admits having committed the crime, the case is dealt with by a single judge. In appeal a court consisting of three lay judges and three professional judges decides about the case.

Tasks

The jury decides about the defendant's guilt without the professional judges and it decides about the sentence together with the professional judges. In deciding about guilt, jurors have a list of questions that they have to answer. A decision of guilt by the jury may be overruled by the professional judges if it is clear that the defendant cannot be punished on the basis of the existing law. Neither the decision about the guilt nor that about the sentence, are accompanied by a rationale. No appeal is possible, except in questions of apparent legal errors, which may be referred to the Supreme Court of Denmark.

Lay judges make all decisions in cooperation with the professional judge or judges. They have the right to ask questions during the trial, but they seldom do so. In principle, the two lay judges can overrule the professional judge should they hold an opinion on the case that differs from that of the chairperson. In such a situation, the chairperson may put the case against a decision that is not correct in his or her opinion. He or she can convince the lay participants that their opinion is wrong and that an appeal may be instituted by the Prosecution. The president may also give a dissenting opinion in writing (Tak and Fiselier 2004).

Selection

Candidates for both service as members of a jury and as lay judges are selected from two lists. One list consists of citizens of the community where the *Byret* is located and the other comes from political parties, which ask their members if they want to sit on a jury. Because the selection is entrusted to committees appointed by local councils, members of local political parties tend to be preferred. Local majority parties and the larger opposition parties have a better chance of being involved (Garde 2001). Members of the committee would tend to nominate persons they know, directly or by reputation, and whom they trust. Garde (2001, 108), a Danish judge, does 'not consider this as a corrupt practice', however. Participants are selected on the basis of their suitability for service as a member of a jury or as a lay judge.

One candidate is chosen for every 300 citizens. Candidates who are selected can be appointed both as a member of a jury and as a lay judge (Garde 2001). The lists that are constructed are forwarded to the presidents of the Courts of Appeal, who randomly select individuals who are requested to serve in the administration of justice. The Danish Law on Judicial Organization stipulates that the lay participants should be able to perform their tasks and should be sufficiently capable of understanding complex cases (Garde 2001; Tak and Fiselier 2002).

The lay adjudicators serve for a period of four years and can be reselected after their term expires. On average they serve on four cases each year. The parties in a case are not informed beforehand on who will sit on it. A judge (lay or professional) or a member of a jury may be challenged in case of doubt about his or her impartiality or lack of neutrality. The lay participant should be between 18 and 66 years of age and should have Danish nationality. Grounds for being excused may include certain forms of employment, such as military service, working for the fire brigade and physicians and midwives. Having a criminal record may lead to disqualification as a lay participant. Several types of civil servant, members of the Prosecution and police, religious leaders and several other categories of persons are excluded by definition from serving as a lay participant.

Representativeness

About 13 per cent of all criminal cases are tried by mixed courts, in which lay judges take part (Garde 2001). The jury deals with a much smaller percentage of cases: about 0.1 per cent. Because a certain assessment of the candidate's potential for serving as a lay participant is made by both the Selection Commission and the President of the Court of Appeal, no fully representative selection from the population of Denmark is obtained (Garde 2001). Teachers and farmers would appear to be overrepresented, while self-employed people and employees of small firms are largely absent. Middle-aged people, especially those in their 50s, are overrepresented and young people are underrepresented (Garde 2001).

Debate

Lay participation as a general principle is not under discussion in Denmark. However, the role and function of the jury is debated at regular intervals, especially the lack of rationales for decisions and the absence of an opportunity for appeal. The new law has redressed some of these points of criticism.

Germany

Germany had juries from 1849 until 1924. At present the *Schwurgerichte* (which resemble a jury court) still try a small number of very serious crimes. The introduction of lay judges in the legal system (*Schöffengerichte*) dates form 1849. During the Nazi regime the participation of lay persons in the legal system was virtually absent. After the war the mixed system with lay judges was restored.

The mixed court of first instance (at the District Court, *Amtsgericht*) tries criminal cases for which punishments between two and four years can be imposed. If a lower penalty is expected, a single judge deals with the case. At the District Court the composition is two lay participants (*Schöffen*) and one professional judge. In more serious cases, as well as in appeal at the *Landgericht*, two or three professional judges try cases together with two lay judges. In certain complex cases the number of professional judges is increased to a total of five judges (*Grosse Strafkammer* of the *Landgericht*). In this court the professional judges are thus in the majority. In extremely serious cases, a *Schwurgerichte* is assembled at the Court of Appeal which consists of three professional judges and six lay judges. Nowadays the *Schwurgerichte* play only a minor role; the rest of this description of the German system is therefore focused on tribunals involving *Schöffen*.

Tasks

Professional and lay judges decide in cooperation about both guilt and the sentence. Each decision is made with a two-thirds majority. During deliberation the case is discussed and the youngest lay judge is the first person to express his or her opinion. In principle, the *Schöffen* can overrule the professional judge(s) in most courts. As will be illustrated in later chapters, this does not often happen. Unlike the professional judges, the lay judges are not allowed to inspect the case file before the trial session. They are allowed to ask questions, but not many lay judges make use of this power.

Selection

Municipal lists are used to construct a list of candidates for service as a lay adjudicator in the legal system. Some municipalities do so by calling on residents to apply; other municipalities approach political parties, religious organizations and trade unions to obtain new lay participants. Methods for selecting lay participants differ between municipalities. The resulting list is sent to the District Court and there a commission decides who can become a lay judge.[3]

Lay judges are appointed for a period of four years, which can be prolonged after its termination. It is expected that lay judges participate about twelve days each year. They must be aged between 25 and 70 years and have German nationality. They must have lived in the municipality where they serve as a lay judge for at least one year. A number of occupations are considered to be incompatible with being a lay judge; these include members of the government, certain civil servants, lawyers, judges, police officials and religious leaders. Some professions may serve as grounds for being excused, such as physicians, dentists, nurses, pharmacists and family carers.

Representativeness

There is sometimes criticism of the *Schöffen* for not being representative of society as a whole. Within the selection procedure there is a subjective element, as there is also when presidents of the court make the final decision with respect to nominating a candidate as a lay judge. The presidents of the courts tend to select primarily those lay persons who would, in certain respects, resemble professional judges (Machura 2001), thereby reducing the representativeness of the lay judges for society at large.

Debate

The participation of lay people in the legal system in Germany is not widely criticized (Machura 2001). However, a number of comments have been voiced. The dominant role of the professional judge is one of the focal points of critique of the system. Other objections are directed at the lack of representativeness of the lay people who participate. In general, the lay people who participate are more satisfied by their task performance and their own influence on the decisions that are made, than are the professional judges (Machura 2001).

3 www.schoeffen.de.

England and Wales

The jury has a long history in England and Wales. The jury system was developed in Norman times and still exists today. A considerable number of criminal cases are tried by Magistrates' Courts, however. Magistrates' Courts have existed since the fourteenth century. In these courts two or three lay persons (the magistrates) decide about a certain category of crimes which are less serious than crimes tried by a jury. The jury, consisting of 12 jurors, is only involved in trying serious crimes, when the defendant does not admit the offence. Jury cases are tried in a Crown Court, which also deals with decisions by a Magistrates' Court on appeal. In appeals this Magistrates' Court is chaired by a professional Crown Court judge.

Tasks

The task of the jury is to decide about the defendant's guilt. It is the professional judge alone who decides the sentence. At the trial the jury is sent out of the courtroom when complex legal issues are discussed among the judge and the lawyers. No appeal is possible on jury verdicts with regard to the decision about the alleged facts. The jury decision must be unanimous, but in extreme situations a majority of 10 members can be sufficient. The jury is not always informed at the beginning of the trial about this possibility. Members of the jury are allowed to ask questions during the court session, but they do not often make use of this power. If they wish to inquire of a defendant or witness, they are expected to give a note to the presiding judge, who then decides about asking the question. Jury pools are composed for a period of two weeks. During these two weeks they should be available full time for trying cases. As a consequence, they may be involved in the trial of several cases.

Magistrates' Courts decide about both the defendant's guilt and about the sentence. These courts consist of three (or in some cases two) magistrates and they are chaired by a senior magistrate. The two other magistrates are called 'wingers'. They have the same powers as the chairperson, except for presiding over the trial. With regard to legal issues, the magistrates are assisted by a legally qualified clerk. Clerks generally give their advice in open court. The magistrates do not play a large role in the presentation of the case and the testing of the evidence. The Crown Prosecution Service presents the case to the court and produces witnesses and expert evidence. The court leaves it to the parties to interrogate the defendant and the witnesses. The common law system discourages the magistrates from asking questions other than those focused purely on clarification. Neither juries nor magistrates are given access to the case file before the trial starts. Magistrates should sit at least 26 half days per year.

Selection

Jurors are chosen at random from the electoral register. This is organized by the Jury Central Summoning Bureau. The lay persons who are selected are randomly assigned to particular cases by the Crown Court. Members of a jury must be between 18 and 70 years of age and must have lived for five years in England and Wales. A criminal record can be a reason for excluding the candidate. The same goes for certain occupations, such as a military appointment. The Defence and Prosecution have no role in jury selection. They can challenge jury members, but since they are not allowed to put questions to the candidates they do not often make use of this power. The judge also has the power to exclude certain candidates, for example because they are not able to read or write.

Methods for recruiting magistrates differ from those for selecting members of a jury. Local advisory committees select candidates for service as a magistrate. These committees are expected to seek out people from a large variety of backgrounds when composing their list. Recently the selection procedure changed: all persons who consider themselves capable of being a magistrate can apply. Local advisory committees spread announcements via the internet calling for candidates to be a magistrate. These announcements stipulate that no formal qualifications are required. However, magistrates need intelligence, common sense, integrity and the capacity to act fairly.[4] According to these announcements, membership should be widely spread throughout the area covered and drawn from all walks of life. Each bench should broadly reflect the community it serves in terms of gender, ethnic origin, geographical spread, occupation and political affiliation.

Until the 1970s little was done to make the magistrates representative of the general population. It was general custom that sitting magistrates took it upon themselves to recruit new members of the magistrature. Since then, this has changed and recruitment has become less informal. The aim is to obtain younger people and people from other ethnic backgrounds and the Magistracy has become more representative than it was before. The candidates now have to undergo two interviews. The key criteria that are used for testing candidates are integrity, fairness, common sense, social awareness, good character and sound judgement. A criminal record can be a reason for excluding a candidate. Level of education is not a criterion for selecting magistrates. However, it remains difficult to recruit people from some ethnic backgrounds, such as, for example, the Chinese community. Those who have a tenured job are underrepresented. Political affiliations, however, are diverse: even Freemasons are represented in the Magistracy. Nevertheless, persons with enough spare time and independent incomes are overrepresented.

---

4 http://www.magistrates-association.org.uk.

Jurors, by contrast, are randomly selected from electoral registers. In the old days it was easy to be excused from jury service, but this has changed. As a consequence juries are more representative now than in earlier times – and they are more representative than the Magistracy.

Training

At the time of writing (2008) there are 30,000 magistrates in England and Wales. Of them, 28,000 are members of the Magistrates' Association.[5] Magistrates receive initial training on the practical aspects of the hearing of cases. They receive basic information on the standard of proof, the order of procedure, case management and the criminal procedure rules. This training is given residentially, in one weekend and two days. This varies between the Benches, however.

A mentor is assigned to them after they begin sitting. They are appraised once a year, by other magistrates. There are magistrates' regional training committees that conduct the training and the appraisals and that make training plans. These committees are all composed of volunteers. There is continuing education on issues such as new legislation, family violence, drugs, mental health, etc. The amount of training given and received has increased over the years. The Magistrates' Association organizes the training. As a consequence of the training they receive the magistrates can to a certain degree be considered professionals, not amateurs. In this sense, they differ from jurors, who generally are involved only once in their lives. Members of a jury are not trained.

Representativeness

Nowadays, when composing lists for jury duty, more explicit energy is invested in trying to reflect the community. Lists of candidates for jury duty, for example, may contain a maximum of only 15 per cent of people with the same type of occupational background. Juries are now less exclusively middle class than in earlier times and they are younger (Lloyd-Bostock and Thomas 1999; de Roos 2006).

About 95 per cent of all criminal cases are dealt with by Magistrates' Courts.[6] Figures from an annual report show that the majority of the magistrates are aged between 50 and 69. Most of them are on the conservative end of the political spectrum. White people dominate on the Magistrates' Courts to the figure of 93.5 per cent.[7]

It is estimated that 1–2 per cent of all criminal cases go before a jury (de Roos 2006). Juries, more than the magistrates' courts, are composed of

---

5 http://www.magistrates-association.org.uk.

6 http://www.hmcourts-service.gov.uk/infoabout/magistrates/index.htm.

7 http://www.dca.gov.uk, *Judicial Appointments Annual Report 2003–2004*, Department for Constitutional Affairs.

representatives of the 'working class'. But juries too do not perfectly reflect the composition of the population; women and ethnic minorities are still underrepresented (Lloyd-Bostock and Thomas 1999).

Debate

England and Wales seem highly satisfied with the participation of lay persons in the criminal justice system: lay magistrates dealing with less serious crimes and the jury for the more serious ones. There is some criticism of the absence of an obligation to give reasons for jury verdicts and of the complicated procedure that is followed in jury trials. However, there is no movement for abolishing the jury to be found in England and Wales.

The Netherlands

In the Dutch legal system the lay element has almost totally disappeared. The system does not make use of juries, and lay judges, as far as they are involved, are all experts in a certain field. Juries only operated in the Netherlands during the French occupation (1811–1813). The jury system was abolished immediately after the country became independent from France again. Juries have never been popular in the Dutch legal system (Bossers 1987; Malsch 2003).

Participants who have no background in law act as judges in a limited number of procedures in the Dutch legal system. These 'lay judges' try agricultural tenancy cases[8] and military criminal cases, or are part of a court that hears cases concerning the execution of sentences.[9] The Netherlands also has a Companies and Business Court[10] and the Plant Breeders' Rights Division.[11] Lay people may also be involved in procedures like arbitration and mediation. All these participants without legal training are experts in a certain field. The Dutch criminal justice system also makes use of honorary judges[12] who participate in 'regular' cases in all legal fields. These honorary judges all have a university degree in law, and they must have had professional experience as a lawyer for at least six years before being allowed a position as a honorary judge. 'Ordinary' lay people, in the sense of persons who have not enjoyed academic education and who are not experts in a specific domain, are not involved in the trial of cases in the Netherlands.

8 *Pachtzaken.*

9 Execution of Sentences Court, *Penitentiaire Kamer, Hof Arnhem.*

10 *Ondernemingskamer Hof Amsterdam.*

11 *Kamer voor het Kwekersrecht*, sitting in both the District Court and the Court of Appeal in The Hague.

12 *Rechters-plaatsvervanger.*

Tasks

The tasks of both experts in the courts sketched above and of the honorary judges are largely the same as those of professional judges with respect to the hearing of the case and decision making. All judges, professional, expert and honorary, read the case file before the court session. In this respect, the Dutch situation differs strikingly from that in other countries, where the reading of the case file is generally restricted to the professional judges only. At the trial session the experts and honorary judges in the Netherlands have the same powers as the professional judges: they can ask questions and they sometimes even preside over a case. During deliberations, generally the judge without legal training is the first person to speak and to give his or her opinion on the case. They may also be involved in the writing of the court decision, but not many of them take part in this task.

Selection

In the Agricultural Tenancies Courts, the Execution of Sentences Court and the Companies and Business Court, the participants are selected on the basis of their knowledge, experience and expertise in a certain field. The experts involved in agricultural tenancies cases have knowledge in the field of agriculture, while the judges without training in law in execution of sentences cases are experts in psychiatry or psychology. The experts involved in the Companies and Business Court generally have positions on the board of directors of large companies or in trade unions.[13]

Some decades ago honorary judges were used exclusively in the event of illness of one of the professional judges. By and large, however, honorary judges have acquired a regular place in the panels at District and Appeal Courts in the Netherlands. The recruitment of honorary judges not officially forming part of the professional judiciary is carried out by a special committee (Selection Committee for the Judiciary[14]). However, many candidates are approached by members of the judiciary, and some candidates express their wish to enter the judiciary to a court, which may then start the procedure for application on its own initiative (Eskes 1996; Eskes and de Groot-van Leeuwen 1996; Loth 2003).[15]

13 More information about ways in which the participants in these specific legal procedures are recruited can be found in the chapters that deal with the interviews which were conducted

14 *Selectiecommissie Rechterlijke Macht (SRM)*; see Chapter 5.

15 More attention is given to the selection of honorary judges and experts and to their representativeness in Chapters 5 and 6.

Debate

In 2006 and 2007 a debate was conducted in the Netherlands on whether the judicial system should allow for more lay participation (de Roos 2006). A perceived decline in confidence in the legal system and a decrease of trust in state organizations in general contributed to this fresh call for lay participation. The media, politicians and certain scholars have publicly drawn attention to the fact that the Netherlands is almost the only country in Western Europe without lay participation in the strict sense of the word. Some politicians opined that the Dutch criminal justice system had become too professionalized. The introduction of lay participation would help to bridge the gap that purportedly exists between the legal system and the citizens. The observation that Dutch judges were too lenient was another factor in this plea for more lay involvement (de Roos 2006). This debate led to a request by the Dutch Minister of Justice to a law professor, Theo de Roos, to write an advisory memorandum on the desirability of the introduction of lay people in the Dutch legal system. This advice concluded that the introduction of lay people in the adjudication of cases cannot be considered as an adequate method for bridging the gap between citizens and the judiciary (de Roos 2006). Legitimacy of the judiciary would not be increased, discrepancies between judges' and citizens' opinions on severity of punishment would not be resolved and confidence would not be enhanced by the introduction of lay people. On top of that, introduction of a jury, or of mixed panels, in the Netherlands would imply too abrupt a break with historical traditions. The advice also points to a growing awareness in the Netherlands that the legal system lacks openness and accessibility with regard to citizens and participants in trials. Nowadays more attention is being paid to an adequate rationale for court decisions, as well as to the availability to the public of more information about the legal system and its decisions (Malsch and Nijboer 2005; de Roos 2006). Both the government and the House of Representatives have followed the advice and debate on lay participation in the Dutch legal system has virtually come to a halt.

Other European Countries

Most countries in Europe have some form of lay participation in their justice systems. Here, lay participation in a number of European countries is briefly summarized, with the aim of providing a wider overview of the situation in Europe.

France

France has a *Cour d'Assises* for the most serious crimes. This jury court consists of nine jurors and three professional judges. In appeal, those numbers are 12 and three respectively.

Electoral registers form the basis for selection of members of this court. These names are selected at random by the mayor, who forwards the names to a committee which checks whether there are reasons to disqualify persons from this list. Thirty days before a jury trial starts the president of the jury court chooses 40 persons from this list, from whom the jury members are randomly selected after the start of the trial session. In view of this procedure, which contains a number of random selections, a comparatively representative body of jurors can be expected.

Challenging candidates for jury service is possible for both the defence and the Prosecution Service. Grounds for disqualification, challenge and excuse are similar to those in other countries discussed previously. Only the most serious crimes are subject to a jury trial. The Prosecution has an opportunity to avoid a jury trial by 'correctionalizing' the crime: giving it another, less serious qualification and thereby handing it over to a court consisting of exclusively professional judges. Less than 1 per cent of all criminal cases go before the *Cour d'Assises* (Bonnieu 2001).

Jurors do not have the right to inspect the case file. The jury may ask questions directly to the defendant, witnesses and expert, but they must first obtain the consent of the chairperson of the court. Deliberation and decision making by the jury court takes place in cooperation with the professional judges and the members of the jury. A majority of eight out of 12 votes is needed for a guilty verdict (Bonnieu 2001). On appeal, 10 votes are needed for establishing the defendant's guilt. A simple majority of seven votes (eight in appeal) is sufficient for a decision about the sentence.

As in Belgium, no further rules of evidence exist than the rule that jurors should reach an individual conviction as to the defendant's guilt (*conviction intime*). The assessment of the evidence thus is up to each individual lay judge. Related to this individual and silent weighing of evidence is the absence of an obligation to justify court decisions, and the secrecy of voting about the decisions that have to be made. The 'lay judges' have to express their individual opinion on the defendant's guilt according to their *intime conviction* and they do so anonymously (Jackson and Kovalev 2006). Decisions are made with the help of a questionnaire that the president of the jury court prepares in advance and that, after deliberation, has to be answered by each member of the panel. The questions focus on the facts and have to be answered with 'yes' or 'no' (Bonnieu 2001). Prior to 2001, appeal against jury decisions was not possible. Since then, appeal has been a possibility. In appeal, another *Cour d'Assises* is assembled, consisting of three professional and 12 lay judges.

In France, it is not only juries who decide criminal matters; there are also *juges de proximités*. These are lay judges sitting on their own to determine cases and having jurisdiction over relatively minor offences (Jackson and Kovalev 2006). They have recently been established to relieve the pressure of increasingly high case loads.

Most French people regard the *Cour d'Assises* as a democratic institution that is a guarantee of a fair trial. No substantial debate seems to be taking place on whether it should be abolished or replaced: most citizens of the country are of the opinion that lay people are just as competent at judging criminal cases as professionals. Some criticism is voiced, however, on how the jury court operates in practice: the system of evaluating the evidence, the *conviction intime* and the absence of an obligation to justify decisions (Bonnieu, 2001). Further criticism concerns the complexity and the length of the procedure.

Norway

In Norway, lay participation in the legal system is extremely important. Lists of citizens kept by the municipalities are the basis for selection of lay participants, but the names that are forwarded by political parties also play an important role in the construction of the final list of candidates.

At the District Courts, the mixed courts consist of one professional judge and two lay judges. In more serious or complicated cases (in which a penalty of more than six years of imprisonment can be imposed) the composition of the panel is two professional judges and three lay judges. In appeals the panel is composed of three professional judges and four lay judges. Lay judges participate for a period of four years. Grounds for disqualification, excuse or challenge are similar to those mentioned for the other countries discussed previously. In the first instance, all criminal cases are dealt with by a mixed court, except for certain cases for which sufficient evidence is available and the defendant admits having committed the crime, which are dealt with by a single judge. As in the other countries discussed, lay participants are not considered to be representative of the Norwegian population (Strandbakken 2001). About 75 per cent of all lay judges are nominated by a political party.

Lay judges have the same tasks and powers as the professional judges. They decide, in collaboration, about both guilt and the sentence. The lay judges are allowed to ask questions during the trial of the case (Mulder and Tak 1993). The professional judge writes the court decision and the lay judges have to give their consent. None of judges sitting on the panel, either professional or lay, consults the case file before the court session. However, the professional judge occasionally asks for the case file from the prosecutor to inform him- or herself about the case before the trial starts. Decisions are made by simple majority. In appeal for a guilty verdict, however, five out of seven votes are required.

Norway also has juries. Selection of jurors takes place from lists of inhabitants of municipalities. The composition of a jury court is three professional judges and 10 jurors. In complicated cases, however, the number of jurors may be increased to 11 or 12. Juries are only involved in cases where more than six years of imprisonment may be imposed. As a consequence the number of cases that are tried by a jury is small. The jury decides the defendant's guilt. For a verdict of 'guilty', seven votes are needed. If the three professional judges feel that the evidence for the defendant's guilt is not sufficient, they may determine that the case should be retried by a mixed panel. When the jury finds the defendant guilty, the three professional judges and a representative from the jury decide the sentence.

A large portion of all criminal cases is dealt with using lay judges. There seems to be no substantial debate about lay participation in Norway. A proposal that is being discussed at present is the replacement of the jury by lay judges. Decision making in cooperation between professional and lay judges is considered to have many advantages over independent decision-making by a jury. Other objections against the jury are heard as well, such as juries not providing a rationale for their decisions, and that jury trials take too long and are complicated. The jury has existed in Norway only since 1887, so the argument of 'tradition' does not have much impact in this country (Strandbakken 2001).

Sweden

Sweden has lay judges who take part in mixed courts. Municipalities and provinces (for the appellate courts) in Sweden select lay judges and members of a jury. Political parties also play a role. In the first instance, the mixed courts are composed of three lay judges and one professional judge. In appeal the panels contain two lay and three professional judges. The term for which the lay judges are appointed is four years. Grounds for disqualification, excuse or challenge are similar to those mentioned for the other countries already discussed.

In principle, all criminal cases in the first instance are tried by lay judges, except for simple and not very serious cases. The latter can be tried by a single judge. In principle, any adult can become a lay judge in Sweden. However, in practice lay judges are elderly, wealthy and better educated. There is criticism of the selection procedures, because being a member of a political party is considered by some to be incompatible with the requirement of independence of the judges. Lay judges decide together with the professional judges about both the defendant's guilt and about the sentence. A simple majority suffices. They have the same tasks and powers as the professional judges.

Sweden also has juries, but only for cases regarding freedom of the press. Jurors are selected by the councils of the various provinces of Sweden. An assessment takes place of the candidate's capability to form an independent judgement. Both candidates with and without former experience as a member of a jury are selected. Only a few reasons for disqualification apply. However, parties have more opportunities for challenging candidates than in many other legal systems. The composition of a jury court is three professional judges and nine jurors (Swedish Code of Judicial Procedure; Diesen 2001).

The jury decides about the defendant's guilt (Jackson and Kovalev 2006). If the jury is of the opinion that the defendant is guilty, the professional judges have to give their opinion as well. They may find the defendant guilty of a less serious crime or even acquit him or her. When the defendant is considered to be innocent by the jury, this is the final decision in the case (Diesen 2001).

We do not have information about any discussion taking place in this country about lay involvement in the legal system.

Finland

Finland makes use of lay judges only. City councils select the candidates. The councils are asked to aim to reflect the community when recruiting lay participants. Characteristics of the candidates that are taken into account in this selection procedure are age, gender, language and occupation. The president of the District Court determines who sits on which case. As a consequence, he or she is able to select the most capable lay judges. Lay judges are called to try criminal cases only in the first instance. The composition of a mixed court is one professional judge and three lay judges. A single judge decides in cases for which the maximum penalty is up to 18 months of imprisonment. Mixed courts are the prevailing composition of panels; single judges are the exception (Godzinsky and Ervasti 1999; Klami and Hämäläinen 1992).

Finnish lay judges are predominantly farmers and retired persons. They often are elderly men, who during their active life have performed a function in a political party when they were younger (Klami and Hämäläinen 1992). Grounds for disqualification, excuse or challenge are largely the same as those mentioned for the other countries discussed above. The lay judges are deployed for a period of four years. They are expected to be available for about 12 days per year. They are not allowed to inspect the case file before the trial session. For the remainder of the procedure they have the same rights and powers as the professional judges. They are allowed to ask questions during the trial of the case, but not many of them make use of this power.

Because the lay judges form the majority in the panel, they are able to overrule the professional judge. This appears to happen only rarely. During deliberation of the case the president gives a summation of the evidence and presents the relevant legal rules. The president is the first to give an opinion. In the event that there is no majority decision, the opinion is taken that is in favour of the defendant.

In Finland lay involvement in the adjudication of cases dates back many centuries. In 1993 the procedure was changed. The seven lay judges who participated in a panel until then, and had one vote between them, were replaced by three lay judges each having one vote. Research has shown that 69 per cent of all judges are in favour of lay participation in the criminal justice system (Godzinsky and Ervasti 1999).

Scotland

In Scotland both Justices of the Peace (JP) and juries are involved in the trial of cases. A JP Advisory Committee has the task of recruiting candidates for the function of Justice of the Peace. They try to find candidates who are both capable and who reflect the community. Justices of the Peace try cases either alone or with another Justice of the Peace, without a professional judge. They are assisted by a legally qualified clerk. In contrast to most other countries, Justices of the Peace are appointed until their retirement; they do not serve for a fixed period of time. Another difference is that lay people who are approached are not obligated to participate as a Justice of the Peace. They may decline involvement. Grounds for disqualification or challenging the lay judge are similar to those in other countries.

Summary offences such as vandalism, theft or speeding are tried by Justices of the Peace. The Justice of the Peace can impose a prison term for a maximum of 60 days. For the trial of criminal cases there are two procedures: the solemn procedure, involving a jury, and a summary procedure. The latter can be dealt with by a sheriff in the Sheriff Courts, or by a panel of either one or two Justices of the Peace. The majority (96 per cent) of all criminal cases are tried in a summary procedure, of which 34 per cent go before the Justices of the Peace. There are about 700 Justices of the Peace in Scotland.[16] After having followed a training course, Justices of the Peace are expected to act as judges once every two weeks. Justices of the Peace decide about both guilt and the sentence. If there are two JPs and they differ in their opinion, the decision that is most favourable to the defendant will be imposed.

Scotland also has juries that are selected from the citizens in the regions where the Sheriff Courts are located. At a Sheriff Court 15 jurors and one professional judge decide cases. At the High Court of Justiciary a panel of the same composition deals with the most serious cases. Members of the jury are not allowed to be present during the whole court session; they can be sent out of the court when a legal issue has to be treated. Questions may be asked by the jury, but they have to put them into writing on a piece of paper and hand it over to the presiding judge. The jury decides about the defendant's guilt by simple majority (Duff 1999). The judge decides on the sentence.

16 'The Review of Summary Justice, Consultation on First Order Issues', March 2002, www.scotland.gov.uk; Jackson and Kovalev 2006.

At present a debate is being conducted in Scotland about whether the system of involvement of lay people should be simplified. The Scottish government considers this system to be too complicated.[17]

Northern Ireland

In Northern Ireland, a small proportion of all cases are tried by a jury, which deals only with very serious crimes. A jury court consists of 12 lay members and one professional judge. The jury decides the defendant's guilt and the judge decides the sentence. Before the jury deliberations start, the judge gives a summing up of the facts and the relevant legal provisions. He or she instructs the jury and formulates the questions that have to be answered. The jury decides in the absence of the judge, however. The jury does not have to be unanimous; a majority of 10, or, if there are only 10 members present, a majority of nine, is sufficient. In Northern Ireland, Justices of the Peace are only involved in the trial of youth cases.

Challenging candidates for jury duty without giving reasons plays a substantial role in Northern Ireland. The defence may challenge up to 12 candidates, while the Prosecution is not allowed to challenge any prospective juror. As a consequence a jury cannot be considered as representative of Northern Ireland's population. A jury is selected for a period of four to six weeks. During this period they may be called to perform jury duty at any time. Jurors are prepared for their task with the help of a video. They are allowed to ask questions during the court session, by forwarding a piece of paper to the president. It appears that, in practice, members of the jury do not often ask questions (Jackson et al. 1999).

Ireland

Ireland does not have magistrates or Justices of the Peace. In 1924 it replaced its magistrates with professional judges. The country does have juries, however, which decide in what are called 'non-minor offences'. Jury trials are held in both the District Courts and the Central Criminal Court in Dublin. The percentage of cases that are tried by juries is about 0.1 per cent.[18]

Members of a jury are selected from the community or county where they live. Because jury trials are never held in some regions of Ireland, and thus no candidates for jury duty are selected, not all inhabitants of the country have an equal chance of participating in the legal system. Grounds for disqualification,

---

17 'Jury Service in Victoria', Final Report, Vol. 2, December 1997, Ch. 6, United Kingdom: Scotland, under 6.88, www.parliament.vic.gov.au/lawreform/jury/jury4/title.html.

18 Statistics, www.courts.ie.

excuse or challenge are similar to those mentioned for the other countries discussed here.

The jury court consists of one professional judge and 12 jurors. The jury decides about the defendant's guilt and the judge decides about the sentence. When deciding about the guilt the jury has a questionnaire at its disposal, which lists a number of issues that have to be answered by the jury. The jury decides by majority: 10 votes are necessary for a decision.

Spain

Spain has both Justices of the Peace, who decide in less serious cases, and juries. The jury was re-introduced in 1995, after having existed from 1812 to 1936 (Jimeno-Bulnes 2004). A long debate preceded the reintroduction of the jury (Thaman 1997/1998). The Spanish legislature chose the French model as its example for designing its juries. Members of the jury thus have to answer a number of questions while deciding about the defendant's guilt. These questions, and the answers that are given, form the basis for the final decision. The jury in Spain is required to briefly give reasons for their decision, which is exceptional in comparison with countries elsewhere with jury systems. The jury decides about the defendant's guilt without the judge, and the judge determines the sentence without the jury's assistance (Thaman 1997/1998). In this respect the 'classical', archetypical Anglo-Saxon model of a jury has been chosen (Jimeno-Bulnes 2004). The jury may request the help of a clerk when making a decision. An appeal against jury decisions is possible at the High Court (*apelacion*). In appeal three professional judges decide about decisions made by the jury.

Juries deal with cases of very serious crime. In 2000 only 425 jury cases were tried (Jimeno-Bulnes 2004). Thus only a very small proportion of all cases are dealt with by a jury. Generally juries consist of housewives, students, manual workers, civil servants and unemployed persons. The composition of the Spanish jury court is one professional judge and nine lay members. Seven votes are needed for a decision that is unfavourable to the defendant and five for favourable decisions. The lay members are allowed to ask questions during the trial, but have to do this by forwarding a piece of paper with the question on it to the president of the court.

Election registers are the basis for selection of candidates for jury duty. Those lists are sent to the courts located in the Spanish provinces. Grounds for challenging, disqualifying or excusing candidates are similar to those in other countries.

Jury decisions are considered to be unpredictable and the legal system is thought too complex for jurors to make optimal decisions (Thaman 1997/1998). Another point of criticism of the newly introduced system is that the professionals, such as judges, prosecutors and defence lawyers, are not well attuned to the new system. Their attitudes, the language that is used and the customs and rituals in court are still highly formal and conventional, and are not focused on a situation with a jury (Jimeno-Bulnes 2004). Nevertheless, the jury is generally considered to represent the Spanish population well and is expected to enhance participatory democracy (Thaman 1997/1998; Thaman 2000).

Italy

In Italy juries decide in cases where people are charged with crimes with a maximum penalty of at least 24 years, as well as on crimes against the state. There are 93 *Assize Courts* in Italy. In the Courts of Appeal there are specialized units such as the Appeal Court of Assize, which is in charge of appeals on decisions by the *Assize Courts*. In courts of first instance the jury is composed of two professional judges and six lay judges. The president of the jury court is a judge at the Court of Appeal and the other professional judge is based in the *Tribunale* (District Court). In the Appeal Court the jury has the same composition. The president of the court in that instance is a judge from the Court of Cassation, and the other judge comes from the Court of Appeal (Fabri et al. 2003).

The lay members of the jury court have the same powers as the professional judges. They are allowed to ask questions to the parties and the witnesses through the president. Together with the professional judges the lay members decide about the guilt and the sentence. A simple majority is sufficient for the decisions that have to be made. Decision making takes place by voting; the youngest lay member is the first one to express his or her opinion and voting ends with the president. When the votes are equally divided, the decision is made that is the most favourable to the defendant. One of the professional judges writes up the court decision (Fabri et al. 2003).

In accordance with the Italian Constitution, which states that justice may be administered with the participation of lay people, the law has established a new Court of Limited Jurisdiction composed exclusively of honorary judges (Justices of the Peace). Justices of the Peace, who decide cases in this court, are appointed by the Higher Council of the Magistracy for a initial term of four years. They can be reappointed for another four-year term. Justices of the Peace must be law graduates. These judges decide both civil cases (small claims) and criminal cases (misdemeanours). The law that introduced the Justices of the Peace made a provision for 4700 new honorary judges, to be allocated in a large number of offices spread throughout the country (Fabri et al. 2003).

Switzerland

Various types of lay involvement can be found in the Swiss cantons (states). In some cantons, three lay judges collaborate with a legally educated clerk. These lay judges are involved in the adjudication of cases on a professional basis, which implies that they have either a permanent or part time tenure. In other cantons lay judges are only involved for a restricted period in either a classical *Schwurgerichte* (jury), or in a mixed court of lay people and lawyers. However, the *Schwurgerichte* has virtually disappeared; most cantons have abolished this type of court and replaced it with courts of three professional judges. In those *Schwurgerichte* that still sit, members of the jury decide cases in collaboration with one or more professional judges. Such decision making takes place in very serious criminal cases in the cantons of Zurich, Bern, Solothurn, Tessin, Waadt and Neugenburg. The jury in Geneva is a combination of the *Schwurgerichte* and a mixed panel (Sträuli 2001). The following section is concerned with the *Schwurgerichte* as it operates in Geneva.

Geneva City councils make lists of residents who meet the criteria for participation as a member of a jury. Via the parliament of the canton this list is transferred to the president of the jury court. During the final stage of composing the jury the parties are given the opportunity to challenge candidates. Reasons for challenge, disqualification and excuse are similar to those in other countries (Sträuli 2001).

The *Cour d'Assises* (jury court) tries cases with a maximum penalty of more than five years imprisonment, and consists of one professional judge who chairs the trial and 12 jurors. About 1.5 per cent of all criminal cases go before such a jury.[19] Only a small percentage of all residents are involved in the administration of justice. In Geneva about 40 per cent of the residents do not have Swiss nationality; they are excluded from jury service.

The jury does not have the right to inspect the case file. They do have the right to ask questions to the parties, witnesses and experts. The jury decides about the defendant's guilt. The president of the court is present during deliberations on this issue and can advise about the legal provisions, but giving any indications as to his or her opinions about guilt or innocence is not allowed. The jury and the professional judge deliberate together about the sentence. The clerk is present to record the rationale for the decision. In 1996 an obligation to give reasons for the decision was introduced in the law. The court decides by simple majority. In case the votes are divided equally, the opinion that is most favourable to the defendant is chosen.

As was mentioned previously, in several Swiss cantons there has been a general tendency to replace *Schwurgerichte* by courts that consist of professional judges only. Another tendency is towards a reduction in the number of lay people participating in courts. In Bern, a clear majority of professional judges seem in favour of continuation of lay participation in the legal system. Defence lawyers are of a similar opinion, because it is believed to improve chances that

19 www.jgk.be.ch, Vernehmlassung vom 16. Juni–9. September 2005, Justiz-, Gemeinde- und Kirchendirektion.

their clients will accept the court's decision. The prosecution, however, is not in favour of lay participation.[20]

Basel Direct election of lay judges by the residents takes place in the City of Basel.[21] The *Dreiergericht* (mixed court) is composed of a president with a legal education and two lay judges. Lay judges are elected for a period of six years. This type of court decides cases in which a maximum penalty of three years imprisonment can be imposed. More serious cases can be tried by the *Strafgericht*, which consists of a president with a legal education and four other judges who are not lawyers by training.

In some cases the chairperson of the court may order that the lay judges have access to certain documents that form part of the case file. All judges have an equal vote. Decisions are made by simple majority. Both questions about guilt and punishment are decided in collaboration by all judges involved, lay and professional.

Hungary

Hungary makes use of lay judges. The administration in the counties selects the lay judges. Political parties have no influence on the selection. There are panels that consist of one professional judge and two lay judges and there are panels of two professional judges and three lay judges. The president is always a professional judge. In criminal cases lay judges participate in cases where sentences of imprisonment of eight years and longer can be imposed. Lay judges participate in about 25 per cent of all criminal cases. They are often retired people. Not many requirements apply to lay judges. They are not often excused from participation.

The rights and obligations of the lay judge are identical to those of professional judges. They decide in collaboration about both the defendant's guilt and about the punishment. Decision making takes place by simple majority. The professional judge can be outvoted by the lay judges, and this in fact sometimes happens. In such a situation, the professional judge may write a dissenting opinion.

Lay judges do not seem to contribute a lot to the trial and to decision making. They are generally more punitive than their professional colleagues. No debate seems to be taking place about abolishing lay participation in Hungary.[22]

20 www.jgk.be.ch, Vernehmlassung vom 16. Juni-9. September 2005, Justiz-, Gemeinde- und Kirchendirektion.

21 The same happens in the canton of Zurich (Jackson and Kovalev 2000).

22 Information obtained from the president of a District Court in Hungary.

Other Eastern European Countries

Many Eastern European countries make use of lay judges. Russia recently reintroduced a jury system. In former Communist countries such as Armenia, Azerbaijan, Bosnia and Herzegovina, Georgia, Lithuania, Moldova and Romania, lay adjudication was associated with the old regime and was considered an ineffective mechanism for the protection of human rights. During the Communist regime in these countries lay or people's assessors were introduced. These lay adjudicators did not, however, play a significant role in the criminal process and were considered to be mere democratic window-dressing for authoritarian criminal justice systems (Jackson and Kovalev 2006). During deliberations, the professional judge who chaired the trial would totally dominate and determine the outcome (Pomorski 1975). Lay assessors in mixed tribunals were ineffective as an independent counterbalance under the Soviet system and, as a consequence, defence lawyers would have almost no chance of obtaining a not guilty verdict (Machura 2003). Proponents hoped that the reintroduction of the jury in Russia in 1993 would serve as a 'school of democracy', in contrast to the Soviet professional judges who had often acted as instruments of the Communist Party, secret service, and later of local political authorities (Machura 2003).

A number of former Communist countries currently in a state of transition have abolished the system of people's assessors introduced during the Soviet era. This has created a vacuum. Some of these countries, such as Russia, Chechnya, Azerbaijan, Georgia and the Ukraine have introduced the classic jury system or have made plans to do so. This trend towards the expansion of lay adjudication in the former Soviet Union countries cannot be observed in all countries, however (Jackson and Kovalev 2006).

The debate on lay adjudication that is being conducted in both established and transitional systems has focused on the merits of the jury versus collaborative models. Proponents of the jury models see them as the best way of promoting strong and independent civic participation in the administration of justice in countries moving towards democracy. On the other hand, proponents of the collaborative model point to the lack of accountability of the jury because juries do not have to give reasons for their verdicts. Decisions about which model to adopt in a country may be influenced by the political and legal environment of each country, and cannot be made without considering these wider cultural and political forces (Jackson and Kovalev 2006).

A Comparison of Jurisdictions with and without Lay Participation

About a quarter of the European legal systems, most of them in the Eastern part of Europe, operate without any lay adjudicators in the sense of people without legal education and without a certain expertise that is the reason for their participation in trials (Jackson and Kovalev 2006). These countries are Albania, Armenia, Azerbaijan, Bosnia and Herzegovina, Cyprus, Georgia, Lithuania, Luxembourg, Moldovia, the Netherlands, Romania and Turkey. The list is dominated by Eastern European countries, with only Luxembourg and the Netherlands drawn from the West. The Netherlands has been discussed in this chapter and will be discussed again in Chapters 5 and 6. Luxembourg abolished its jury system in 1987 (Tak 2006). The reason for this was that no appeal of jury verdicts was possible, which was considered to be incompatible with the European Convention of Human Rights, Article 6.

Trials in which lay people participate can be distinguished from trials with only professionals by a greater orality and immediacy. In principle, all evidence should be presented in its most direct form to the lay judges or jurors. Written materials are used to a reduced degree in such systems. The decision makers spend substantially less time prior to the court session reading the case file. In most systems that make use of lay adjudicators, inspection of the case file is not offered to them and sometimes it is not even offered to the professional judges involved. The absence of prior judgements on the part of lay people is valued highly in such systems. It is remarkable that absence of preconceptions seems almost to acquire the level of a 'principle' in the case of juries – members of a jury are not expected to know anything about a case before they enter the courtroom – whereas it has more the nature of a 'convenience' in the case of lay judges collaborating with professionals. In systems of that sort it is considered to be time-consuming and impractical to provide inspection of the case file to the lay judges, and thus it does not often happen. Such systems however often are not *in principle* against letting the lay judges familiarize themselves with the case before the trial session.

As a consequence of a greater immediacy and orality, court sessions in systems with lay participation take substantially longer. All witnesses and experts have to appear in court and give evidence, in the case of witnesses repeating statements already made to police or investigators. They have to do so in a way that the lay people understand what they say. The language that is used by the officials in court is thus simplified to a greater extent than in systems without lay people. Experts are more often requested to explain their findings and they are not allowed to present ambiguous expert evidence.

Jury decisions concerning the defendant's guilt are not usually accompanied by a rationale. This reduces the comprehensibility of court decisions for the public at large. However, in countries without a jury system, the obligations for professional judges to provide a rationale for their decisions are not very strict either, leading to decisions which may not be fully comprehensible in these countries as well.

Lack of representativeness is an aspect that unites all systems described in this chapter. Some systems, like in England and Wales, try harder than others to find people from all segments of society or, like France, primarily employ the method of randomly selecting candidates. But none of the systems under review is exempt from criticism about the resulting selection of lay participants. Grounds for excusing or for challenging candidates often contribute to a biased composition of panels and juries. In many countries criticisms are heard about the way selection takes place and the fact that some groups of occupations or jobs are not represented because of the opportunities that are offered for excusing themselves. Systems of adjudication that make use of lay participation are much more inclusive than systems that are primarily or exclusively professional in nature.

Chapter 4
The Expertise of Professional Judges and Lay Adjudicators

The preceding chapters have touched upon the question of the sort of expertise provided by professional judges., They have also explored the contribution offered by the various types of lay and expert adjudication. This chapter further elaborates on these issues. First, the expertise of professional judges is examined, followed by a discussion of the types of knowledge that lay people may introduce into the system. The chapter ends with a graphic representation of the various types of involvement of professionals, lay people and experts in the jurisdictions discussed in the preceding chapters. Two dimensions of 'professionality' are distinguished. One of these dimensions encompasses legal knowledge and the various forms it may take. The second dimension relates to experience in the trial of cases. The various types of tribunals presented in the previous chapter are arranged in a space that is determined by the two dimensions. Within the figure, countries under review in Chapter 3 have been given a position on the two dimensions. The decision as to where each country is placed on the figure is based on the data and other information collected for the previous chapter. This implies that further research might shed new light on the position of each country in the figure. The figure, therefore, can be considered primarily as a starting point for further research and discussion.

The Expertise of Professional Judges

Professional judges can primarily be characterized by their formal training. They possess an academic degree in law and in most countries judges receive additional training beyond that. This extra training is aimed at teaching the candidate capabilities in presiding over court sessions, knowledge about how to deal with cases, about the composition of the case files, the types of tasks executed by various law officers, etc. In the Netherlands, depending on the candidate's background, this extra training takes either six years or one or two years, should the candidate have previous experience in a legal function outside the judiciary. An important element of the curriculum is the need to obtain experience in legal practice: candidate judges have to follow in-practice training in various posts, so that they can acquire more detailed and comprehensive knowledge of the various legal fields dealt with in court. During this training they perform the tasks of a clerk at the court session, have a post in a law firm and act as a prosecutor. After having accepted a permanent position in the judiciary, professional judges continue to enjoy training. A special institute, the *Stichting Studiecentrum Rechtspleging*,[1] provides courses that can be followed by professional judges although participation is generally not obligatory.

This type of continuing education for judges exists in other countries too. In France, Sweden and the US taking part in continuing education may be compulsory or otherwise encouraged, or the culture within the judiciary is such that participants feel committed to follow the training that is offered (Baas 2000). In the Netherlands and Germany participation seems to be compulsory less often and is less common than in France, Sweden and the US.[2]

Two important characteristics of judges in advanced legal systems are their independence and their impartiality. The training of judges pays substantial attention to the development of this professional judicial attitude. Judges are independent of the legislative and executive bodies. In the Netherlands, judicial independence is protected in the Dutch Constitution; judges are appointed for life and they cannot be discharged as a result of the decisions they make (Article 117). At a transnational level, the ECHR (Article 6, section 1) and the IVBP (Article 14, section 1) both stipulate the independence of judges. Court decisions have elaborated on the demands that are put on independence and impartiality. This jurisprudence is not further discussed here, but it is important to emphasize that such demands exist, and that they constitute an important element of a professional judiciary. Lay adjudicators too are expected to be independent and impartial. In their case, the emphasis is generally placed on whether they have known the defendant or a witness before the trial, and to what extent they can be expected to judge in an unprejudiced way in the cases they have to deal with.

Another area of judicial expertise is the experience gained as a result of involvement in the administration of justice. During their practising career judges learn how to deal with cases, how to question defendants and witnesses, how to assess various types of evidence and how to come to a conclusion regarding the defendant's guilt and a possible penalty. Professional judges who sit both as a single judge and in panels learn how to compromise, but also how to reach a decision independent of others.

Continued involvement in the trial of cases provides a more focused and intense experience which may become routine. Having come to recognize certain patterns in the large volume of cases dealt with over years on the bench, an experienced judge knows in advance what can be expected when handling

1 SSR, Dutch Training and Study Centre for the Judiciary.

2 In France, where the judiciary has a clear career structure, non-participation in courses can have direct impact on possible promotion opportunities. None of the countries involved in the Baas study (2000) have systematic controls of the quality of either the initial, or this continuing education. In the Netherlands only professional, and not honorary judges take part in the continuing education.

certain types of cases. In the long run there is a risk that the judge may tend to neglect specific aspects of cases because he or she is inclined only to perceive the patterns and schemes that have become established. The probability of this happening increases if the judge's career has never gone beyond the judiciary. This tendency grows further when judges' professional and private lives revolve around other judges and lawyers. As a result, beyond the courtroom, they rarely come into contact with people with socio-economic, educational or cultural backgrounds that differ from their own.

Cultural and sociological issues are also relevant for assessing professionality. Judges with a permanent position in the judiciary learn what sort of behaviour is expected from professional judges, as well as the lines of thought or the types of statements, whether public or in the inner circle of the court, that are acceptable to colleagues. Each organization, institution and group of professionals has its own norms and values and adheres to certain customs, attitudes and expectations that are shared by the members of the group. It has been contended that an important objective of the extra training that candidate judges and prosecutors receive is to bring about a specific 'judicial attitude' (Köhne-Hoegen 2006). Such a 'judicial attitude' can be expected to include such – often implicit – norms and customs.

Meritocratic factors may strengthen an already existing tendency to adhere to a professional attitude (de Groot-van Leeuwen 2006). When a judiciary only seeks new judges of high quality in the sense of being an expert in the legal field and having experience in the trial of cases and the primary focus is not on seeking judges who reflect the population at large, this can be expected to increase this meritocratic concentration. Meritocracy can be expected to flourish if the members of a certain circle are able to choose their own successors. This happens in many judiciaries around the world: a certain aspect of co-option is present in the procedures of many national legal systems (de Groot-van Leeuwen 2006).

The judiciary can be considered as a semi-autonomous social field (Falk Moore 1973; Köhne-Hoegen 2006). This concept refers to groups of people who work together or are related in other ways on a permanent basis. Such groups develop their own rules and have their own methods of enforcing these rules. These groups come into contact with the outside world as well and there are reciprocal influences with this outside world. It is for this reason that they are called *semi*-autonomous; they do not act in full isolation (Falk Moore 1973; Köhne-Hoegen 2006). The judiciary, being such a semi-autonomous field, can be expected to have certain behavioural norms, both explicit and implicit, that apply to each judge. The formal attitudes and ways of behaving towards the outside world and the typical juridical use of language, both in writing and in speech, have been suggested to be examples of these norms (Köhne-Hoegen 2006). These norms, however, may differ between various divisions of the judiciary. The culture and ways of interacting with colleagues are not the same for each team or sector within a court. Some divisions enjoy their lunch together, in others the members eat alone. In some teams the clerks and secretaries join in at social activities, while in other teams judges restrict such activities to themselves (Köhne-Hoegen 2006). Newly arrived aspirant judges start to internalize such implicit behavioural norms and values, and try to avoid negative reactions. They conform to the typical juridical language that is customarily used in court, and take care to dress in such a way that no negative attention is attracted. The older colleague judges and other employees working within the court or in the judiciary may exert a certain pressure on individual judges to conform to such norms (Tan 1981; Köhne-Hoegen 2006).

In the Netherlands, pressure to conform, as described here, was under discussion a couple of decades ago (Tan 1981). It has been observed that some candidates drop out of the training for professional judges without finishing it because they find it difficult to accept the norms and attitudes that are adhered to within the courts. The ways of thinking and acting within the judiciary are not theirs, and even after two years they do not feel at home in the courts (Köhne-Hoegen 2006). The socialization process gives some candidates the impression that there is little space for dissenting opinions. They feel compelled to choose either to conform or to leave the judiciary (Köhne-Hoegen 2006). As a consequence, it would seem that the least extreme candidates remain in the judiciary; the eccentric and more marked personalities are filtered out or leave on their own initiative (de Groot-van Leeuwen 1991; Gommer and Meuleman 2007).

The Expertise of Lay People

The participation of lay people in a legal system is encouraged for totally different and sometimes even opposing reasons to those that apply to professional judges. These reasons include, among others, the fresh view on cases, democratic arguments, the wish to introduce a human element in the trial of cases, and the bridging of the gap between the judiciary and citizens. These reasons have been discussed in earlier chapters and are not repeated here.

Beyond these characteristics, which all seem to point to ordinary people *not* being professionals, lay people are supposed to possess various types of 'expertise' that differ from, but sometimes also overlap with the types of expertise found in professional judges. Lay people are often considered to have knowledge of the world. Or, to put it differently, they generally come from different walks of life from the professional judges. They are expected to bring their knowledge and experience of society to the legal system. A lay judge who has worked as a taxi driver may tell professional judges about this occupation and the individuals performing it. Lay judges working in hotels or restaurants or having a job as a teacher may inform the professional judges of these sections of society. Professional judges cannot be expected to have knowledge and experience of *all* domains of society and the involvement of lay people may help them to orient themselves outside their own confined circle.

Furthermore, lay judges who, unlike professional judges, have not been 'taught' what justice is, might be thought to possess a genuine feeling for justice that would give them the opportunity to act as a fair judge. It could also be argued that they would be equally good at judging the facts in a criminal case as the professional judges. As most members of a jury are involved in only one case, it could be said that they are less likely to look for patterns or particular types and this would, to a large degree, prevent them from being prejudiced. Emotions are expected to play a substantially greater role in the lay participants' judgements and some people indeed attach considerable value to the introduction of emotions in a legal system they characterize as 'formal'; it could be argued that the system would be softened by certain emotional elements that are brought in by lay people. These characteristics point to the extras benefits that may be introduced into the process by lay adjudication.

Lay people who are involved over an extended period of time, thereby acting as a judge in a large number of cases, acquire some type of expertise that resembles that of professional judges. By and large, they learn about how to make decisions, when to trust or to mistrust statements made by defendants and witnesses and what scientific expertise is and how it should be evaluated. They also acquire knowledge about legal matters and about the norms, values and customs that prevail within the judiciary. Some lay judges even internalize this knowledge. Experienced lay judges may align themselves with the professional standards even more than the professionals themselves do.

To what extent this happens depends on how often individual lay judges participate. At the one end of the spectrum stands the member of a jury who takes part in only one case in his life. They only know from television and, incidentally, from the accounts of family members, friends or colleagues who have previously been members of a jury, how the legal system works and what is expected from them. Sitting in the jury box is an intense experience for such an individual, especially because cases tried by juries generally concern very serious offences. At the other end of the spectrum is the honorary judge who is involved on a regular basis in the adjudication of cases, as happens in the Netherlands. This judge has a university degree in law. Depending on how often he or she sits and how many years he or she has been a judge the difference from professional judges becomes increasingly less. The honorary judge internalizes the professional norms and values and is aware of the customs that are prevailing in court. The only remaining difference with the professional judges is that this honorary judge has his or her main function elsewhere, and this ensures some kind of input from outside the judiciary.

Categorization of Tribunals

As indicated at the beginning of this chapter, we now introduce a graphic representation of the various types of legal systems under review in this book and how lay adjudicators are (or are not) involved. Two dimensions are distinguished. The first dimension covers legal knowledge and the various forms it may take. The second dimension relates to experience in the trial of cases. Not all types of expertise presented previously are included in these two dimensions. The expertise that is considered as typical for lay adjudication is excluded. This means that aspects such as the presumed 'fresh view' of lay persons, or their knowledge of the wider world, have not been included. The reason is that these factors are extremely difficult to assess. It is also unclear whether lay persons always distinguish themselves from professionals on these points.

Before presenting the figure, the various types of involvement of lay people are first described in words.

1. The classical jury (CJ). Members are only involved in one case or a very small number of cases in their lives. This tribunal decides about the defendant's guilt without a professional judge and plays no role in the decision about the sentence. No collaboration with professional judges takes place. The classical jury can be found in most English-speaking countries.
2. The Belgian jury (BJ). This jury is involved in only one case, but differs from the classical jury in that the jury decides about the sentence in collaboration with the professional judges.
3. The Swiss jury (SJ) who tries cases in Geneva. As in Belgium, this jury decides about the sentence together with the professional judge. Furthermore, the jury is involved over an extended period of time (three months), which implies that, in general, several cases are dealt with by the same jury.
4. The lay judges in a *Cour d'Assises* in France and Italy (A). This panel, consisting of lay judges and professional judges, cooperates in deciding both guilt and punishment. The lay judges are hired for a fixed period and may sit on several cases during this time.
5. The Danish and Norwegian jury (DNJ). In these countries the jury decides about guilt. The sentence is decided by the jury (or, in the case of Norway, part of the jury) and the professional judges in collaboration. Members of a jury are involved for a period of at least four years, which implies that they are able to collect a substantial amount of experience.
6. The lay judges in Germany (*Schöffen*), Hungary and Scandinavian countries other than Denmark and Norway (L). The panel, consisting of lay judges and professional judges, decides about both guilt and

punishment. The lay judge may be involved for a period of several years or even until the age of retirement.

7. The lay judge in England and Wales, and in Scotland (magistrates and Justices of the Peace) (M/JP). These lay judges sit alone or with one or two other lay judges and only in some cases with a professional judge. They are generally involved for life and they have a relatively large number of sittings each year.
8. Judges who do not have a legal background but who are involved for reason of their expertise in another field (EJ). They are generally involved for life, but their main professional occupations are elsewhere (experts).
9. Honorary judges in the Netherlands (HJ). These judges have a university degree in law. They are appointed for life, but their main professional occupation is elsewhere.
10. Professional judges (PJ). These judges are lawyers by training and they have, in most cases, a full-time and permanent position in the judiciary.

The X-Axis: Legal Knowledge

The position of each type of panel or judge on the X-axis (legal knowledge), is determined by whether a university degree in law is required and whether other formal legal training has been given. Having a university degree in law was considered the most relevant criterion for legal knowledge. But other types of training are important here as well. The English magistrate, for example, receives training *before* starting in court. Judges may also receive continuing training while in post. The very act of taking part in the administration of justice also leads to an increase in legal knowledge. The same occurs if a lay judge collaborates with a professional judge, as in the Scandinavian countries and Germany. The professional judges give explanations to the lay participants about legal provisions and the way the law should be interpreted and applied; the legal knowledge of the lay participants is enhanced by this. It is difficult to measure the various types of knowledge and to make comparisons between them. The resulting position in the figure, therefore, is based on an assessment (see Figure 4.1).

Y-Axis: Experience in the Trial of Cases

The number of trials served in a judge's lifetime is a criterion for the position of each type of decision maker or tribunal on the Y-axis. A magistrate having worked for one year and a lay judge as can be found in Scandinavian countries, Hungary and Germany, who has been involved for a period of two years, can be considered to have compiled a comparable amount of experience in trying cases. The reason for this type of weighting of the two types of lay judges is that magistrates generally sit more often than the others. While locating the tribunals on the Y-axis, various amounts of experience are taken into account (see Figure 4.1).

Some types of tribunal or decision maker appear in more than one place in Figure 4.1. This is the case for magistrates and Justices of the Peace, lay judges and experts. These varying positions reflect the numbers of cases they have been involved in during their career as a judge. The same applies to honorary judges and professional judges, who have been located more to the right and to the top positions in the figure: they all have a more extensive amount of legal training and are, in principle, able to collect lots of experience in dealing with cases (see Figure 4.1).

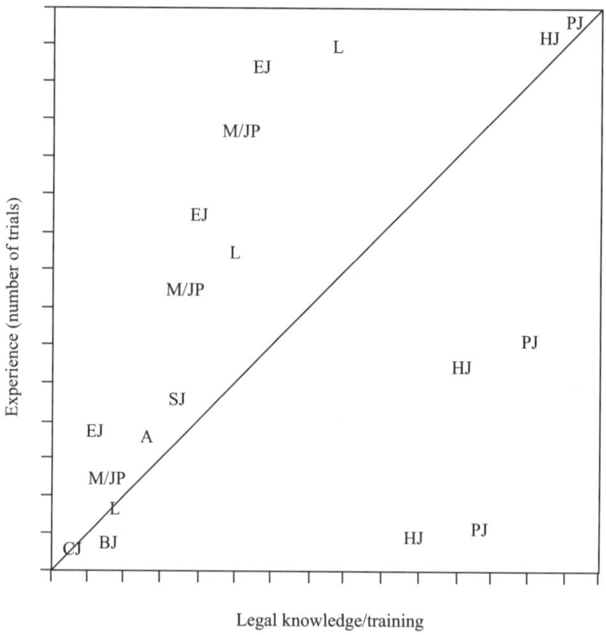

Figure 4.1 Degree of legal knowledge and experience of tribunals

Conclusions

The analysis presented in this chapter serves as a a background for interviewing the lay adjudicators in the following chapters. What are the elements of their expertise? How do they perceive the expertise of the other group of decision makers?

Two dimensions of expertise of a professional nature have been explored in this chapter and the various types of tribunals presented in Chapter 3 have been placed in a figure that is determined by these two dimensions. The results are, therefore, primarily of relevance for *professional* decision making: the elements of lay decision making have not been involved in this analysis. The following chapters have a stronger focus on aspects of lay decision making, either without or in combination with professional decision making.

Chapter 5
The Netherlands: The Involvement of Honorary Judges

The Dutch legal system was briefly outlined in Chapter 3. It does not make large-scale use of decision makers who do not have a background in law. 'Real' lay people, in the sense of citizens who are picked randomly from the community, do not take part in trials in the Netherlands. Adjudicators who lack legal education function as judges in a limited number of procedures in the Dutch legal system, however. This notwithstanding, all these participants are experts in a particular field, so they cannot be considered to be 'real' lay people. Chapter 6 deals with these procedures and the involvement of experts in them. The Dutch criminal justice system also makes use of honorary judges[1] who participate in 'regular' cases. These honorary judges all have a university degree in law, and before being allowed a position as an honorary judge they must have at least six years of professional experience as a lawyer.

Consent was obtained from the Dutch Council for the Judiciary[2] to contact courts for interviews with professional judges, honorary judges and experts without legal training. Four courts from different areas in the Netherlands were selected: two District Courts and two Courts of Appeal. The researchers contacted the presidents of these courts and asked them for the names of professional and honorary judges who could be approached for an interview. All courts consented and forwarded names to the researchers. None of the judges, experts or honorary judges refused to cooperate. The interviews conducted with the selected respondents generally took one to one and a half hours. Use was made of a questionnaire that had first been pre-tested and fine tuned in three pilot interviews. Seven professional and seven honorary judges were interviewed.

This chapter begins with observations that were made during the trial of a criminal case by a three-judge panel, after which the results of the interviews are presented.

1 *Rechters-plaatsvervanger*.

2 *Raad voor de Rechtspraak*.

A Dutch Criminal Case: Aggravated Assault

When entering the court, located on the outskirts of a large city in the Netherlands, visitors have to pass security. Showing ID is not required, however. The security services seem rather relaxed. The courthouse is large. It is about 20 years old, and houses various types of courts, among them the District Court.

The courtroom where the hearing of the criminal case is to take place is small but modern. There is seating for the public located at the back of the room on the same level as where the trial takes place. The courtroom itself is divided from the public gallery by a glass wall that allows an almost unobstructed view of what happens in the courtroom. Visitors have a clear view of all participants in the trial, but they see only the backs of the defendant and his lawyer.

A three-judge panel will decide the case that is being handled today. The bench sits on a slightly elevated dais, together with the prosecutor. The judges and the prosecutor each have their own door through which they enter and leave the courtroom, symbolizing the judges' independence of the prosecution. In this courtroom these two doors are located directly next to each other. It is not clear whether behind these doors judges' and prosecutors' rooms are divided from each other. All judges wear black robes and white bands, as do the public prosecutor, the defence lawyer and the clerk. The bench consists of a male judge in his 60s who chairs the trial and a male and a female judge sitting on each side of him. The female judge is the youngest of the panel. She is in her 40s. During the hearing of the case she takes a rather prominent role in the interrogation of the defendant. There is also a clerk who takes notes and types these directly into the computer. The prosecutor is a female of about 40 years of age.

The first count against the defendant, a young black male, is of growing cannabis, and the second count is of attempted homicide or attempted aggravated assault. The trial focuses mainly on the second count. The chairperson of the bench first asks a number of open questions to the defendant about what exactly occurred on the day of the crime. A fight took place between two groups of young men. All the participants in the fight had been drinking heavily. The victim suffered from two wounds, one just above his hips, the other on the inside of his thigh. He was taken to the hospital and received treatment. However, no medical report had been drawn up. It is therefore not clear how deep the wounds had been. Some of those present observed the defendant with a knife in his hands, whereas others did not see this. The defendant admits having fought with the victim, but denies having had a knife in his hands. He contends that a large quantity of broken glass had been lying on the ground where the fight took place which could have caused the victim's injuries.

After having asked a few open questions, the chairperson turns to the case file and starts reading aloud parts of the reports that have been drawn up of the interrogations that took place before the trial. During the interrogations by the investigative judge[3] at an earlier stage the defendant had already indicated that the victim's injuries could have been the result of the glass on the ground where they had fought. When reading this part of the dossier aloud, the chairman clearly demonstrates his doubt about the likelihood of what the defendant has suggested about the glass and the injuries incurred by the victim. The defendant has been interviewed by the police several times. The chairman picks sentences from these reports and reads them aloud. He sometimes inquires of the defendant whether what is included in the reports is accurate. After that, several witness statements, included in reports drawn up by the police and by the investigative judge, are dealt with in the same way. These statements contradict one another on several points: there are witnesses who are convinced that the defendant had a knife, and there are witnesses who state that he did not. Later in the hearing the prosecutor and the defence lawyer start discussing the witnesses' trustworthiness, accusing each other of using obviously unreliable statements. Neither of the sides at trial seems to be inclined to request that certain witnesses be heard again in open court, which would provide the bench with the opportunity to test their reliability themselves.

Considerable time is taken up in discussing the defendant's personal background. The reason for this is probably that, as it appears from his list of previous convictions, he started committing crimes at a very early age. Moreover, the defendant has problems with alcohol consumption and has been treated at length for his addiction. As with the alleged crimes, the participants receive an opportunity to ask questions about the defendant's personal circumstances. All judges make use of this opportunity, as does the prosecutor.

The prosecutor requests acquittal on the count of raising cannabis (the first count), but asks for a conviction for the violent crime the defendant is charged with. She gives a summary of the items of evidence that are available and requests a punishment of 30 months imprisonment. The defence lawyer asks for an acquittal. The bench retires for about 20 minutes and, on returning, announces an acquittal for the defendant. The acquittal is briefly justified by the court. The court is not convinced of the defendant's guilt, in view of the contradictory witness statements, certain reactions of the bystanders and the absence of a medical report on the injuries incurred by the victim. The fact that the victim mentioned the name of the alleged offender only several weeks after the fight also plays a role in the court's decision. The lawyer and his client happily shake hands. The prosecutor collects her files and other belongings and leaves the courtroom. The hearing of the case, including deliberations and the announcement of the verdict, took about two hours.

The defendant spoke rather inaudibly during the hearing of his case. The other participants could be heard better, but they too sometimes did not speak

3 Judge who is involved in a case during the pre-trial investigation.

into the microphones, or spoke inarticulately. The hearing relied heavily on the case file, which did not make the hearing of the case very comprehensible either. Not everything that was said by bystanders, witnesses and other people involved in the alleged crime was read aloud during the trial, only bits and pieces of the numerous reports that had been drawn up. No witnesses were heard in open court. The participants were already familiar with the case and with the various statements, having read the case file prior to the court session, but visitors were quite unacquainted with what the case was about. Surprisingly, none of the participants at the trial took the initiative of requesting that the court hear the witnesses themselves, which could have contributed considerably to establishing the truth. During the hearing of the case a legal discussion took place about the defendant's intent regarding the alleged attempted homicide or aggravated assault, which probably was difficult for lay visitors to understand.

What helped a great deal in clarifying the case for the public is that both the prosecutor and the defence lawyer (separately from each other) came to the public gallery while the bench retired for deliberations and after the closing of the trial, and asked the visitors whether they had any questions about the case. The presence of a group of visitors may have encouraged them to do so. Their explanations were highly helpful in clarifying the roles of the participants and the way the Dutch system works. However, it happens only rarely that the lawyers take the time to discuss the case with the public. In this sense, this case seems an exception.

After pronouncing their verdict, on leaving the court one of the three judges, now in his street clothes, passed through the public gallery without greeting the visitors. Naturally, he did not join in the discussions between the public and the defence lawyer, who were sitting in the public gallery.

Honorary Judges in the Netherlands

Originally intended to fill gaps in panels in case of a sudden illness or holidays of one of the salaried judges, honorary judges have now become an established fixture in the trial of cases in Dutch courts. Discussions about their role and function have been ongoing for many years (van den Haak 1997, 5–9).

Since the 1970s honorary judges have played an increasing role in the trial of cases (Eskes 1996; Eskes and de Groot-van Leeuwen 1996). Statistics from 1994 show that the number of honorary judges who were on the lists of Dutch courts was twice the number of salaried judges. This seems a lot but these statistics are probably inflated because it is not known how many honorary judges are on the list of more than one court. Furthermore, not all honorary judges are involved in the trial of cases on a regular basis. The research by Eskes (1996) sheds no light on the proportion of all cases in which honorary judges participate; he has computed the totals of the cases in which they were involved, but does not present the number of cases in which no honorary judges participated, so the proportion of all cases cannot be established. The 2006 Annual Report on the Judiciary[4] and the 2006 Statistics on the Courts[5] do not contain any information on the percentage of all criminal cases handled with the help of honorary judges in the Netherlands either.

There is a recurrent debate in the Netherlands about whether there is a conflict of interest between the honorary judges' regular jobs and positions and their work for the courts.[6] Such a conflict is not inconceivable, for example, if the honorary judge works at a law firm and his colleagues' clients, or even his own, appeared before the court. Naturally, such conflicts of interest are most likely in civil law or administrative law. However, in criminal cases involving a company or firm as a defendant such situations may occur as well. This debate has over the years moved from a total rejection of the involvement of all types of honorary judges to proposals for advance warnings to the honorary judges and the court, to alert them to potential conflicts of interest and a call to withdraw if this seems to be the case. A heated contribution to this debate has come from certain groups of 'concerned citizens' who have drawn attention to cases where such conflicts of interest were potentially present (Ruijs 2001).

For several years now honorary judges, like professional judges, have had to list their positions, jobs and other relevant occupations for inclusion in a national register. The register, which is kept up-to-date by the courts themselves, can be consulted by anybody who is interested in the backgrounds of judges. Over recent years, as a consequence of the on-going debate, some courts (but not all) have become more hesitant about making use of the services of honorary judges. Previously the majority of all honorary judges worked at a law firm as their regular job. This, however, seems to have changed and now a smaller proportion of the honorary judges do so. Dutch legislators are presently drafting a new law to regulate the involvement of honorary judges. Some courts, however, simply would not be able to deal with their heavy caseloads without their help. Honorary judges will therefore remain a regular feature in the Dutch legal system, although their actual involvement may change in the future (Eskes and de Groot-van Leeuwen 1996).

Judges' Representativeness of the Community

A number of studies have examined the question of whether the Dutch judiciary reflects the population at large and whether its members' views, daily activities and lifestyle differ from that of 'ordinary citizens'. In 2001, 52 per cent of all Dutch judges indicated they believed in God. Most of the

4 *Raad voor de Rechtpraak, Jaarverslag 2006* (Council for the Judiciary, Annual Report, 2006).

5 Source: Council for the Judiciary, 2006.

6 See the various contributions in *De plaatsvervanger*, Prinsengrachtreeks, 1997/2.

professional judges live in a traditional family (husband, wife and children) and only a minority are not married or have a different type of household (Bruinsma 2001). The judges' political preferences have changed over the years; there has been a decline in Christian Democrats and a rise in the more left-wing Liberals, which peaked in 1991. In general, a movement from the right to the left can be discerned within the judiciary, which runs counter to Dutch society as a whole. Women are increasingly involved in the judiciary, but they are still relatively underrepresented at the top of the legal pyramid (Bruinsma 2001; de Groot-van Leeuwen 2006; de Rooij 2007).[7]

Studies have also looked at the social backgrounds of judges. The Dutch judges' fathers' occupations often involved professions like mayor, medical doctor or judge. The judiciary has thus been drawn primarily from the higher social strata, without significant change over the past 30 years (Bruinsma 2001; de Groot-van Leeuwen 2006). De Groot-van Leeuwen (2006) concludes that the Dutch judiciary seems to have an elite character and that in the recruitment of new judges the meritocratic element dominates (de Groot-van Leeuwen 2006).[8] One study has been conducted regarding the participation of minorities in the adjudication of cases. Exact figures regarding the participation of minority groups in the administration of justice in the Netherlands are not available, but more and more young people from minority groups are studying law. However, only a very small minority of legal officers, including judges, are member of an ethnic minority (Böcker and de Groot-van Leeuwen 2007). There probably is no large difference between the professional and the honorary judges on these questions of representativity.

Previous research has explored the reasons for the use of honorary judges who do not plan to move over to the formal judiciary.[9] Keeping decision-making from becoming too isolated, as well as the risk that judges may operate too exclusively in their own private circles, have been mentioned as advantages arising from the contribution of honorary judges. Moreover, the honorary judges' specialization may be helpful for the courts (Eskes 1996; Baauw 1997). For lawyers who work at a law firm, the position as an honorary judge provides an opportunity to gain insight into how the courts work. The increase in the status that being a judge entails would be an important reason for applying as well (Baauw 1997, 16; Zwemmer 1997). The disadvantages have also been discussed in the literature. They include the risk of partiality, the risk that the professional judges would be overruled by external specialists

---

7 Surprisingly, the Dutch Council for the Judiciary is composed of males only, see de Rooij 2007.

8 On meritocracy and democracy, see Bovens 2006.

9 Some of the honorary judges intend becoming full-time judges. They are also called 'honorary judges'. For them, being an honorary judge allows them to become acquainted with the work of the professional judiciary. This group is not the focus of this chapter.

and an increase in the workload with which judges are confronted, because the honorary judges do not assist in writing the court decisions.[10]

The reason why this book looks at honorary judges is that they can provide a perspective on cases from outside that of the salaried judiciary. In this respect honorary judges share certain similarities with the lay judges and jurors participating in other countries. The striking difference with those other lay adjudicators is, of course, that honorary judges are lawyers by training. This means that their distance from the professional judges is less than in countries where 'ordinary' citizens participate. Another difference is their appointment for life: honorary judges offer their services to the court on a permanent basis, whereas lay judges in other countries generally are appointed for a restricted period of time.

The Recruitment and Actual Involvement of Professional and Honorary Judges

In the Netherlands a special committee has been charged with recruiting and selecting judges, including the honorary judges (Selection Committee for the Judiciary[11]). Previously members of the judiciary outnumbered those coming from outside the field by about two-to-one on this committee (Loth 2003). Since a change in the law 50 per cent of the committee's members come from within the judiciary (judges from various courts) and the other 50 per cent come from outside the judiciary. Besides representatives of the Public Prosecutors Department, scholars and representatives from the Bar, universities, the corporate sector and other social institutions are included.[12] It has been argued that this committee should be sufficiently representative for the judiciary as a whole, and that a substantial number of its members should have a background in areas outside of the judiciary (Loth 2003).

Selection criteria for the recruitment of young lawyers include analytical capacity and balanced judgement. 'Orientation towards cooperation' is added as a criterion for those lawyers who wish to enter the judiciary later in their careers (de Groot-van Leeuwen 2006). The procedure for selecting and recruiting new judges, including the honorary judges, has been characterized as 'closed' (Loth 2003). It has also been characterized as co-option, because of the important role that the judiciary itself plays in the procedures (Bovend'Eert 2002). In 2005/2006 courts took the step of asking those honorary judges who were on the role but had never actually made themselves available for a day in court to withdraw. As a consequence, the honorary judges who remain are involved in the trial of cases on a regular basis.

10 For the special risks presented by attorneys acting as honorary judges, see Ingelse 1997.

11 *Selectiecomissie Rechterlijke Macht (SRM)*.

12 Source: information provided by the Council for the Judiciary, 2007.

The actual involvement of honorary judges in the trial of Dutch cases continuously changes. Influenced by the criticisms that have been made over past decades regarding the risk to honorary judges' impartiality, it is now planned that the placement of individual honorary judges in panels be given more careful consideration than was previously the case. At the national level consensus has been reached on procedures that should be employed in this respect.[13]

The group of honorary judges under discussion in this chapter, specifically those who want to remain in their current job, as well as acting as an honorary judge, includes lawyers who enter the ranks of the judiciary after at least six years' experience in some other legal work, for example in a law firm or at the Ministry of Justice (de Groot-van Leeuwen 2006). Many candidates are approached by the courts to take up a position as an honorary judge (Eskes 1996). Some lawyers who wish to become honorary judges contact courts themselves. An increasing number of retired judges also become honorary judges. Honorary judges sit an average of four to 10 days each year. They generally form part of a three-judge panel that decides serious criminal cases. However, cases that are extremely complicated or serious, where there is an expectation that they will take more than one day in court, generally are not tried by panels including honorary judges. Some experienced honorary judges also act as single judges, but this is more unusual.

Honorary judges receive little or no instruction before starting. Being lawyers by training, who will have already collected a certain amount of experience, they are expected to participate from the outset. Dutch literature provides some indication as to how honorary judges experience participation. The motivation for some is to become acquainted with judicial work, to learn about how deliberations are conducted and how cases are tried. Honorary judges generally describe their experiences as 'positive'.[14] However, not all of them applaud the way the professional judges involve them in the trial of cases. Some honorary judges have observed that their participation is, to a certain extent, frustrated because the two other judges on the panel who work as professionals have already decided certain points in advance and present the honorary judge with the outcomes of their deliberations (Arisz 1997).

The Interviews

Of the 14 interviews that were conducted for this part of our research, 11 were conducted face-to-face and three by telephone. Of the professional judges involved in our study (seven), five were male and two female. All honorary

13 Sources: *RechtspraaQ*, www.rechtspraak.nl, *Agenda voor de Rechtspraak*, 2005–2008.

14 See various papers included in *De plaatsvervanger*, Prinsengrachtreeks, 1997/2.

judges interviewed (seven) were male. Most of the professional judges had worked elsewhere before becoming a judge: three had held a position at a university, two had been working for a law firm and one had had various occupations before entering the judiciary. Only one respondent could be considered as a career judge. This sample, thus, is not representative of the Dutch judiciary as a whole.[15]

The professional backgrounds of the honorary judges included teaching at university (3), being an independent advisor, working for a bank, being in business and having worked for the Public Prosecutor's Office (each mentioned by an honorary judge). On balance, most functions seem to be related to the respondents' backgrounds as an academic lawyer.

The numbers of years experience as a judge varied among the respondents, both professional and honorary. For both groups the least experience was less than one year and the greatest 28 (for a professional judge) and 25 (for an honorary judge). The mean number of years of experience was exactly the same for the two groups: 11.7. This substantial amount of experience gained by both types of judges reflects the importance that is attached to professionalism and experience in the Netherlands.

Advantages of Participation by Honorary Judges

The respondents were asked to indicate the advantages of the involvement of honorary judges. A total of 41 advantages were mentioned: 17 by the professional judges and 24 by the honorary judges. Each respondent could list more than one advantage, and each advantage could be brought up by several respondents. In total, 12 different advantages were identified. The professional judges listed an average of 2.4 advantages per respondent, and the honorary judges an average of 3.4 per respondent. The honorary judges thus mentioned relatively more advantages than the professional judges (see Table 5.1).

The advantages mentioned most often included the ease of having honorary judges participate (filling gaps), the different perspectives of honorary judges and the honorary judges' expertise in certain fields. The argument that honorary judges represented an easy way of filling gaps in panels relates to the original reason why honorary judges were introduced in the judiciary: in case of illness or other unforeseen situations, honorary judges may be approached to fill in the gaps in a panel. It is surprising that this argument is mentioned most often by the honorary judges themselves: they seem very modest about their own task performance.

The 'different perspective' argument was mentioned more often by the professional judges than by the lay judges. The argument of expertise was brought up relatively more often by the honorary judges themselves. 'Input

15 About 28 per cent of all Dutch judges have exclusively followed a career as a professional judge after having left university (de Groot-van Leeuwen 2006).

Table 5.1 Advantages of participation by honorary judges, mentioned by professional (7) and by honorary (7) judges (the Netherlands)

	Professional judges	Honorary judges	Total
Filling gaps in a panel	2	5	7
Different perspectives	5	2	7
Honorary judges' expertise	3	4	7
Input from outside the judiciary	4	2	6
Against routine	2	2	4
Widening honorary judges' horizons	–	2	2
Introduction of human feelings	–	2	2
Honorary judges' experience in society	–	2	2
Experience with other methods of working	–	1	1
Interesting to do	–	1	1
Honorary judges need to think less about career	–	1	1
Lunch is nicer with honorary judges	1	–	1
Total advantages: 12	*17*	*24*	*41*

from outside the judiciary' was valued more by professional judges (4) than by honorary judges (2).

The other advantages were mentioned less often. Two professional judges and two honorary judges presented the advantage that honorary judges prevent professional judges from falling too deeply into routine. The honorary judges mentioned several advantages that the professional judges did not bring up, such as a broadening of their own horizons, the introduction of emotions and of different kinds of experience into trials (each mentioned twice) and the chance to obtain experience of other methods of working, for example, 'it is very interesting to be involved', 'unlike the salaried judges, I do not have to think about my own career' (each mentioned by one honorary judge). One professional judge listed as an advantage that he enjoyed lunches with the honorary judges much more than with professional judges only.

Explanations

The respondents gave various explanations for the advantages that were mentioned. In particular, the 'different perspectives' and the 'input from outside the judiciary' arguments received substantial attention. Two professional judges remarked that the circle of persons with whom they work is small and of a private nature. Including someone from outside this circle every now and then could lead to a fresh input. Some felt that the judiciary is a very closed group, or even elite. A good honorary judge may alert you to relevant points in a case that might otherwise be overlooked. Honorary judges have not been affected by the daily routine of dealing with cases. 'When you have worked for years in the professional judiciary, you become immune to things that go wrong in the organization or with the trial of cases. An honorary judge may make you aware again of what happens and what goes wrong', a professional judge remarked.

Honorary judges are not expected to participate in the 'formalities' that have to be taken care of by the court. Their contribution is valued most by the professional judges at the fact-finding stage. The heavy caseload with which professional judges are confronted brings certain risks with it. 'Some professional judges have too little life experience. When they are confronted with particular problems, they tend to ignore them. Honorary judges may prevent this happening', a professional judge observed. Professional judges would too easily think, 'This is the way we do such things'. In the long term, they tend to forget why they do certain things the way they do them. An honorary judge inquiring why certain things are dealt with in a particular way may force the professional judges to question themselves as to why they use certain procedures, and if they are carried out correctly. As with the professional judges, several honorary judges mentioned the restricted circles within which professional judges operate. Honorary judges consider themselves as more 'streetwise' than the professional judges.

The advantages for the honorary judges themselves lie primarily in broadening their own horizons. They indicate that individuals come before them as defendants who they would never meet outside of their court life. Others emphasize that they bring expertise to the trial of cases that the court lacks or which the court has no time to collect. Some honorary judges make overviews of judicial decisions in certain types of cases. The professional judges are clearly helped by these surveys because they have too little time to do such things themselves.

One honorary judge held the view that he was more independent than the professionals, because he did not have to take his own career into consideration. According to this respondent, professional judges are part of the 'system' and they would, as a consequence, constantly feel watched by their colleagues. Honorary judges do not experience that pressure and would thus be more free to say whatever they want about a case. On this point, differences can be observed among the honorary judges. Younger honorary judges seem to experience more pressure from the system to perform correctly, to ask the right questions and to make the right remarks than older honorary judges. In general, professional judges seem to want to account for their decisions in the first place to *other* judges, while honorary judges do not think in such a directly hierarchical line. This view was endorsed by one of the honorary judges.

Disadvantages of Participation of Honorary Judges

A smaller number of disadvantages than advantages were noted: 18 compared to 41. A total of nine different disadvantages were identified, with professional judges mentioning exactly the same number of disadvantages as the honorary judges. Both groups of respondents, the professionals and the honorary judges, mentioned an average of 1.3 disadvantages per respondent (see Table 5.2).

The most noted disadvantage by far was the lesser input that honorary judges have in the trial of the case. Four professional judges and three honorary judges indicated this as a disadvantage. Lack of knowledge was mentioned by three professional judges but by none of the honorary judges. The involvement of honorary judges was considered impractical by two honorary judges: because they are not always present in court, they can less easily be involved in handling cases. They generally do not assist in writing the verdict, nor do they generally preside over court sessions (see Table 5.2).

Table 5.2 Disadvantages of participation by honorary judges mentioned by professional (7) and by honorary (7) judges (the Netherlands)

	Professional judges	Honorary judges	Total
Less input by honorary judges	4	3	7
Lack of knowledge	3	–	3
Impractical	–	2	2
Risk of inequality of law	1	–	1
Takes more time	1	–	1
Takes relatively more time for myself	–	1	1
Unfamiliar with what happens in organization	–	1	1
Risk of partiality	–	1	1
Honorary judges sometimes want to change system	–	1	1
Total disadvantages: 9	*9*	*9*	*18*

The remaining disadvantages include the following: uniformity of law may decrease if too many persons from outside the judiciary participate; trials take more time because honorary judges need more explanation (both mentioned by one professional judge). Other disadvantages included it taking a relatively large amount of time for the honorary judges themselves, as a lot of work is involved in preparing for the trial; honorary judges not being familiar with general customs within the judiciary; the risk of partiality; and that some honorary judges may, incorrectly, have the feeling that they can change the system (all mentioned by one honorary judge).

Explanations

Respondents were requested to give explanations for why they considered a certain aspect to be a disadvantage. According to the professional judges interviewed, efficiency is reduced when one of the three judges in the panel is not as experienced as the others, leading to a higher workload for the other two judges. In general, honorary judges do not know how certain problems are solved and how formalities have to be dealt with. They cannot make a useful contribution on such aspects. A professional judge indicated that in a situation where he sits with both an inexperienced judge and an honorary judge on a panel, he feels as if he is trying the case alone.

Some of the honorary judges have the feeling of being superfluous. 'I sometimes feel like a piece of furniture. I have never presided over a court session. That is not because I would not be able to do that, but because I know too little about how that is generally done.' In some types of cases honorary judges have the impression that they are only called to complete the panel, and not because of their expertise. This is, for example, the case in trials where preventive custody is prolonged. The law stipulates a panel consisting of three judges. However, the honorary judge does not receive copies of the case file in advance, and thus is not fully acquainted with what the case is about. Only the chairperson of the panel is expected to ask questions during these procedures. As a consequence, honorary judges feel they are being used for 'filling robes' rather than for hearing cases in collaboration with the professional judges.

One honorary judge made a comparison with the company where he works. There he is appraised at regular intervals. He has meetings with his superiors at least once a year about his own performance. That does not happen in court regarding his work as an honorary judge; he never receives feedback about how he functions as a judge and whether the court is satisfied with the way he performs his duties. He blames the professional judges for not helping and stimulating the honorary judges to perform better.

Cooperation between professional and honorary judges

Most professional judges interviewed indicated they enjoyed working together with honorary judges, but not all of them were highly enthusiastic. Two of them added that they would not mind working with professional judges only. In their experience honorary judges did not contribute very much to the decision that had to be made. The degree of the honorary judge's experience and expertise can make a difference; the professional judges favour having experienced honorary judges on a panel. Sometimes the enjoyment of having them on a panel depends on the honorary judge's personality. But when highly complex cases, or a great many cases on one day have to be tried, it is more efficient not to have an honorary judge on your panel. One professional judge, however, emphasized that he does not always want to collaborate with professional judges only. He has a clear preference for working with judges from outside the salaried judiciary.

Honorary Judges' Input

All professional judges were of the opinion that honorary judges provide less input in the trial of cases. Three out of the seven honorary judges however thought that their input was equal to that of the salaried judges; the other four assessed their input as smaller. The honorary judges thus have a more positive view of their actual contribution. The respondents made clear that honorary judges ask fewer questions than their professional colleagues during the hearing of the case. With respect to the deliberations about the case, after the hearing in open court, the general opinion was that the actual participation between professional and honorary judges is about equal.

More often than their salaried counterparts, honorary judges have the impression that they make the professional judges see a case in a different light.[16] Some of them gave examples in which they had been more aware of the legal implications of certain states of affairs than the professional judges were. Others recounted how, by going against the judges' general customs and the regular way of thinking of the court, they were able to influence a discussion. Still others pointed to their own expertise; when issues arose in a specific field during a case, they were able to steer the deliberations in a certain direction and influence decision making. However, two honorary judges stated that they had never been able to make the court see the case in a different light.

A professional judge recalled the years when he had been an honorary judge himself, preparing for the time that he would be a full-time judge.

> In the beginning, I behaved terribly as an honorary judge. But by doing so, I was able to set things in motion. There is a danger, as in all professions, that the salaried judges know too well how things work. Some things have become too self-evident for them; they take things for granted which in fact aren't. Since I have become a full-time judge, I try to remain alert that the defendant understands the case. We sometimes attend cases tried by our colleagues, to have a look how others deal with cases.

Five out of the seven professional judges were of the opinion that it is easy to reach consensus when dealing with cases together with the honorary judges. If there are differences of opinion, they are mostly on the point of sentencing. Honorary judges, by their restricted experience, lack a frame of reference on

16 The respondents were asked whether honorary judges sometimes do make the professional judges see the case in a different light. Two out of the seven professional judges and five out of the seven honorary judges have experienced this at least once in their career.

this point. The professionals can, by referring to other cases, easily convince the honorary judge of their standpoint. The professional judges made it clear that most honorary judges are prepared to accept the sentences that are generally imposed for certain crimes and to adjust their views to those of the professionals. It is general custom that during deliberations about a case, the least experienced judge gives his or her opinion first. Often honorary judges are asked to present their views first. Many honorary judges interviewed expressed their uncertainty regarding the level of punishment that they might propose in such situations. Their lack of experience on this point is reflected in their lack of confidence about what to propose regarding the sentence. This means that many honorary judges are rather reticent about presenting their views.

Most professional judges asserted that the honorary judges sentence with about equal severity as the professional judges. On the other hand four out of the seven honorary judges had the impression that they tended to sentence more leniently than the professional judges who more frequently want an unconditional sentence. Two honorary judges made it clear that in drug cases, in particular, they tend to punish more leniently than the professional judges. They noted that in drug cases there are few opportunities to discuss each case in depth, simply because of the volume of them. In these cases honorary judges believed they were more sensitive to personal circumstances than the professional judges, which led to less severe sentences.

One honorary judge observed that the use of sentencing guidelines that circulate within the courts is not always clear and unambiguous. Those guidelines are not, as a general rule, handed over to the honorary judges. With respect to disclosing case files to the honorary judges, it is not always clear which types of documents should customarily be given and which not. This particular honorary judge was of the impression that such issues could be better organized by the courts.

A number of respondents observed that too little time is set aside for dealing with cases. Judges have to work under extreme time pressure; they are increasingly expected to deliver 'product': court decisions that bring the case to an end, at least in that instance. One consequence is that they cannot spend lots of time on each case. One honorary judge stated that professional judges are less confident and courageous now than they used to be. They have become more afraid that when they regularly express a view on a case that differs from those of their colleagues, they will be seen as out of step with their peers. They might be treated as outcasts, and their career prospects might be hindered. He is of the opinion that judges should be less afraid to say what they think about a case and to come up with their own, independent judgement.

An honorary judge remarked that he was happy that honorary judges have a background and experience in law. He does not understand the current desire to involve lay people in the trial of cases. But he accepts that this is in line with general tendencies in society: citizens wish to have influence. After a number of miscarriages of justice, the public fears that other cases may go wrong as well. It is felt that judges do not sufficiently explain their decisions. Therefore, citizens want to participate. Speaking personally, this honorary judge thought that the solution would be better sought in improving the legal system. Increasing the quality, giving a rationale for decisions, the apparent fairness of the trial and the integrity of the judges would seem to be a better solution.

The Influence of Experience

Do the opinions of honorary judges change over the course of time as a consequence of gaining experience as a judge? A difference emerged between the professional judges' and the honorary judges' views on this issue. Four out of the seven professional judges had the impression that the honorary judges' opinions change as a consequence of experience, whereas only two out of the seven honorary judges held that view. Honorary judges thus emphasized the continuity in their own views, where the professional judges recorded a change.

The inclination to conform with the professional judges was stressed by several respondents. 'You adjust to the system. And you create your own frame of reference. Extreme candidates have already been filtered out by the Selection Committee that recruits new judges', a professional judge observed. Over the long run, honorary judges accept the way procedures are shaped and followed. They learn while practicing. As several honorary judges made clear, that does not necessarily imply that their views on cases changed; they merely adjust to the frame of reference that is used within the professional judiciary.

The honorary judges stressed that they had learned a lot since they began: they see the people who are tried before them in court, and they realize the sadness of so many lives. Some honorary judges thought that the system had moderated, becoming more human. The interaction with the defendant is now less formal; less distance is maintained in communicating with the defendant now than was formerly customary.

Some of them expressed their admiration for the professional judges, and the great efficiency and skill with which they deal with their heavy caseloads. In the morning they may try a burglary and a number of smaller cases, and in the afternoon a high profile murder case may be dealt with. And after that, they still have to deliberate about the defendants' guilt and the sentences. This may go on late into the evening. Many people outside the salaried judiciary, including the honorary judges, are impressed by the heavy caseloads of the courts and the burden that trying such serious cases forms for them.

Emotions

Six out of the seven professional judges observed that honorary judges are about equally emotional during the hearing of cases as they are themselves. The majority of the honorary judges (four out of the seven) however felt that the honorary judges are more emotional. The professional judges made clear that no obvious emotional differences exist between professional judges and, as far as emotions might play a role, this would be diminished and counteracted by the other members of the panel. A number of respondents pointed to the selection procedure for honorary judges: those persons selected are impartial and independent. They are expected to be able to act with distance. In the same vein, honorary judges would not be more influenced by media reporting than the professional judges.

One professional judge recounted that when he started as a judge he had suffered from headaches at regular intervals. He had difficulties with locking offenders up in prison. Others too acknowledged that the court sessions increase tension for the judges on the panel. They have to get used to this tension. In general, honorary judges are not involved in very serious cases that fill more than one day; those cases are dealt with exclusively by professional judges. But nevertheless, the hearing of cases is strenuous and it consumes the energy of both the honorary judges and the professional judiciary.

Several honorary judges admitted that they had certain emotions when dealing with cases. But these must not prevail during the handling of a case; all respondents agreed on that point. A professional judge observed that he was glad that he was not sitting as a lay person, not knowing anything about the legal system: 'real', inexperienced lay persons probably would suffer too much from their emotions and would not sufficiently understand what the cases were about.

Acceptance of Court Decisions

Most of the respondents were of the opinion that court decisions are not better accepted because of the participation of honorary judges. The reason most often mentioned is that participants and the public are simply not aware an honorary judge is sitting on a panel, because all three judges wear the same robes and bands. What counts is that correct procedures are applied in court, not the composition of the panel. And even if the public knew, most thought it would make no difference either. According to the respondents, it is far more important that the judges, prosecutors and the defence lawyers listen well to the defendant and the other participants at trial and that the hearing of the case takes place according to the law and in a fair manner.

One honorary judge thought that participation by honorary judges might exert a certain influence on the acceptance of court decisions. He felt that if people knew that judges with certain relevant posts outside the judiciary participate in a trial, they would accept the decision better. The input of such participants should therefore be made more visible. Experience in society has to be used in court and the participants who possess that type of experience should let their voice be heard more loudly in the panel.

Importance Accorded to the Participation of Ordinary Citizens

The respondents were questioned about their views on participation by 'ordinary' lay people in the administration of justice. None of the professional judges interviewed attached any importance to the participation of ordinary citizens in the criminal justice system, whereas three out of the seven honorary judges considered this important. Various arguments were given for *not* introducing lay adjudication in the legal system. Among them were that the quality of the handling of cases would decrease if lay persons participated. Others were that it would be too time-consuming, that the Dutch in which the indictments are phrased is far too complicated to be understood by lay people and that the changes in the system which would be required for introducing a lay element would be too radical. The complete Code of Criminal Procedure would have to be rewritten if lay persons were requested to participate. Moreover, lay people would not have had a different opinion on cases such as the *Schiedammer Parkmoord*.[17] In general, it was felt that it would not be efficient to have lay people on a panel – and it did not fit Dutch legal culture.

The professional judges insisted that they are not out of touch with the real world, so lay people are not necessary to give them insight into how society operates. It was felt that openness and transparency are more important than including lay adjudication in the legal system. Furthermore, professional judges would be more critical towards defendants who deny their guilt than inexperienced judges. Lay people would not be able to acquire sufficient experience for developing such a critical attitude, because they only sit every now and then.

Many respondents expressed their adherence to the professionalism of the Dutch legal system. 'Trying cases is a real profession; weighing interests, considering the legal consequences of the facts. But also, listening to the statements, being alert that sufficient time is given for dealing with cases', a professional judge explained.

There were also professional judges who, while not favouring lay adjudication, did acknowledge the risk that professional judges might become too isolated and create their own incontestable image of the world. These respondents observed that it could not be ruled out that such judges become insensitive to views other than their own. Professional judges sometimes have

17 A high profile Dutch case concerning the murder of a little girl. The man convicted in the case later appeared to have been innocent, after another man confessed and was convicted for the crime.

their own language. Care has to be taken that this does not escalate, these respondents warned.

The respondents who were not entirely against lay participation were found only among the group of honorary judges. But none of them was fully in favour of lay adjudication either. They generally took the position that there are no serious objections against lay participation in minor cases, or they were proponents of more involvement of expertise in the trial of cases. But they did not expect miracles from the introduction of the lay element into the legal system.

Other honorary judges were strictly against participation by lay people. One of them stated:

> Lay people would, in such a situation, be dominated by the professionals. They would be tolerated, but would be expected to adjust to the professionals at the same time. You have to be a member of the 'club' to become accepted by the judiciary. And lay people have no expertise. They have no insight in cases. Expertise is much better than the *Gesundenes Volksempfinden*.

Another respondent said:

> Trying cases is a profession. You go to the bakery for bread, and to the judge for a legal decision. When you are not happy about the bread you are not going to bake it yourself, and the same applies for the law. I do not understand why lay judges would be desirable. I do not become a lay doctor myself either. I would not go to lay doctors. You must have studied law to become a judge, you must collect experience, talk about it, update your expertise. Then you reach quality. We should never introduce lay people!

Ivory Tower

The majority of the respondents were of the opinion that Dutch judges are sufficiently in touch with the real world: six out of the seven professional judges and five out of the seven honorary judges. Nevertheless, respondents gave certain examples where a judge seemed to live in an ivory tower. Some judges only communicate with members of their own, private circle. They lack a connection with other parts of society.

One professional judge felt that some judges clearly are out of touch with the community. They are vain, and would not tolerate other opinions. He observed that they can primarily be found among the group of career judges who never worked outside the judiciary. Career judges were more likely to be out of touch with real life than judges who had first had occupations outside the judiciary. They were perhaps naïve because of their lack of experience outside the system. 'You can identify them by the fact that they never let other people end their sentences when they speak. They remain in their own circle and never come into contact with other people. Someone from outside the judiciary, like an honorary judge, can help to overcome this defect.' Another professional judge contended that it was important for professional judges to have activities outside the judiciary, such as sitting on Boards of Directors, or fulfilling other duties. Many judges only have their position as a judge and they sometimes develop strange views that are not corrected by the people surrounding them.

Some honorary judges stressed the social connections of judges. Most judges have children, which makes them more open to developments in society. They are generally on the left of the political spectrum, or at least they are not conservative.

In the 1960s there were more judges living in ivory towers than there are now, an honorary judge maintained. They were colourful people, but not in a positive sense; in a way these judges were too eccentric. Such judges are no longer found in the judiciary, the respondent made clear. 'The selection procedures and the training of judges has contributed to their disappearance. Earlier, the element of co-option was more dominant than it is now. The selection has been streamlined. Eccentric persons have been filtered out.' The judge indicated that he was happy with this development. The eccentric views on specific types of crime, for example, or certain types of defendant, have disappeared. There is now a more open debate during deliberations on the cases than there used to be.

Dissemination

All the honorary judges indicated that they talk about their experiences in court to their families, friends and colleagues. They spoke mostly about the cases they tried, but also about their cooperation with the professional judges and about their own dilemmas and emotions while trying cases. Their experiences as a judge produced interesting stories that could be told at home. When colleagues said something negative about the system, the honorary judges could inform them about how the system works in reality. In doing so, they tried to educate the people they talk to. Some had taken their partner with them to a court session. Beyond their direct family and friends, they were more reserved in telling what happened in the cases they tried. The trial of cases was not a theatre or an exhibition. The deliberations are secret and no dissenting opinions are allowed to be made public in the Netherlands. When speaking to students, the honorary judges passed on a lot about how the system works, and how judges operate. Some honorary judges only talked about their experiences within the family; they did not share it with friends, because they could never be certain where they would go with the information they received.

Being Kept Awake at Night

Surprisingly, more professional judges recounted being kept awake at night by the decisions they have to make in court than honorary judges: three out of the seven professional judges compared to only one honorary judge. Those who indicated *not* being kept awake said that nevertheless they were regularly concerned about the decisions they had to make. This is a good sign, because it shows that they are committed to their work.

Some of the professional judges indicated that they were kept awake when they started as a judge, but that they learned to be professionally detached in due course. Of all types of criminal cases, those regarding sexual crimes or those with small children as victims produce most concern for the judges. One honorary judge was glad that he had to travel for some time after a court session before arriving home. This gave him the opportunity to reflect on the cases he had decided and to gain distance from them.

Others emphasized the defendant's opportunity to appeal. This reassured them; there is still a higher court that might examine the case and make the final decision. In the beginning, some honorary judges found it hard to send someone to prison; they found the decision to lock someone up onerous. But someone has to make these decisions and if they did not assume this responsibility, someone else would have to do it. 'If you are too deeply bothered by the decisions you have to make as a judge, you have chosen the wrong job, you better not have a function in the judiciary or the prosecution. We reflect on a case and make a decision. After that decision is made, you have to stop thinking about it', an honorary judge said.

Conclusions

The views presented in this chapter reveal that no insurmountable differences exist between the professional and the honorary judges. Most respondents were reasonably happy with the involvement of honorary judges. Collaboration generally goes well and the perspectives of the two groups do not seem to diverge greatly. With respect to the emotions that are experienced by the two types of judges, no large differences were observed either. The reason for that may be that honorary judges can also be considered as 'professionals' due to their legal training and their experience in functions similar to those of a judge or at least requiring a certain degree of formal education. The public is unaware that one of the members of a panel is not a salaried judge. Acceptance of court decisions thus is not influenced by the participation of honorary judges. It would seem that neither professional nor honorary judges are often kept awake at night by the decisions they have to make.

As far as discrepancies between the two groups can be discerned, they relate to the issue of perceived advantages and disadvantages of the participation of honorary judges, their actual input during trials and the importance they attach to opportunities for participation by ordinary citizens. Honorary judges more often think that the reason for their involvement is that it is easy, practical and cheap. Some honorary judges feel superfluous and consider that not all salaried judges do their best to dispel the impression that their input is not valued. When it comes to the actual hearing of the case and the forming of a judgement, honorary judges largely remain in the background. They ask fewer questions and they lack a frame of reference regarding the sentences that are generally imposed. More honorary judges than professional judges are in favour of participation by 'ordinary citizens' in the trial of criminal cases: none of the latter group is a proponent of involvement of 'real' lay people, while three honorary judges think that this possibility might deserve more attention.

It is surprising that topics such as a potential risk to the bench's impartiality caused by the involvement of honorary judges went almost unmentioned by the respondents. By contrast, this topic was the most frequent in the literature and in the previous discussions that have been conducted. Apparently the judiciary, both professional and honorary, presently is less concerned about this aspect of the participation of honorary judges than they were in the 1990s.

The literature suggests that aspects such as the status that is derived from being an honorary judge and, on the other hand, the lowering of the professional judge's status when he or she has to sit with an honorary judge, do play a role in the views of judges.[18] Such issues hardly came up in our research. Respondents in a face-to-face interview, however, probably are more reluctant to touch upon such issues than when writing an article or a contribution to a book.

One of the conspicuous issues that emerged during our study is the severe time pressure under which Dutch judges have to deal with cases. Both the professional and the honorary judges remarked on this point. The heavy caseload stands in the way of a thorough and serious treatment of all cases. Not all cases seem to receive the attention they need. Related to this point is that Dutch judges seem to work under considerable psychological pressure from their colleagues. There is an explicit and implicit pressure towards unity of law. Guidelines are increasingly used in courts and there is a pressure to reach 'targets' and to pronounce as many sentences as possible. Perhaps the honorary judges, who are not in court every day, are better able to sense such pressure than the judges who spend most of their time there. Respondents also perceive a pressure to adjust to what is customarily decided and to accept the procedures that are regularly used in court. In particular the honorary judges highlighted this pressure, both on themselves and on the 'regular' judges. By the same token, the professional judges with whom they work notice that the

---

18 See the various papers in *De plaatsvervanger*, Prinsengrachtreeks, 1997/2; Eskes 1996; Eskes and de Groot-van Leeuwen 1996.

honorary judges adjust to this pressure, especially when forming an opinion on the sentence.

This type of pressure can be expected to be even stronger if the size of the group is strictly limited and, at the same time, has relatively little contact with people outside their own circle. That, however, seems not to be the overwhelming picture of the Dutch professional judiciary: most respondents indicate that Dutch judges do not live in an ivory tower. A few respondents remarked, however, on the risks that operating in a small, exclusive group may have for the forming of judgements in individual cases. The lack of experience of life was noted as contributing to this risk. A number of professional judges stressed the importance of having responsibilities outside the judiciary, or first working elsewhere before accepting a post as a permanent judge.

Scholars have observed that in the Netherlands the circles in which lawyers operate are interwoven to a large extent (de Groot van Leeuwen 2005). Participation by minority groups in these circles remains limited. In principle, most judges are in favour of a judiciary that reflects the community, but actual practice has shown that this is, at this time, not the case, either in the Netherlands or in other countries (Böcker and de Groot-van Leeuwen 2007). Research has revealed that there is at least some – and increasing – diversity in the judiciary with respect to characteristics such as occupation of parents, political preferences, occupations and gender. But on the point of the balance between white and non-white judges, the judiciary in most countries is not diverse at present (de Groot-van Leeuwen 2005). Thus, although some changes can be observed in the homogeneous composition of the Dutch judiciary over the past decades, there remains a risk of a certain isolation from the outside world. On the one hand, the Dutch judiciary has reached an extremely high level of professionalism and specialization; on the other, it still allows for relatively few audits and evaluations of the judges' work by the outside world.

Several respondents referred to the various procedures that are generally used in court, of which the honorary judges are ignorant. Formalities and customs play a large role in the trial of Dutch criminal cases, and it is considered impractical that honorary judges are unaware of them. It seems that the criminal justice system has been organized in such a way that it cannot flexibly adjust to the input of non-professional judges who are not fully knowledgeable about how things are generally done, even though the honorary judges share an equal background in legal training with the professional judges.

Nevertheless, the contribution of honorary judges in the administration of justice is generally positively valued. As mentioned by the professional judges, it provides an 'outsider's' perspective which is generally viewed as an advantage It will in the future remain an important part of the work done in the courts.

Chapter 6
Expert Participation in Dutch Procedures

The previous chapter discussed the participation of *lawyers* who are not a formal part of the judiciary in the administration of justice – the honorary judges. This chapter focuses on the involvement of *experts* in the hearing of cases in the Netherlands. Three types of court are explored: the Agricultural Tenancies division of the District Court,[1] the specialized court that hears cases concerning the execution of sentences (Execution of Sentences division of the Arnhem Court of Appeal[2]) and the Company and Business Court in Amsterdam.[3] Our study is restricted to these three procedures involving experts, because the main emphasis in this book is on criminal law and the involvement of people whose participation is *not* due to a particular expertise. This being the case, no notice is given to procedures like arbitration, mediation and disciplinary law in their varying forms.

The following sections describe the three courts and the ways experts are involved in them. Face-to-face interviews were conducted with both the professional judges and experts involved in these courts. For each of the three procedures, four participants consented to an interview. This chapter starts with a discussion of the Company and Business Court, after which the Execution of Sentences Court and the Agricultural Tenancies Courts are dealt with.

The Companies and Business Court

As an independent judicial authority, the Companies and Business Court (hereafter: Companies Court) that forms part of the Amsterdam Court of Appeal has specific jurisdiction on legal disputes on all sorts of business-related issues. It deals with, among other things, the setting up of inquiries into the conduct of companies, rulings on takeover battles, matters concerning annual reports and financial statements, buyouts of minority stakeholders, private law expropriation by one shareholder of the shares of another shareholder in cases where there is an 'irretrievable breakdown' between the two, mergers, divisions of companies and the participation of works councils in the process of corporate decision making (Josephus Jitta et al. 2004). Among disputes of this sort, three come before this court most frequently. The inquiry procedure

1 *Pachtkamer.*
2 *Penitentiaire Kamer, Hof Arnhem.*
3 *Ondernemingskamer van het Hof Amsterdam.*

is the most visible and most often requested type of process. Procedures instigated by works councils when a company's board has not complied with the legal rules concerning the works council's right of advice make up another significant proportion of all cases before the court. A third quantitatively important type of dispute is one in which a company's accounts and audits are at stake.[4]

In an inquiry procedure the Companies Court gives specified powers to experts and investigators to examine how a company is run by its Board of Directors and Supervisory Board.[5] If this inquiry demonstrates that mismanagement of the company has taken place, the Companies Court has a wide variety of powers at its disposal to intervene in the company and its affairs. The court cannot only declare that the company was badly managed, it can also establish who among the directors is to blame and it can, if it thinks that this is appropriate, dismiss executive and non-executive board members, appoint executive and non-executive board members, annul decisions of the board or of the general meeting of shareholders, alter the articles of association and suspend voting rights (Willems 2004). The law grants the right to request an inquiry to a number of distinct categories of applicants: holders of shares or depositary receipts who represent a certain percentage of the issued share capital of the company, persons who are authorized by law to do so, trade unions and the public prosecutor of the Court of Appeal in Amsterdam (Josephus Jitta et al. 2004).

A slightly different type of jurisdiction of the Companies Court is laid down in the 1971 Statute on Works Councils. Every enterprise employing more than 50 people has to set up a works council[6] with whom the management must discuss a number of specified matters and which has the right to advise the board of the company how to decide on matters of 'strategic importance'. For example, if the board of a company has decided to shut down one of the company's plants contrary to the works council's advice, the latter can request a decision by the Companies Court. If this court considers the complaint of the works council well founded, it can declare the company's decision null and void and prevent the board from executing it (Willems 2004). This type of law ('co-determination law', see Kemperink 2004) reflects the Dutch social model of consensus. Strategic decisions in Dutch companies are usually not the result of direct, top-down management actions and decisions. On the contrary, they often result from lengthy and exhaustive discussions among stakeholders in the company (management, strategic shareholders, works council and labour unions). This notion of consensus can also be found in the governance of large Dutch companies. The board of supervisory directors is regarded as a

4 Annual Report of the Companies and Business Court, 2005.

5 This procedure is very rare in the world. See Josephus Jitta et al. 2004, 1–42.

6 *Ondernemingsraad.*

cohesive body which is obliged to serve all interests that are present within the company, including shareholders and employees (Kemperink 2004).

The way the Companies Court reaches its decisions reflects this culture of consensus as well. The court assesses whether the varying interests affected by a proposed management decision have been properly considered. By doing this, the court tests the contents of the management decisions. It touches on the business rationale of the decision in its judicial review (Kemperink 2004).

The Companies Court was established by parliament in 1971. This law not only created a new type of court, but also a new set of legal rules; one might even say a whole new branch of law has emerged since (Willems 2004). The court is composed of not only professional judges. 'Lay' judges, such as former members of the boards of listed companies like DSM NV or Akzo Nobel NV and chartered accountants, take part in the decision making by this court. The composition of the court is five judges, among whom are three professional judges and two from the group of 'lay judges'. These 'lay judges', however, have been primarily selected and appointed to this court because of their specific knowledge and expertise relevant to the Companies Court. In reality they are to be considered as 'experts' who generally do not possess legal training.

Although this Companies Court is part of the Amsterdam Court of Appeal, it is a first instance court. There is no 'regular' appeal available from the decisions of this court, but there is the possibility of an appeal to the Dutch Court of Cassation.

Observations

The Companies Court sits in one of the courtrooms of the Amsterdam Court of Appeal. In the session that was attended by the researcher, the panel was composed of elderly males only. Indeed, all participants in this trial were males, with the exception of one of the lawyers for the defendant and the clerk; they were both females in their 30s. The judges wear black robes and white bands and the experts are in their everyday clothing. Apart from the members of the court, only lawyers for the parties are present at this type of trial. The trial is not easily comprehensible for a visitor who is not well acquainted with the sort of procedures dealt with in this court. The president spoke rather softly. The lawyers for the parties, who take the most prominent role during the lawsuit, were much more audible. The public seemed not to be interested in this particular case. However, other trials of this court certainly do attract attention; indeed some cases it deals with have been widely covered by the media.

Views of Judges and Experts

In total, the Companies Court has seven professional judges and 15 experts at its disposal. The researchers approached the chairman of the court to request the court's cooperation and he gave names of potential respondents. One judge and three experts participated in an interview. The topics of these interviews included the way in which the experts are recruited and how they are prepared for their post, their experiences while performing their tasks and their views regarding the participation of experts and lay persons in legal procedures.

The professional backgrounds of the experts interviewed varied. One was a financial expert who has been a Chief Financial Officer (CFO) in a large company. One had been a chartered accountant at one of the largest accountancy firms in the world and has also had a position at a university. One had been member of the board of the largest national trade union. All were male.

The judge characterized this court as an institution that has no equal in the world. The court '"runs" companies and acts as a "company doctor" at the same time'. Apart from the court itself, there are 120 experts, advisors, investigators and others working in companies all over the country. They conduct investigations and temporarily take over the governance of companies. The judge further enumerated the powers of the Companies Court: 'We can discharge directors and members of the supervisory boards. We intervene in companies. We take care of the case law regarding company law, as well as in the field of co-decision procedures and worker participation'.

The Companies Court can be regarded as a judicial body with specialized experts in it. Most of the decisions that are made by this court are not juridical in nature, the judge explained. The court decides on the balance of power within companies and on corporate governance. 'Our level of decision-making is intellectually high, we work multidisciplinary. We have many powers. We can send the top of the company home.'

The Appointment and Actual Participation of Experts

In the interviews, attention was given to how the experts are recruited, the role they played in the handling of the cases by this court and how they and the professional judges perceived their participation.

The number of years that the interviewed experts had formed part of the Companies Court were 19, eight and six years, respectively. All had been asked to become involved in the court and thus had not applied on their own initiative. One respondent explained:

> When I retired from my regular position in a company, I was instantly asked to come here. Now I have to retire from the Companies Court as well. It is usual that each expert, when retiring from the court, takes care of finding

> someone who can take his place. It is expected that you deliver someone who is 'better than you are yourself'. A candidate first has a meeting with the Companies Court's chairman and then with the president of the Court of Appeals of Amsterdam. I have myself suggested two persons to the chairman as a candidate to succeed me, and the first one was chosen by him.

The other two experts interviewed confirmed this procedure for recruiting new members for the Companies Court. They entered the court in a similar way.

Generally the experts have about eight to 10 sittings each year. In large and complex cases, experts who have gained considerable expertise in the Companies Court are placed on the panel. But for the remaining cases, no explicit choice is made as to who sits on which case. In principle, one chartered accountant has to be part of each panel in the Companies Court.

Experts are not instructed at all before having their first sitting at the Companies Court. The experts only have a brief meeting with the chairman of the court before their first sitting; there is no further preparation. During the interviews, all three made clear that they were not concerned about the lack of prior instruction. Coming from the world of large companies and trade unions themselves, they already knew a lot about what is going on in this court and the types of disputes that are resolved.

However, reading the case files – customarily sent to all participants in the court a couple of weeks before the trial – and acquiring an adequate overview of what the specific cases are about, appears to be difficult at the beginning. 'When I started, the case file was a mess to me. All types of documents are in it. It was difficult to detect a line in it. It seemed a jumble of facts to me', one of the experts related. The respondents made clear that over time they learned how to read a file and how to form a judgement on a case.

The judge confirmed that new members of the court are not instructed beforehand.

> That is not necessary. They belong to the top in their own field. They sit on the bench as if they have not done anything else in their lives. Sometimes they ask me a question about a legal matter. I then say that they do not have to know anything about the legal aspects, the professional judges take care of that. They do not have to master the legal details. We do that. Thanks to the experts I, in turn, have learned a lot about accountancy.

Opinions on the Involvement of Experts

The advantages of the involvement of the experts, as described by the respondents, centre around the expertise and experience that they introduce into the procedure. The professional judges lack practical knowledge; they only have the case file at their disposal and they have to base their judgement exclusively on that. They generally do not know what goes on during shareholders meetings, or in boardrooms of big companies, but the experts do. The experts have knowledge of how companies are run. When it comes to writing the court decision, the judges have to do that. They take care of the legal framework of the decisions. One of the experts explained, 'It is the cooperation between the professional judges and the experts that is so beneficial and satisfying. We work in a team, we know each other well, we like each other, we are aware of each others' strengths and weaknesses'. The judge was of the opinion that the experts are indispensable for this court.

The disadvantages that are mentioned mirror the advantages: experts have no part in resolving the legal issues. There is a certain risk in having the two types of professionals enter each other's domain. However, none of the respondents seemed to consider these disadvantages a serious impediment to the adequate functioning of the Companies Court. The expertise of the non-legal members of the court is considered to be complementary to that of the legal participants, so there is little risk of role confusion. In general the input of the experts does not differ in volume from that of the professional judges; all experts ask questions of the parties during the hearing of the case, and all experts participate fully in the deliberations.

During deliberations reaching consensus is easy; all the respondents agreed on that. Initially there are often differing opinions, but they never lead to a persistent conflict. 'One-and-a-half hours of deliberations is long. Generally, the way a case is presented during the hearing already determines the opinions of the panel. The only issue that is sometimes more thoroughly debated is the question whether the state of affairs is sufficiently serious for an inquiry', one of the experts explains.

It is a generally accepted custom during the secret deliberations in Dutch courts that the member who has entered the judiciary the most recently gives his opinion first and the others follow.[7] The chairman gives his views last. The judge who was interviewed made it clear that this court deviated from this general custom. In the Companies Court it is not necessary to protect the younger members from the opinions of the 'older' and more experienced judges; anyone can and does say what he or she wants to say about the case and the less experienced participants would not need any incentive or protection to do so.

The respondents were asked whether the Companies Court's decisions are more readily accepted as a result of the participation of the experts. Their answers made clear that the acceptance by 'insiders', who are familiar with the court, is large. However the outside world does not always know who the participating experts are. Journalists who lack knowledge about the legal system would be simply unaware of the expertise that is involved in the Companies Court. They would thus not accept the court's decision more

7 This practice was formerly stipulated by law, but that legal provision has been repealed.

readily for this specific reason. The judge was confident that the Companies Court has substantial authority. Many lawyers would rather bring their case before this court than before a regular court. The chairman was often invited to give lectures. The court's decisions are scrutinized by exchange markets all over the world. The court receives lots of media attention, and is often in the spotlight.

The Outside World

Upon being asked, the experts indicated that they did not feel that Dutch judges were out of touch with the real world. However, they cautioned that their experience was limited to this special court and that they knew nothing of other judges in this respect.

Two of the three experts indicated that they talked about their experiences in the Companies Court with their family, friends, colleagues, or in clubs they belong to. The third expert stated that he never talked about the Companies Court, except when somebody explicitly asked for information.

None of the respondents indicated being kept awake at night by the decisions they had to make in the Companies Court. However, one expert explained that in the beginning, he sometimes simply did not know what to do with a case, or how to read the case file. He sometimes sat reading the files until midnight.

The respondents fiercely objected when the suggestion of participation of 'real' lay people in the legal system was put to them. They felt that, especially in the Companies Court, such an involvement of ordinary citizens would not be a good idea. Even lawyers sometimes find the cases of this court difficult and incomprehensible; lay people would have insurmountable problems understanding them. But the introduction of lay people in other legal fields was open to objection too. Within criminal law *Gesundenes Volksempfinden* (common sense) and the ordinary citizen's inclination towards revenge would be too prevalent. For example, juries would be prejudiced if a famous soccer player appeared before a court. The process would become too emotional with the participation of lay people. Lay adjudication was, thus, not supported by our respondents. They felt that expertise was one of the good things in life and should be cherished. One expert explained: 'I understand why there is this call for lay adjudication at present. It is because of the miscarriages of justice. But our system is not appropriate for lay people taking part'. The judge was the most outspoken in denouncing lay participation. 'That should not be made possible. The administration of justice is not a democratic institution. It should be done by people who are selected for it, well-qualified people. Experts must be offered the opportunity to participate. But lay people not.'

Conclusions

From the interviews, the Companies Court can be portrayed as a court that attaches considerable value to the expertise that is introduced by its members. The selection criteria for recruiting new experts for this court are fully meritocratic.[8] In fact, the selection is left to the non-legal members of the court themselves. They are requested to administer their own succession, and the main criterion seems to be that the replacement member must be 'even better than yourself'. The final decision of whether this is the case is made by the chairman of the Companies Court. The corollary of this view is that there is little consideration of the potential input of people who do not possess legal knowledge and who are not an expert in the fields covered by the Companies Court. Such an input is simply not considered feasible.

All respondents were satisfied by the way the court operates. The different types of expertise presented by the court's members seem to lead to a synthesis at a higher level. The chairman of the court takes a dominant place in the course of affairs within the Companies Court. All respondents underscored this central position and it does not seem to lead to second thoughts on the part of other participants in this court.

Execution of Sentences Division of the Arnhem Court of Appeal[9]

The Execution of Sentences division of the Arnhem Court of Appeal (hereafter: Execution of Sentences Court) consists of three judges and two experts in the mental health domain: a psychiatrist and a psychologist who are knowledgeable in the forensic field. Most cases heard by this court concern the prolongation of the 'tbs measure',[10] that is, mandatory confinement of a convicted offender who has committed a very serious crime and suffers from a serious mental disorder to a closed psychiatric clinic, when it is established that there is both a relationship between his or her mental condition and the crime for which he or she was convicted and that he or she poses a continuing danger to society. This measure is imposed by a District Court and its prolongation can be appealed at the Execution of Sentences Court. The prolongation of a similar measure for minors can also be appealed at this court, as can a measure imposed on recidivists who have repeatedly reoffended. Mental health experts are involved in all these procedures. About 300 appeals against the District Courts' decisions regarding prolongation of the tbs measure (including

8 On the meritocratic character of the selection of Dutch judges, see de Groot-van Leeuwen 2004. See Chapter 4 for the characteristics of professionalism.

9 *Penitentiaire Kamer, Hof Arnhem.*

10 *Terbeschikkingstelling (tbs)*, detention at Her Majesty's Pleasure, or in the United States, civil confinement of offenders.

those for minors and recidivists) are dealt with each year by the Execution of Sentences Court (Otte and Vegter 2004). Not all cases heard by this court include mental health experts on the panel. A minority of cases concern the conditional release of defendants or the transfer of a Dutch national serving a prison term in another country back to the Netherlands to complete his sentence; in such cases the addition of experts in the field of mental health is not deemed to be necessary (Otte and Vegter 2004).

The judges sitting in this court are involved in these procedures on a regular basis, in addition to their regular work in the Arnhem Court of Appeal. The court makes use of about 10 mental health experts who participate in turn (Otte and Vegter 2004). No appeal to the Dutch Court of Cassation is possible for decisions made by the Execution of Sentences Court.

The relevance of this court's work for society is high. The tbs measure, and the question of at what point these people may be released back into society, are hotly debated topics in the Netherlands. In recent years a number of convicted offenders who were subject to tbs commitment and who had been temporarily released as a trial in preparation for their definitive release have committed serious crimes while on leave. In one case, one of them slipped away from his guard and committed a new murder. This led to a public outcry for more safety and for a more stringent regime for the leave of tbs patients. As in many other Western countries, there is in the Netherlands a general and increasing concern about public safety and security which in turn influences discussions about the tbs measure as well. Over the last few decades courts have increasingly prolonged tbs committals[11] and have become more hesitant about releasing offenders. This general reluctance reflects the advice of the clinics where the offenders are being treated, which frequently oppose their release. The clinic's recommendations are generally followed by the courts. As a consequence, the time offenders spend in institutions under tbs committals has increased (Otte and Vegter 2004). In cases where a serious violent or sexual crime has been committed affecting the victim's physical well-being, and the threat exists of a repetition of a similar crime, the tbs measure can be prolonged after four years. In the most extreme situations the measure can last for the rest of the offender's life, although every year, or every two years, a court has to authorize its prolongation.

The Court's decision regarding a prolongation of the measure is extremely important for the offender. The contribution of the two mental health experts is of great relevance. It is the court that makes the final decision about whether the offender has to stay in the clinic or whether he can be released, now or in the near future, but this legal decision is based on both legal considerations and on insights from mental health expertise. In this court a bridge is thus built between legal and psychiatric and psychological expertise (Otte and Vegter 2004).

11 Prolongation of a tbs measure is legally possible for one or two year periods.

An academic debate has been conducted on the question of whether the deliberations between the professional judges and the experts should take place in public instead of in chambers after the public hearing of the case, as happens at present. The Dutch law professor Paul Mevis is of the opinion that, at present, the influence exerted by the experts on the court decision is not transparent. Due to the secrecy of the deliberations about the court's decision, the content of the debate that is conducted on the prolongation of the tbs committal remains veiled. This lack of openness becomes problematic if the court makes a decision that deviates from the clinic's advice regarding the danger to public safety that is posed by this offender (Mevis 2004). Mevis (2004, 888) believes that the experts should have their place in the *courtroom* and not on the *bench*, so their views can be questioned. In many cases the experts who work in the clinic where the offender is a patient are not summoned to appear before the Execution of Sentences Court, which does not serve to stimulate an open debate on the merits of the advice and the danger that is posed by the offender either. Others disagree with Mevis and emphasize the value that is added by the cooperation in this court between lawyers and mental health experts (Otte and Vegter 2004, 488). This debate has not as yet led to any changes in the law.

The court sits one day a week. The researchers visited for one full day. On the day of the visit the panel was composed of five males: three judges and two experts. All of them were in their 50s or 60s. The judges wore black robes and white bands, the experts were in their everyday clothes. Several cases were dealt with in the course of the day. One of the applicants appeared before the court was surprised by the large number of judges behind the bench. The chairman then explained each judge's background. The two experts were active during this court session, in the sense that they asked many questions of the offenders who appeared before them. Their participation was seen to be at least as extensive as that of the professional judges.

Interviews with Judges and Experts

Two professional judges and two experts, a psychiatrist and a psychologist involved in the Execution of Sentences Court, were interviewed. As in the interviews for the other courts, the topics included the ways in which the experts are recruited and how they are prepared for their post, their experiences during the performance of their task and their views regarding the participation of experts in legal procedures.

Of the judges, one had four years' experience in this special court and the other had nine years. The psychologist had participated in the court for 16 years and the psychiatrist for nine years. Both experts had worked in the forensic field in various positions before entering the court. One of them was a professor at a university. All respondents were males.

The Appointment and Actual Participation of Experts

The judges who were interviewed explained how the recruitment and selection of new experts for the court works. One judge explained that:

> There are ten experts. When we need a new member, we inquire of the other experts as well as among some former judges if they know someone who is suitable for the court. Upon receiving a new name, we investigate whether there are any contraindications, whether their intellectual level is sufficiently high, whether they are sufficiently acquainted with the forensic field, and whether they have won their spurs in this domain.

The other judge interviewed confirmed this procedure. 'As with the honorary judges, the selection and recruitment is very informal. Most of the experts are slightly older, most of them are over 55 years of age. They have lots of experience in the field concerned.'

The new candidate has a meeting with the chairman of the Execution of Sentences Court and with the president of the Court of Appeal of Arnhem. Their appointment by the government is for five years and is extended automatically. Each expert has about six to eight sittings per year. The court is careful that the experts involved are not related in any way to the clinic where the offender is committed. Many experts still work or have had a post in the forensic field and it is thus not inconceivable that they may be acquainted with the case in one way or another. 'While recruiting and selecting new members, the court aims at obtaining a reflection of the various schools and traditions that can be found in the mental health field', one of the judges explained.

On each day in court about 10 cases are dealt with. In about one third of these cases an expert from outside – for instance, from the clinic – is summoned and testifies in court. Over the last three or four years experts have been summoned to appear less frequently. Now, however, experts from the clinics are again testifying more often and decisions by the court are reasoned more extensively and in more detail than a couple of years ago, one of the judges explained.

It is recommended to new members of the court that they attend a sitting of the Execution of Sentences Court first and they are invited to listen to the deliberations about the cases in chambers. They are also encouraged to have a meeting with one of the other experts. The experts who were interviewed indicated that there is no specific instruction for new members of this court. However, most experts have been in this court before, albeit in a different capacity, because they come from the forensic field themselves. Thus they know the types of cases the court deals with, and the way hearings are conducted.

Once a year all the judges and experts in the court gather somewhere outside the court for an informal discussion of how the court functions and the general state of play. The issues debated have included the extent of the court's discretion, the legal framework, opinions regarding, for example, the new school of risk assessment, and so forth. During this meeting the judges make a point of explaining the legal framework to the experts. Not all the experts seem deeply interested in this aspect.

The focus of the experts differs from that of the judges. In hearing cases, the expert judges often examine the experts representing the clinic where the applicant is confined. Questions may relate to the medication, plans that the clinic may have regarding prevention of new offences, the offender's treatment, etc. Or they ask the applicants whether they are able to detect for *themselves* when a psychotic episode is coming up. One of the judges explained:

> Experts sometimes extend their task as far as to cross-examine the clinic's expert. That is not what our court is meant for. On the other hand, they sometimes make highly useful suggestions to the clinic that can be involved in the court's decision. Those remarks have a very beneficial function in instructing the clinic and the offender's supervisors there.

During deliberations in chambers, the experts give their opinions first, before the judges do, and they do so from their expertise in mental health. The participants in these deliberations do not always agree on all points, but it is not difficult to reach consensus. All respondents agree that the experts participate fully in all aspects of the process. During the hearing of the case the chairman asks the most questions, but the experts ask more questions than the other two judges.

Opinions on the Involvement of Experts

Both judges were highly in favour of participation by the experts in this court. One judge explained that

> In most cases there would not be a different outcome. But they contribute to better deliberations. They have more insight in the tbs field and how the clinics work. If they think that the clinic is not applying the right treatment for this offender, they sometimes write a recommendation which is included in the written court decision. The clinics often take these recommendations into account, and at the next trial for prolongation of the measure, the District Court will examine what the clinic has done with the experts' suggestions. Their expertise has lots of added value.

The other judge supported the involvement of experts as well. However, he was aware that the experts generally have less distance from the case than the judges do:

> Their body language sometimes reveals their views on the case. But some of them are very good in directly communicating with the applicant. They have a wide insight into human nature. They are good at talking with the offenders, even in the case of very serious mental disorders, and they succeed better in obtaining information from them than we do.

Specific knowledge of the forensic field is the advantage of expert involvement that was most often mentioned by the respondents. Experts know how clinics work and they have knowledge about different types of treatment for offenders who suffer from mental disorders. They introduce a different type of thinking that provides a useful contribution to the legal decision-making. Their opinion on a case is taken very seriously by the judges, and has a profound influence on the final decisions. Moreover, all the respondents indicated that they enjoyed the collaboration between the lawyers and the experts. There are no difficulties in the communication because the experts generally do not use mental health jargon. Legal issues generally do not have to be explained. Most legal issues dealt with by this court are not highly technical in nature and can be resolved without an extensive discussion with the experts.

As to disadvantages of expert involvement, the respondents mentioned the expense, which is greater than it would be without their participation, and the lack of transparency that is the result of non-public deliberations between the lawyers and the experts in chambers.[12] There might be a risk of partiality if the expert involved was related to the clinic in which an applicant was being treated. However, the court is very concerned about such risks and avoids them by scrutinizing the files beforehand and contacting and questioning the expert.

One respondent (an expert) mentioned the risk that experts might make too much use of their authority within the panel and that, as a consequence, their opinions would prevail over those of the lawyers. He stressed that it is important that the judges continue to take care of the legal framework, preventing the experts from becoming too dominant. But overall the respondents did not see many disadvantages to the experts' participation.

There are few differences between the experts' and the professional judges' views on the content of cases. The experts are sometimes more focused on the offender's reintegration into society and are more inclined to end the tbs measure than the lawyers. They look more at the applicant's personal development and at ways for better treating and supporting him or her. Judges, out of a concern for safety risks, are generally more in favour of a prolongation of the tbs measure. One of the experts explained this by use of a fictitious example: when an offender, during his stay in a tbs clinic, demolishes a television, judges react differently to that. 'We take that less seriously', the

12 See the introduction on the Execution of Sentences Court in this chapter for this debate.

expert explained. Judges tend to feel that such incidents are predictive of future violence, while experts consider them more as boasting and not as an immediate risk to society or to the personal safety of others. The experts can also make the judges see a case in a different light on other points. 'Judges do not always notice when the offender is under the influence of a psychosis, or when he has delusions, and we do see that', one expert remarked.

The two judges had the impression that the experts' views do not change over time as a consequence of their participation in this court. The experts do not sit sufficiently often for that to happen. The experts themselves, however, observed an evolution in how they look at cases. 'I have become more interested in criminal law. I have reached the insight that criminals are not only assholes. They often are losers, who have suffered misfortunes in their lives ... For the rest, I have not become more like the judges. Our decisions do not come from the computer anyway, they remain the result of human judgements', one of the experts told us. The other expert explained that now, more than when he began, he was of the opinion that offenders should be offered the opportunity to have their 'day in court'.

> You have to protect them from what happens in the courtroom. The forensic field is under strong political pressure as a consequence of the safety concerns in society. Clinics have become highly rigid. I want to give more space, more freedom to the offenders, give them the opportunity to tell their own story. They have to fight against the Ministry of Justice, against the system. And that is difficult, especially when you do not have a good lawyer to defend you.

Neither of the experts interviewed felt that over the course of time their views on cases had become more like those of the judges, but they did think that the lawyers and the experts by and large understood each other better after having collaborated over an extensive period of time.

The Outside World

A couple of questions were asked about relations between this special court and its members with the outside world. Three out of the four respondents felt that acceptance by the outside world of the court's decisions was enhanced by the experts' participation. Most of the offenders were aware of the experts' presence. Some of them probably had the impression that the experts listened to them more than the judges did. The experts presumed that offenders were positive about the fact that during the hearing of the case experts often asked critical questions of the clinic's staff. Sometimes the media report that experts form part of the panel. But in general the public at large do not know that experts are involved. The only reason why people attending the hearing of a case would know, is that the experts do not wear robes whereas the professional judges do. However, few people attend sittings. It is not generally the custom to inform the applicant that two experts have seats on the panel. Sometimes the offender is surprised that the panel is so large and inquires about its composition. The chairman then explains about the two experts who are taking part .

Mixed views were presented with respect to the question of whether 'ordinary citizens' should be offered the opportunity to participate in the administration of justice. None of the respondents was in principle *against* lay involvement. However, before taking this step they felt that all pros and cons should be thoroughly considered from every angle. One of the judges said:

> The point is that we, the judges, lack a democratic legitimation, because we have been appointed and we are not elected by the population of a country. Openness and transparency in a trial is not sufficient to replace lay involvement. There is nobody in the public gallery in most cases. However, lay participation does not fit into our legal culture. But that is not a strong argument. Nothing would ever change if you adhere too much to that view. However, everything will go slower with ordinary citizens. We now have an efficient system.

The other judge gave the example of the UK Sentencing Guidelines Commission. Ordinary citizens who meet certain requirements take part in this commission. Their opinions are taken into consideration when drawing up guidelines for sentencing. This respondent would support such an involvement in the Netherlands as well. He also made it clear that he felt at least some degree of affinity with the system of lay magistrates that is in use in the UK.

The two experts were less in favour of lay participation. 'Not in regular criminal law', one expert clearly stated. The other expert interviewed was of the opinion that the involvement of lay people would not contribute anything to the trial of cases.

One of the experts acknowledged that, although judges generally are not out of touch with the real world, to a certain extent courts have the characteristics of a private circle. Both experts thought that it would in general be a good idea if judges were encouraged to take more positions in society or to develop other activities in addition to their work for the court. For instance, they should visit a caravan camp every now and then, just as the experts sometimes do. Some judges should acquaint themselves more with the tbs clinics as well; that happened more often in the past than it does now. Unfortunately, due to the ever-increasing caseloads there is insufficient time for such useful initiatives which might provide more insight into social circumstances different from their own.

It was extremely rare for either expert to speak about their experiences in court at home or to friends and colleagues. If they did, it was mostly in general terms, or about funny events that had happened in court. With colleagues they sometimes talked about classification of offenders and difficulties arising from that.

None of the respondents indicated being kept awake at night by the decisions they had to make. One of the experts did say that he was concerned about certain developments in the tbs field. He felt that in society, but also in the tbs field itself, there is too strong an emphasis on security matters and the prevention of risk (see also Gonzales 2007). Offenders are too easily being sent to the 'long stay' department of tbs clinics and they are given too few opportunities to get out. Further, psychiatric institutions do too little to offer places to offenders who are mentally disturbed. As a consequence of the closing down of psychiatric institutions over the last decades, the tbs field is now exploding. Former psychiatric inmates walk the streets. They are not able to live their lives without help. They begin committing crimes and, as a consequence of the mental disorders they suffer from, get drawn into the tbs field. This respondent was deeply concerned about these developments.

Conclusions

In this court, expertise in the tbs field is the most important reason for the involvement of the experts. Experience gained and knowledge of the relevant area are prominent among the advantages of expert participation most often mentioned. The meritocratic element dominates the selection procedure of experts for this court. In general, all respondents were highly satisfied with the way this court operates and how professional judges and experts collaborate.

The decisions made by the Execution of Sentences Court bear a stronger resemblance to the criminal law domain than are the decisions made by the Companies Court, which is primarily concerned with the affairs of businesses and corporations. This difference is reflected in the opinions of the respondents. The 'lay' members of the Execution of Sentences Court were more concerned that judges might be out of touch with the real world. They were of the opinion that some judges should accept posts outside the judiciary more often. Such opinions were not encountered at all at the Companies Court. Finally, most respondents in the Execution of Sentences Court were more open to lay participation in one form or another than those from the Companies Court.

The Agricultural Tenancies Division of the District Court[13]

The Agricultural Tenancies division of the District Court (hereafter: Agricultural Tenancies Court) decides disputes regarding agricultural tenancy contracts. Conflicts between landlords and tenants about, for example, the prolongation of the lease of land, whether a lease contract exists or not, and

13 *Pachtkamer.*

questions about the replacement of tenants by other tenants are decided by this court. For example, while a farmer is ill, someone else may use his land, till the soil, set up fences around the land and otherwise invest in it. Does this imply that a lease contract now exists? It may happen that with the farmer's death his heirs want to sell the tenancy, but now there appears to be a lease contract. The heirs may base their claims on their right to use the land themselves. The Agricultural Tenancies Court then decides whether such a right exists and if the specific claim is valid in the specific situation. Each District Court in the Netherlands has an Agricultural Tenancies division.

In this court, two experts sit together with a professional judge[14] who chairs the hearing of the case. These experts have been delegated by organizations of farmers and landlords. In the trial of each case, a representative of each type of organization must be included on the bench. Most judges, and most experts, are involved in this court over considerable periods of time. This ensures that they are able to obtain a wide expertise in the domain of agriculture and the relevant law (Heisterkamp 2004).

Originally the Agricultural Tenancies Law was part of the Code of Civil Law, but later a distinct Agricultural Tenancies Law was created. In the near future this law will again be incorporated into the regular Civil Law legislation. A court consisting of five judges, including two experts, tries agricultural tenancies cases on appeal. This court forms part of the Arnhem Court of Appeal. No appeal of its decisions at the Court of Cassation is possible.

There are three reasons for the participation of non-professional judges in the Agricultural Tenancies Court:

- professional judges are insufficiently knowledgeable in this field;
- regular civil law is too bound to formalities, leading to long and complicated procedures, and this makes its application in the agricultural field undesirable;
- by the participation of farmers and landlords in this type of law, procedures are made more accessible for those who want to file a complaint (de Visser 1971).

Some citizens, especially among farmers and landlords, would prefer that the trial of disputes be kept entirely among themselves, rather than delegating it to professionals. Although the jury system was abolished after the French occupation of the Netherlands ended in 1813, there seems to be some evidence that the call for specialized courts making use of non-professional judges

14 A *kantonrechter*, a single judge dealing with small and non-complex cases in the first instance.

still exists, according to de Visser (1971).[15] Such panels could deliver more convincing decisions, thanks to the experts' contribution.

Participation by experts in the Agricultural Tenancies Court differs in certain respects from that in the courts discussed previously in this chapter. In the Agricultural Tenancies Court the experts who participate to a certain degree represent the organizations of farmers and of landlords from which they are recruited. A number of studies have been conducted into the situations in which members of a court represent certain constituencies. At the Appeals Court for Social Security Matters,[16] which existed until 1992, representatives participated in the trial of cases regarding social security. Roos investigated the views of these representatives and the judges on their participation (Roos 1982). From the results of this study it appeared that the contribution of the lay members to this panel was slight. The professional judges did most of the work and had the largest influence on decision making. Nevertheless most lay participants appeared to be quite satisfied by their own participation. However, because applicants were generally unaware of the lay participation in the panel, it could not be expected that the court's legitimacy would be enhanced by this fact. Specialized knowledge of how certain branches of industry operate was almost never introduced into the panel's decision-making. There was, thus, scarcely a role for *expertise* brought in by the lay members of this court (Roos 1982). Dissatisfaction with the actual contribution of the 'lay' members on the part of the judges was the reason why this court was abolished and its role taken over by administrative courts that operate without lay participants (Roos 1982).

A Belgian study is also relevant to the issue of participation by representatives on benches. Like many other countries in Europe, Belgium has labour courts[17] that make use of lay judges. Representatives of employers' organizations and trades unions take part in these courts. In contrast to the Dutch experience, these courts appear to provide great satisfaction through the participation of its non-professional members (Franssen et al. 2005). The majority of both professional and lay judges in this court (>90 per cent) are in favour of a continuation of lay participation. As in the *Raden voor Beroep voor de Sociale Verzekeringen* discussed above, many members of this court have a position in organizations for employers or in trade unions. It appears that being a representative does not imply that the experts only defend the standpoint of the organization they are recruited from; they are able to keep a certain distance from the interests of their own organization. Lay participants do not play a highly active role during the hearing of cases; they generally remain in the background. In the long term, the lay members undergo some

15 As de Visser was writing in 1971, further research would be required to verify if this view is still wholly accurate.

16 *Raden voor Beroep voor de Sociale Verzekeringen*. See Roos 1982.

17 *Arbeidsgerechten*.

form of professionalization; they become less of a lay person. The authors conclude that, despite the satisfaction it produces, the participation of the lay members has a certain symbolic function (Franssen et al. 2005).

It can be generally concluded from these two studies that the lay participants in these courts do not act and decide strictly as representatives of the organizations they are recruited from. Their input in the trial of cases is considered to be weak. The Belgian and Dutch studies show a difference in the level of satisfaction with the experts operating in the courts: in Belgium this satisfaction is substantially greater than it was in the Netherlands.

Interviews

Interviews were conducted with two judges and two experts from two Dutch Agricultural Tenancies Courts. The topics discussed in the interviews were similar to those for the other two courts discussed previously in this chapter. Attention was also given to the question of to what extent the experts in a court of this type consider themselves as representatives of their organizations.

The two Agricultural Tenancies Courts that were visited for our research were both located in small Dutch towns. They are both in courthouses that are annexes to the headquarters of the courts in larger cities nearby. One of the buildings where the court sat was located in a narrow shopping street in a small town in the Western part of the Netherlands. Anyone could enter the building. There were safety devices at the entrance of the building, meant for scanning bags and people, but it was abundantly clear that they were never used. In both locations the court was easy-going and informal. The professional judge wore a black robe and white bands and the experts were in their everyday clothes. During the interview with one of the judges in her office after the court session, the clerk entered to take the judge's dog out. It had been sleeping under the table in her office during the hearing of the case.

One of the judges interviewed had formed part of the Agricultural Tenancies Court for 18 years, the other for seven years. All respondents were in their 50s or 60s. The two experts had participated for 15 and seven years respectively. All respondents, thus, had gained considerable experience in the Agricultural Tenancies Court. One of the professional judges was a woman; all other respondents were men.

The Appointment and Actual Participation of Experts

The experts are appointed to the Agricultural Tenancies Court by the Government from a list made up by the Provincial Executive. In the past, the influence of the agricultural boards on the recruitment and appointment of the experts was larger than it is now. One of the judges interviewed explained that there are not many differences between the experts from organizations of farmers and those from organizations of landlords; they have many interests in common and their views do not differ strikingly. The experts are appointed for a period of five years, which can be, and most often is, prolonged.

One of the experts reported being recruited via the agricultural organization of which he was a member.

> It was announced that the court was looking for an expert out of the circle of tenants. I called the court and asked whether I could attend a trial. Naturally that was possible, court sessions are open to the public. I was then selected. What may have played a role is that I am a member of a commission for start-up entrepreneurs in the small town where I live.

The other expert cannot remember by whom he was asked to enter the court. 'I already had lots of experience in governance and in being member of boards', he explained, 'I was a member to the National Land Consolidation Commission. You have to mediate between parties on a regular basis in that commission. To do that, you have to have a considerable knowledge of human nature'.

The two judges had worked together with the same experts for many years. The two experts in one of the courts indicated that they did not feel themselves to be or to make decisions as 'representatives'; in most cases they held the same opinion. When they had a sitting, one of them picked up the other by car and they travelled together to the courthouse. In the car, they discussed the cases that would appear before the court that day.

As in the other courts discussed in this chapter, the experts were given little preparation for their function before entering the court. This was not necessary because they had ample knowledge of the agricultural field. The experts made it clear that they were not in need of an extra introduction before starting; they had collected considerable experience and had wide insight in the issues pertinent for the court's decision making.

Surprisingly, both experts interviewed stated that they had different powers from those of the president. 'We advise the president, but she decides.'[18] The two judges, however, indicated that the lay participants had the same powers and opportunities to ask questions and make decisions as the professional judge. All participants in the panel received copies of the case file well before the trial so they could prepare for the sitting and the issues that need further clarification.

One of the judges remarked that 'his' experts often asked questions of the parties. He encouraged them to do so and is happy that they participate on a wide scale. 'They ask slightly different questions than I do. They often inquire about the actual running of a farm. I do not know a lot about that aspect.

---

18 The experts legally have the same powers as the judge, except for chairing the hearing of the case.

The experts run farms themselves and thus they know about the agriculture in practice.'

The judge writes the court decision. The experts read the draft and suggest modifications. In general the panel comes to an agreement easily. Serious differences of opinion seldom emerge. The experts indicate that their opinions are based on their expertise. They are sometimes able to make the judge see the case in a different light.

The deliberations are very informal. The experts give their opinion first, the judge follows. In most cases, the facts are clear. The two experts sometimes come to a different conclusion. However, all respondents agreed that it is not difficult to reach a consensus. After having reached a conclusion, the experts leave it to the judge to prepare the verdict. Both judges who were interviewed had an agricultural connection either directly or through their families. The field thus was not completely new to them. One of the experts prepared himself by buying and reading the Agricultural Tenancies Law.

Opinions on the Involvement of Experts

The two judges considered the input by the experts as absolutely indispensable. One of them gave an example. If a tenant wanted to have his new wife replace him as a tenant and the court is asked to decide, one of the experts may ask the woman, 'At what temperature should potatoes be saved in winter in the barn?' If she did not give the right answer, the court did not allow her to take over as tenant. The experts know how agriculture operates in practice. Their knowledge and common sense is an advantage. All respondents greatly enjoyed the collaboration between the lawyers and the experts. Few disadvantages were mentioned by the respondents. Perhaps the trial takes a little more time, and the larger number of participants on the bench may lead to slightly higher expenses, but in the opinion of the respondents those disadvantages are only of minor importance.

In the long term the experts' views on cases do not become more like those of the professional judges; they retain their own individual input. All respondents agreed on that.

The Outside World

A few questions were asked about the relations of this court with the outside world. Three out of the four respondents thought that the participation of experts did not make any difference to the acceptance of the court's decision. One judge felt that the questions asked by the experts were better accepted because they were so well informed and familiar with agriculture.

Despite being strongly in favour of the participation of experts in the trial of cases, the respondents were not in support of 'real' lay people taking part in the administration of justice. The reason for this rejection of lay adjudication is that the Dutch system is professionalized to such a high degree. Lay people would not be able to contribute anything to the trial of cases.

Both experts indicated that they did not often talk about their experiences in court at home or with friends. None of the respondents was kept awake by the decisions they had to make in court. None of the respondents considered Dutch judges to be out of touch with the real world.

Conclusions

As in the other two courts examined in this chapter, all respondents were highly satisfied with the way experts collaborate with the professional judges. The type of expertise used in this court is rather specific in nature. It is practice-based and has been handed down from parents to their children. The experts involved have learned from first-hand experience; their knowledge is not primarily the result of formal education and has not been obtained from books. In this sense the expertise involved in this court differs in certain respects from the types of expertise used in the other two courts discussed in this chapter. Through their lack of formal training, the experts who take part in the Agricultural Tenancies Court are closer to 'real' lay people than those involved in the other courts.

But there are also many similarities with the other courts in this chapter. Expertise is the obvious motive for allowing the experts to participate. There seem to be no other considerations equally relevant for their involvement in this court.

Final Remarks

The most conspicuous similarities among the three courts described here are the satisfaction with the way in which the courts operate and the considerable degree to which the experts actually participate in the hearing and decision making. In the three courts there is a great emphasis on expertise, which can be most clearly identified in the way experts are recruited. There seem to be few formal rules or criteria for selection, other than that the candidate must have knowledge and expertise in the relevant field. Fully meritocratic standards are used for selecting the candidates. The decisions on who to contact for a post and who to recommend for an appointment are almost exclusively left to the judges and the experts themselves, at least in the Companies Court and the Execution of Sentences Court. For the Agricultural Tenancies Court the situation seems slightly different, although insufficient information has been obtained on this to be able to make a definitive statement.

The courts described here seem to rely to a large extent on their members' expertise in other aspects as well. When starting out, the experts receive almost no preparation for their duties. Like the professional judges, they receive the case file in advance and have to find their way through it. No formal training is provided and obtaining further information about how the court operates is largely left to the experts' initiative. None of the respondents seems to find this a problem, however.

The types of expertise held by the lawyers and the experts do not seem to overlap greatly in any of the courts under review here. The experts know about the substance of the decision that has to be made and the lawyers are aware of the legal rules, the boundaries of the court's discretion and know-how to write a decision. The different disciplines seem quite happy with each other and all enjoy the collaboration. There was hardly any dissent from the respondents on this point. Experts exert a considerable influence on the decisions that are made. Having input during the trial and in the deliberations seems far more self-evident in these courts than in many courts abroad that use 'real' lay people.

The way in which the courts dealt with in this chapter function reflects the Dutch focus on professionalism. Whereas many other countries strongly adhere to giving ordinary citizens a place in the many institutions a country has, among them the legal system, such an argument does not seem to play a role in the Netherlands. Its adherence to professionalism and to the input of professionals is to a large extent interwoven in the legal system. With respect to the courts described in this chapter, the question may be asked whether it would reasonably be possible to introduce a lay element; most probably it would not. The general idea that with the help of lay participation the community might be better represented in court decisions is absent in the Netherlands. This being the case, the participation of experts does not appear to be seen as providing a sense of or increasing the legal system's legitimacy within the eyes of the public. As a judge of the Companies Court contended, the administration of justice is not a democratic institution. The courts aim is to improve the quality of their decisions and that seems impossible with the involvement of 'real' lay people.

It is remarkable that all three courts operate almost exclusively with male judges and experts, most of whom are in their 50s and 60s. The only female was the judge chairing one of the Agricultural Tenancies Courts. Clearly, the increasing involvement of female judges in the trial of cases has not yet reached these specialized courts.

None of the experts interviewed seemed to talk a lot at home, at work or with friends about what is going on in the court. In that sense, dissemination of knowledge about how the courts operate can be expected to be meagre. The Companies Court's decisions receive much more media attention than those of the other two courts. The Agricultural Tenancies Court's decisions remain virtually invisible to the outside world.

Only in the Executions of Sentences Court did there appear to be some criticism of the 'private circle' in which judges (not necessarily of this court) operate. It was suggested that judges should broaden their circle by going to clinics or to visit places they would otherwise not come into contact with. That would expand their knowledge of the field they are working in. At the same time, the respondents realized that judges have little time for this, because of the heavy caseloads they are confronted with. Such options are not voiced on the other courts. The respondents there generally hold the view that judges are sufficiently in touch with the real world, or they do not consider this issue to be important.

In conclusion, these courts fit very well in the Dutch professionalized legal system, and the participants are very contented with the way they operate. No difficulties seem to exist in the cooperation between the lawyers and the experts.

Chapter 7
Denmark

Introduction

In Denmark both juries and lay judges take part in the administration of justice. This chapter outlines the results of several observations in the *Byret*, the District Court of Denmark, where panels consist of one professional judge and two lay judges. The researchers also made observations at court sessions at the *Østre Landsret* (Court of Appeal). No full trials were observed there, however. Apart from these observations, a number of interviews were conducted with both professional judges and lay judges.

The Dutch Council for the Judiciary contacted the Danish Council for the Judiciary to obtain consent for the study to be carried out in Denmark. This consent was granted and two courts in Denmark were contacted by the researchers. The court organized a two day programme for the researchers which involved both visits to court sessions and interviews with judges. In total seven cases were observed and 12 interviews conducted, six with professional judges and six with lay judges. Jury cases were not observed. In the following sections the observations will first be summarized, after which the results of the interviews will be presented.[1]

Observations

Seven criminal cases were observed, five at the *Byret* (Court of First Instance) and two at the *Østre Landsret* (Court of Appeal). At the *Byret* one of the judges explained what was happening and translated what was said into English for the researchers.

The *Byret* is located in a vast neoclassical building in the centre of the city. The building previously served as the city hall. Anyone can enter the building without being checked or monitored. There are no security services that check bags and nobody asks what you are doing in the building, which is quite astonishing for a Dutch visitor. The only part of the building that cannot be

---

1 The observations and the interviews were conducted prior to the implementation of new legislation in Denmark that changed the composition of the panels in both types of courts (January 2008). However, in the type of panel that was observed, the experience of the lay and professional participants would not be altered as a result of the new legislation.

entered by the public is the section intended exclusively for the judges. Judges walk through the building with large bunches of keys. When they enter the building they have to find their way through defendants and their families and other people waiting for a trial in order to reach the door that gives access to the part meant for the judges only

Denmark has a large number of small courthouses in the numerous small towns spread throughout the country. There the judges, in the late afternoon or early evening, walk home after having delivered a number of court decisions. All the residents of the small town or village know the judges. The researchers inquired whether this situation might present any dangers for the judges. The judges answered that the only thing they could remember that had ever happened was that a party in a case had once attacked a judge *inside* a court building. This had not led to any damage, however. The judges we spoke to did not seem to have any fears in this respect. The atmosphere during court sessions of the *Byret* is very relaxed and informal. During a short break in one of the cases we observed, a defendant walked over to his mother sitting in the public gallery and hugged her. His mother cried. Although this was a case that was attended by the security services, they did nothing to prevent this happening, nor did they seem alarmed or concerned.

The courtroom in which we began our observations had many large windows, light furniture and looked almost like an office. The behaviour of the court officials was easy-going and pleasant. At regular intervals laughter could be heard, although the defendant did not join in. The judges did not wear robes, nor did the defence lawyers and prosecutors. Seen from the public gallery, the prosecutor, a young woman, sat at a small table at right angles to the higher table occupied by the judges at the right hand side of the courtroom. In all cases that we observed at the *Byret* the prosecutor was a young woman and the president of the panel was in all cases a middle-aged woman. The defence lawyers, sitting to the left at a separate table, were all men in their 40s or 50s. During the breaks, the defence lawyers stayed in the courtroom, talking loudly on their mobile phones.

The president and the clerk both had a computer before them. The public gallery consisted of a number of uncomfortable, free-standing small chairs at the back of the courtroom. One of the cases observed was attended by a large number of members of the defendant's family. The security services were of the opinion that there were too many chairs in the courtroom. For reasons of fire safety several of these chairs had to be removed. Three chairs were taken away without objections from the people occupying them, who had to leave as well. Half an hour or so after the session started, a man holding a motorcycle helmet in his hands entered, laughing sheepishly. Since the doors of this old building cannot be opened and closed without lots of noise, it seemed as if he burst into the courtroom. He was politely asked to leave the courtroom because all the chairs allowed were occupied. After he closed the door, the clerk walked over and locked the door from the inside with her key. As a consequence, anyone wishing to leave the courthouse had to request the key.

One of the cases we observed had to be postponed. It appeared that six court hearings had previously been held on this case and that on the day of our observation the panel was not composed of the same judges as on the previous court days. During deliberations about whether the trial should proceed or whether it should take place at a later date, one of the lay judges entered, an elderly man who blushed with shame because of his late appearance. It was decided that the trial would be postponed.

As there was no trial taking place in the courtroom we had been in, we moved to another courtroom. This room had walls that were painted a warm shade of orange and small lamps that would not have been out of place in the home of an elderly couple. It looked quite different from the one we had been in before: cosy and comfortable. The president of the court was a woman in her 40s, as were the two lay judges. The only men were the defendant and two defence lawyers. One of the lawyers defended an accused who was not present at this session.

The defendant was accused of burglary. As was the case in other trials, most of the interrogations were conducted by the prosecutor. The president only asked a question every now and then and the defence lawyers asked almost no questions. The lay judges asked no questions at all. All three judges were writing for a large part of the trial. After the interrogations, the president read the defendant's statement aloud and the clerk typed it directly into the computer. This took a lot of time. After this was finished, the president inquired of the defendant whether his statement had been correctly reproduced. He confirmed that was the case. The judge who assisted us in understanding what was going on made it clear that this reading aloud of the defendant's statement is a general custom in Denmark.

When a witness had to be heard, the defendant left his chair and took a seat next to his lawyer, near the side wall of the courtroom. The witness then sat down in the defendant's seat. The witness interrogation was again started by the prosecutor, who apparently plays a central role in criminal cases in Denmark. The defence lawyers, by contrast, say almost nothing during the court session. During one of the short breaks one of the defence lawyers in this case walked over to the female judge who translated and explained things for us and hugged her. They talked together for a while. Apparently, they knew each other well. There seems to be no objection to this type of contact between a lawyer and a judge.

One of the few formalities that are observed in the trial of criminal cases in Denmark is that the public stand when the judges enter and when they retire to deliberate about decisions that have to be made. Both the prosecutor and the defence lawyers make their arguments standing. Furthermore, everyone, including the public, is expected to stand when the sentence is pronounced. Aside from these moments, very few formalities seem to apply.

We returned to the light courtroom in which we had started the day. Two boys in their 20s were on trial. They sat next to each other, only about seven yards away from the first row of chairs of the 'public gallery'. They were accused of having robbed a man. The two defendants had been remanded into pre-trial custody and thus there were security guards present at this trial. One of the two defendants had a bottle of coke. He gave a sip to the other defendant every now and then. The two lay judges were both men, one young man and one slightly older. Neither of them was formally dressed: they wore no tie or suit. The younger lay judge wore jeans.

There were no microphones in the courtroom. They were not necessary either, because the room was rather small. Again, the prosecutor played the leading role in handling the case. It seemed as if she was the only one in the courtroom who knew the case well. This was confirmed to us later by the judges. There are judges who, out of principle, do not read the dossier themselves, or only glance at it briefly before the trial, because they feel that, just as the lay judges, they should be unprejudiced when the trial starts. In all cases, as a general rule witnesses are heard again and all the evidence is examined at the trial, and thus it is not necessary to be acquainted with the case beforehand. The present case illustrated this 'principle of immediacy': although it seemed not to be an extremely complicated case, it took all day. Several witnesses were heard. The speed at which the case was handled was, at least to the researchers who were used to the Dutch way of dealing with cases, extremely slow. The judges who guided us during our stay told us that they almost never have cases that go on into the evening. Apparently, the cases are scheduled in such a way that a day in court more often ends *earlier* than planned, rather than later. In this respect, there is a huge difference with the Dutch system in which very often cases go on to far after five o'clock in the evening.

The victim of the alleged robbery by the two young men in this case did not want to make a witness statement in the presence of the two defendants. Actually, he wanted to testify in the presence of the judges only. After substantial deliberation, he made a statement in full court from which only the two defendants were removed. One of the defendants was sentenced to 40 days in prison, the other was acquitted.

On the second day of our visit, at the *Østre Landsret*, we observed two cases, both appeals of a decision by the *Byret*. The *Østre Landsret* is, like the *Byret*, located in the city centre in an old, majestic building. Unlike the *Byret*, this building seems quiet and empty. This court sits with three professional and three lay judges. The professional judges wear robes and the lay judges do not. The robes are slightly open at the front, which gives the impression of informality. During the court session the president plays the most important role and the lay judges remain passive for most of the trial.

The general picture that was gained from these observations in the two courts is that of a criminal justice system that is informal and easy-going, and that attaches much importance to a full discussion of all evidence at trial.

Participants in this system do not seem deeply concerned by crime, rushed to obtain 'targets', or indeed to have any great sense of urgency.

Tak and Fiselier (2004), who made comparisons between Denmark and the Netherlands on the basis of a number of criteria used by Hofstede (2002), observe that Danes generally feel less threatened by insecure situations than the Dutch do. The findings of our research seem to confirm these observations: the Danish judges pay only minor attention to potential safety threats. The procedures employed in Danish criminal courts are characterized by informality. The prosecution plays an important role, not only in the preparation of the case for trial, but also at the trial itself. During the treatment of the case in open court, lay judges generally remain silent. No visible contact takes place between the professional and the lay judges during the court session.

Interviews

On the two days that were spent in the *Byret* and the *Østre Landsret* interviews with professional and lay judges were also conducted. The researchers were introduced to a number of professional judges, and were afforded time to speak with them in their offices. The lay judges who were sitting on these days had been asked in advance by the professional judges whether they would be prepared to participate in an interview after having fulfilled their duties. As far as known to us, nobody refused. All interviewees took the time to discuss matters with us. They all spoke English sufficiently well for an interview.

The interviews were conducted with the help of questionnaires that were designed for the Dutch study, but subsequently revised for the Danish situation. Each interview took about one hour. In the following, we will first look at the respondents' backgrounds, after which the results of the interviews are presented. The respondents' answers are presented anonymously.

Respondents' Backgrounds

Of the professional judges (both of the *Byret* and the *Østre Landsret*), three were females and three were males. Four of them can be considered as 'career judges', having worked all or most of their lives in the judiciary. Two of them had different professional backgrounds: one had worked at the Ministry of Agriculture and taught criminal law at a university prior to becoming a judge, and the other was previously an attorney at law.

The lay judges' backgrounds showed a wide variety. The following occupations were mentioned by the respondents: software engineer, secretary, taxi driver, librarian, law student and teacher. Obviously, not only highly educated lay people are involved in the trial of cases in Denmark. Of the lay judges, four were male and two were female. The number of years they had participated as a lay judge ranged from two to 11.

The Recruitment and Involvement of Lay Judges

For the most part, the recruitment and selection of lay judges takes place through political parties. Selection from political parties is proportional to their size: large political parties nominate more candidates than small ones. In recent years political parties have faced a substantial reduction in their membership. On top of that, they seem less able to motivate their members to accept a position as a lay judge. As a consequence, other ways of recruiting candidates, for example, from municipal voter registration lists, have become relatively more important. A few of the professional judges remarked that they preferred lay judges from political parties because they were better motivated to contribute to the common good by participating in the administration of justice. Lay judges who are picked randomly from election registers may be less motivated in this respect.

Selection procedures seemed not always to be applied in a strict manner. For example, one of the respondents became a lay judge in an unusual way. A friend of his with whom he shared a house was approached to become a lay judge. As fate would have it, it was our respondent who picked up the phone instead of his friend. This respondent was then asked and agreed to become a lay judge as well.

Lay judges are appointed for a term of four years. This term is extended automatically. The lay participants can be called for duty both in the *Byret* as a lay judge and as a member of a jury or as a lay judge in the *Østre Landsret.* There is not a separate list for each type of court. If lay judges want to sit more often than the three to five days each year they are expected to, this is possible. They may also replace other lay judges who have fallen ill. Some lay judges sit eight to 10 days each year and there are also lay judges who only sit as few as one or two days per year.

The involvement as a lay judge may be problematic for those with certain occupations, such as businesspeople. If a trial takes more than one day, it may conflict with the requirements inherent in this type of occupation. A professional judge interviewed recounted an occasion when, for this reason, he had relieved a businessman of his duty to act as a lay judge. One of the lay judges worked for a private company and feared he might be fired if he were absent too many days for duty as a judge. In theory, employers are obliged to give days off if you are called for service in the administration of justice. However, some firms are not happy about doing so and try to find reasons to end your contract if you are away too often. Some lay judges thus request that they not be called for jury cases, because these may last longer than one day in court. Trials in which lay judges sit generally do not take more than one day.

The instruction that the novice lay judges receive is not very detailed. Before their first court session they have an evening meeting in which a professional judge explains how the legal system works and what is expected from lay judges. In between the court sessions there are no instructional meetings planned, and no supervision takes place. Professional and lay judges come together 10 minutes before each trial. The president of the panel then explains the crimes the defendants are charged with and asks whether the lay judges know the defendant personally. The judges' impartiality is thus checked; they have to sign a form that they are not personally acquainted with the defendant.

One professional judge interviewed explained that candidates receive a booklet with information about their duties and the problems that have to be faced. This judge has been present at introductory meetings with lay judges and has spoken to them. He was of the opinion that lay judges should not receive too much education as a judge: they act as lay persons and thus should not become too professional. Further instruction and education would therefore not be desirable.

Personal Experiences of Lay Judges

During the interviews attention was paid to lay judges' experiences regarding their service in the judicial system. Before starting as a lay judge, the respondents held preconceptions of what it would be like to act as a judge. Some expectations were fulfilled, others were not. Five out of the six lay judges who were interviewed indicated that they were pleased to be in the position of a judge. The remaining respondent made clear that he was rather indifferent towards his role as a judge. Court sessions were sometimes exciting, he felt, and he was aware that he was doing the system a favour. These were his motivations for serving as a judge.

Reasons for enjoying participation centred around being able to become acquainted with the legal system and having the opportunity to decide cases together with professional judges. Some respondents were proud to be able to act as a lay judge and happy to be able to have an input from a lay perspective. One lay judge had, before starting, been convinced that courts sentenced too leniently and found it illuminating to see how judges come to their decisions in practice. He now understood better why courts do not sentence as harshly as he had previously thought proper. Before taking up her position as a judge, one young female had wanted to influence society. This wish was fulfilled: she was actually able to make relevant decisions and to exert influence.

The expectations regarding what it would be like to take part in the trial of cases differed between the lay judges. One lay judge was a little disappointed that he was unable to put forward his own opinions as he had expected. In most cases, presidents of the panels give their own opinion first and then ask the others. The views of the lay judges are usually asked last. However, there are also presidents who give the floor to the lay judges first and only give their own opinion after having heard the others. Other lay judges, on the contrary, were surprised by the amount of input they could have, both in determining the defendant's guilt and in sentencing. On this point, experiences between the lay judges differed, probably caused by the variety of ways in which professional judges supervise the court session, communicate with the lay judges and chair the deliberations afterwards.

Advantages of Lay Participation

The judges, both professional and lay, were asked to indicate the advantages of lay people participating in the administration of justice. Altogether, 16 different advantages were mentioned. Each respondent could mention several advantages and each advantage could be mentioned by one or more respondent (see Table 7.1).

The professional judges mentioned by far the largest number of advantages (18), whereas the lay judges mentioned nine different advantages. Lay adjudicators having a perspective that differs from that of the professional judges was the advantage mentioned most often, by four professional and one lay judge. The expectation that the criminal justice system would deal more fairly with cases as a result of lay judge participation was mentioned by three professional judges and by one lay judge. Being educated on how the legal system works was mentioned as an advantage by two lay judges and one professional judge (see Table 7.1). Other advantages mentioned more than once were lay participation enhancing the acceptance of court decisions (by two professional judges), and it leading to more confidence in the system (one lay and one professional judge).

The respondents gave various explanations of the advantages mentioned, The lay judges stressed that the type of input they have differs from that of the professional judges. 'I do know more about how youngsters live and about their behaviour in certain situations than the professional judges do,' said one of the younger lay judges. 'I know how they talk to each other, I can recognize when they must have been drunk when committing the alleged crime, and I know when to take them seriously and when not.' The possibility of presenting views from an angle that differs from that of the professional judges was voiced by other respondents as well.

Some lay judges felt that it was an advantage that more groups in society were offered the chance to participate. Lay judges indicated that they now had more trust in the legal system than before, because they had seen how it operates. They often agreed with the professional judges on cases and decisions that had to be made. However, because they do not sit every day, they retain their fresh and unprejudiced view on cases. This is strengthened by the fact that they do not read the case file before the court session.

When ordinary citizens participate, they are able to discuss cases with the professional judges. Both professional and lay judges attach value to

Table 7.1 Advantages of lay participation mentioned by professional (6) and by lay judges (6) (Denmark)

	Professional judges	Lay judges	Total
Different perspectives	4	1	5
Fairer treatment of case	3	1	4
Education of lay people	1	2	3
Acceptance of court decisions	2	–	2
Increased confidence in the system	1	1	2
Better connection with society	1	–	1
Lay people see we do it correctly	1	–	1
More discussion with lay people	1	–	1
Common sense of lay people	1	–	1
Beneficial for the system	–	1	1
Judgement by peers	–	1	1
Against drawbacks of routine	–	1	1
Three know more than one	–	1	1
Helps to make your arguments more clear	1	–	1
Dissemination of knowledge system	1	–	1
Lay people become more moderate when taking part	1	–	1
Total advantages: 16	*18*	*9*	*27*

this opportunity. They suggested the system's legitimacy would be increased by lay participation. It was important to hear the public's voice when the defendant's guilt has to be established. The same would apply in determining the sentence.

Both professional and lay judges made clear that lay participation could also have advantages for the defendants, such as an enhanced chance of receiving a fair trial. The opportunity of becoming acquainted with the legal system was one of the advantages most often expressed by the lay judges who were interviewed. It was felt that insight into the operation of the system is increased, as is the understanding of the complexity of judicial decision making. Through participation, lay judges were able to gain an understanding of how difficult it is to be a judge and to form an opinion on a case.

All in all, the respondents, both lay and professional, seem to feel that lay adjudication is beneficial for the legal system. Most respondents indicated more than two advantages of lay participation. In total, the professional judges mentioned a larger number of advantages per person than the lay judges (three vs 1.5).

Disadvantages of Lay Participation

On request, the respondents also indicated the disadvantages of lay participation. The number of disadvantages mentioned was smaller than the advantages. As with the advantages, each respondent could mention several disadvantages, and each disadvantage could be mentioned by one or more respondent (see Table 7.2).

Table 7.2 Disadvantages of lay participation mentioned by professional (6) and by lay judges (6) (Denmark)

	Professional judges	Lay judges	Total
Jury sometimes incorrectly acquits	3	1	4
Some lay judges reluctant to punish	3	-	3
Lack of expertise	-	2	2
Trials take longer	1	1	2
Juries decide out of their emotions	1	-	1
Lay judges don't have their own room	-	1	1
Difficult to reach correct decision	-	1	1
Difficult to get days off from work	-	1	1
Lay people differ too much from each other	-	1	1
Higher expenses	-	1	1
Total disadvantages: 10	*8*	*9*	*17*

The number of disadvantages mentioned were about equal for both groups: eight for the professional judges and nine for the lay judges, This implies that a mean of 1.3 disadvantages was mentioned per professional judges and 1.5 per lay judge.

Comments by professional judges often focused on the way the jury functions. In some cases, the jurors might be inclined to acquit the defendant while the professional judges would be convinced of his guilt. Members of a jury might be driven by their emotions and that would not be the case (or would be less the case) with lay judges, because the latter could be advised by the professional judge.

Some professional judges remarked that lay people can have strange opinions and make illogical decisions. Some lay judges hold very strong opinions against the imposition of prison sentences. It seems they are, in principle, against incarceration. It may happen that all lay judges on a panel are opposed to the prison system, so that there is the risk of acquittal even when the defendant has obviously committed the alleged crime. Professional judges sometimes felt that it would be easier to decide cases on their own. In a panel with lay judges, decision making takes longer which increases the costs of the judiciary.

In the wider society, there is a regular criticism that judges are too lenient. However, these lenient punishments are generally due to the influence of the *lay* judges and not the professional judges. According to one professional judge, it would be very difficult to explain this to the politicians who want the courts to punish more harshly. Politicians are convinced that the public wants more severe penalties, but they are not aware that it is, in fact, the lay judges who are the cause of the lenient climate in criminal cases.

The respondents indicated that there are serious differences among lay adjudicators. One respondent gave the example of a lay judge who thought that the defendant's guilt had already been established before the trial had started and wanted to proceed directly with determining a penalty. He obviously was not aware that the court first had to make a decision regarding the defendant's guilt before proceeding with the questions about the sentence.

One disadvantage put forward by lay judges was the fact that they do not have their own room in the courthouse where they could retire after the conclusion of the deliberations. It may happen that they leave the court building together with a criminal who has just been convicted. 'To keep this from happening, we generally wait some time before leaving. Nevertheless, it may happen that you come face to face with the convicted person when leaving the building. About 70 per cent of all cases are about violent crime, so you can imagine that this is not a very pleasant situation', a lay judge remarked.

An important disadvantage is the lay judges' lack of routine. In the opinion of some lay participants, it is very difficult to actually form a judgement on a case. They consider it extremely problematic to form an opinion on guilt, culpability and a possible sentence without having experience.

Collaboration between Professional and Lay Judges

Almost all the professional judges enjoyed collaborating with lay judges. Lay judges have a fresh view on the cases and their perspective differs from the views of the professionals. However, collaboration is not always without difficulties. One professional judge recounts that she once had a lay judge who appeared drunk. Sometimes lay judges do not behave correctly. And once they are appointed, you cannot get rid of them. She sometimes thought to herself when she saw the name of a particular lay judge on her lists, 'Oh no, not that one again!' But that is an exceptional situation; most cases go well.

Professional judges sometimes have to get used to working with lay persons. In the beginning they find it difficult, especially in complicated cases. In the long run they get used to it and become more positive about collaborating with lay judges. Some cases, however, are so complicated that lay judges are not able to have effective input. A professional judge remarked that in complicated cases it would be good to be able to choose your own lay judges.

That, however, is not allowed; you have to take the person who is at the top of the list. Two professional judges made it clear that they would not mind if the lay system was abolished. The others, however, preferred to retain lay input.

Lay Judges' Input

The actual input by lay judges during the trial of cases is, according to all respondents, substantially smaller than that of the professional judges. If they want to ask a question, they generally do this by writing it on a piece of paper and giving it to the president, who subsequently poses the question to the defendant. When deliberating over the verdict and the sentence after the court session, lay judges generally give their opinion first. The president generally indicates the boundaries within which the sentence can be chosen and leaves it to the lay members to give their opinion first. In a trial before the *Østre Landsret*, some presidents first ask the opinions of their professional colleagues and then those of the lay judges. The reason is that the professional judges know more about sentencing and current trends; lay judges lack such a frame of reference.

It clearly appeared from the responses in the interviews that, contrary to general expectations, the lay judges preferred lenient sentences more often than the professional judges. They were more often in favour of conditional sentences, and they were more sensitive to personal circumstances. Because of their more extensive experience, professional judges would be less empathic and have more distance from the defendant. They are better able to compare a case with former cases. Therefore, they focus more on the case itself and have less personal involvement than lay judges.

All respondents stressed that it was generally easy to come to an agreement on the various decisions that have to be made. One respondent estimated that in about one out of 10 cases the panel did not reach an agreement. If that happened and she, as a professional judge, was in favour of an acquittal, she wrote a dissenting opinion. She did not want to reach an agreement at all costs. Professional judges stress that they enjoy deliberating with the lay judges. It is stimulating and they like to communicate about a case and how all judges, lay and professional, perceive it.

The respondents estimated that the lay judges' contribution during deliberations was about equal to, or slightly less than, that of the professionals. Generally the professional judge starts post-session discussion of the case by presenting a summary and then leaves it to the lay judges to give their opinions on the defendant's guilt and the sentence.

Lay judges sometimes make the professional judges see a case in a different light. They emphasize circumstances that may lead to a different judgement on a case. In some cases they introduce specific knowledge. One professional judge gave an example of a hotdog seller who was accused of tax fraud. One of the lay judges sitting that day had sold hotdogs herself. She was able to make clear that the defendant was right in saying that it was not possible to sell the numbers of hotdogs he was accused of. If this lay judge had not participated, the outcome might have been different. In another example, a young lay judge who was familiar with the youth culture in the city where he lived was better able to assess the way youngsters interact and what type of behaviour could be expected in certain situations. Most of the professional judges recalled having experienced that a lay judge made them see a case in a different light, but most of them could not come up with concrete examples.

The Influence of Experience

Respondents were asked whether the opinions of lay judges changed as a consequence of gaining experience as a judge. Four out of the six professional judges had observed this happening and two did not know. Four out of the six lay judges were of the opinion that their opinions had *not* changed since they had started acting as a judge. The reasons suggested for a perceived change in the lay judges' opinions included that the lay participants increasingly felt part of the judicial system after having acted as a judge in a number of cases. This greater involvement was evident in the fact that the lay judges gradually showed less empathy towards the defendant and that they distrusted the defendant more. They were able to keep more distance from the cases they had to try. The professional judges felt that it was easier to collaborate with lay judges who have obtained some degree of experience than with 'new' lay judges.

Two lay judges also observed that they had become harsher in the course of participation. In the long run, their opinions become more similar to those of the salaried judges. Their sympathy for the defendant decreased and they now focused more on the case characteristics. On top of that, the lay judges indicated that they were now more involved in the investigation of the case, by more frequently putting questions to defendants, witnesses and experts. One lay judge remarked that she had become less convinced of the effectiveness of imposing a prison sentence. She had noticed that many convicted persons reappear in court after having served a prison term.

Emotions

A majority of all respondents (10 out of 12) felt that lay judges were more emotional than professional judges. Only one professional judge took a position in the middle ('lay judges are slightly more emotional, especially when the media are present in the courtroom'[2]) and one lay judge felt that lay judges were not emotional at all, because they learned not to be.

2 The respondents made it clear that journalists and cameras do not often attend criminal trials in Denmark.

The ways in which this emotion is shown include a greater sensitivity to what the defendant says and how he or she looks. Lay judges more often want to impose conditional rather than unconditional sentences. Personal circumstances, such as a father who is addicted to alcohol, receive more attention from the lay judges. The lay participants often have more empathy with the defendant, or with witnesses and victims.

These emotions may lead the lay judges to give greater credence to what the defendants say. The professional judges, on the basis of their experience in dealing with cases, take a more critical view towards the defendant's statements and they are inclined not to believe what he or she says. They make comparisons with other cases and keep more distance. Their personal involvement is smaller.

Most lay judges admit to being influenced by their emotions to a larger extent than the professional judges. When deliberating about a case lay judges are more often angry and they are more sensitive to what happens during the trial than the professional judges are. But that is, they note, the very reason why lay people are involved: they introduce a human factor in the administration of justice.

The reason that respondents give for their greater emotional involvement is that they are not used to sending people to prison. However, there are discernible differences between people from varying backgrounds. Some would, as a result of their professional background, be more likely to impose punishments than others. It was also remarked that after having participated in the judiciary for some years this emotional sensitivity decreases: lay judges become less impressed by crime and by certain suspects, and become better able to step back from their own emotions.

Acceptance of Court Decisions

Respondents were asked whether they felt that court decisions would be more readily accepted because lay judges were involved in making the decisions. Eight out of the 12 respondents thought that this was the case, three took a middle position and one thought that such an influence was negligible.

Some felt court decisions would be better accepted because the lay participants would tell their families and friends about how the system works. Knowledge of the system is, thus, disseminated among the public. Lay judges are often people who want to serve the common good. The public, when aware of this motivation, would thus more readily accept the decisions. Defendants, while making a statement, regularly direct their attention primarily towards the lay participants. Professional judges use too much legal jargon and as a consequence defendants experience a certain distance from them. Defendants are less likely to feel that the verdict is a foregone conclusion when lay people participate. They also generally assume that their chances are better with benches involving lay adjudicators.

The general public too finds it easier to accept court decisions when lay people are involved. Acceptance is increased because lay participation allows the professionals to show that they are independent and unprejudiced. The public feels that these decision makers are more impartial. Professional judges to a certain degree live in an ivory tower, while lay participants do not. According to one respondent, citizens love the idea that ordinary people participate in the judicial system. With professional judges only, there would be a greater probability of mistakes being made. Lay people have a different focus from the professional judges, and that is the very reason that they are engaged. They can ensure that the professional judges do not act and make decisions from routine, which may lead to defective decision making.

The lay judge who was of the opinion that lay participation would *not* influence acceptance made it clear that the system has existed for such a long time that people do not really think about it, and would not let their acceptance be affected by it. Two judges who took a middle position (no overriding influence on acceptance) were of the opinion that two or more decision makers are better than only one, irrespective of whether they are lay people or professionals. When three people reach a decision, it has more legitimacy and this would be the main reason for greater acceptance.

Importance of Ordinary Citizens Participating

Respondents were asked whether they personally felt that the involvement of ordinary people in the administration of justice was important. Ten out of the 12 respondents did. Various motives were mentioned.

Several respondents pointed to the long tradition that exists in Denmark regarding the involvement of lay people, not only within the judiciary, but also in other fields in society. Lay participation fits very well in the country's legal culture. It is considered as natural that ordinary citizens should participate at all levels of society. The image of the judiciary that is created in society by the participation of lay people is important. On top of that, lay people may prevent decisions being made without deep reflection. 'If I were to decide with professional judges only, we would very easily and quickly come to conclusions. Now, we have to think and explain why we have a certain opinion', said a professional judge. The requirement to give reasons to the lay participants for certain of their standpoints would thus lead to more thorough and robust decisions than would be made by an exclusively professional panel.

Respondents were aware that the decisions are not strikingly different from those which would be made if no lay people participated: in general, few differences of opinion emerge during deliberations about a case. The reason for lay participation would then primarily lie in the increase of trust, the acceptance of decisions and the transparency of the system. The participation of lay judges demonstrates that no decisions are made in secret. Many respondents indicated that it is important that citizens know what is going on in the courts.

Ivory Tower

Most respondents were of the opinion that Danish professional judges were sufficiently in touch with the 'real world'. They stressed that judges participate in society like any other citizens, and that they are no different from other people. One professional judge stated that, although the judges do not live in ivory towers, they actually come from a different social strata than the 'general public'. One lay judge noted that the risk of not being fully in contact with the 'real world' may lead to too much routine and professionalism. There is a risk that professional judges become too aloof, and no longer open to arguments brought forward by other people outside their own group.

Dissemination

Lay judges were asked whether they spoke to others about their experiences as a lay judge and, if so, what they talked about. Four out of the six lay judges answered that they did so. Most of them talked about their experiences with friends and family. There was a certain variety in the topics: most of them only talked about the case itself and said nothing about the system, others primarily talked about the operation of the criminal justice system without saying anything about the case that had been tried in court. Those who talked to their friends and family about the system explained that they were generally positive about its operation. The public's general knowledge of the legal system in Denmark is inadequate and therefore these respondents explained how the system works. Those who talked about the case in hand remarked that people generally were interested in the individual cases; they were eager to know what crimes were committed and how these crimes were dealt with in court.[3]

Being Kept Awake at Night

None of the respondents said that they were kept awake at night by the decisions they had to make in court, but most of them emphasized that they often kept thinking about a case after it had been decided. One professional judge explained that during the first period that she worked in court, she was sometimes kept awake at night by the decisions that had to be made. Now she was more experienced and had stopped being concerned about the cases she dealt with.

3 One lay judge stated that he refused to talk about individual cases: it was nobody's business what happened in court.

Conclusions

Satisfaction with the system of lay participation seems high in Denmark. The distance between the professional and the lay judges is small and they generally reach an agreement quite easily. In the Danish legal culture the participation of lay people in the various institutions in society is self-evident; nobody seems to question it.

The respondents seemed aware of the risks of one-sidedness in decision making: too much professionalism and too much routine may lead to a lack of thorough investigation of a case and to a lack of transparency. The involvement of lay people helps to overcome the negative effects of routine. The lay judges are drawn from a variety of backgrounds. It is not only highly educated people who take part in the administration of justice.

Negative aspects of lay participation were not neglected by the respondents however. They commented on some of the lay judges who did not act professionally and were not able to preserve sufficient distance. They noticed a change in the composition of the group of lay judges, who were more often being recruited from voter lists used for municipal elections and less often from political parties. The latter group were better motivated to perform tasks of a public nature than people randomly selected from the municipality. It is also noted that exigencies in daily professional life for lay participants may conflict with their participation in the judiciary. Insufficient remedies exist to deal with these. However, the overriding picture in Denmark is one of general satisfaction with lay participation in the criminal justice system.

Chapter 8
Germany

Introduction

The German legal system makes use of various types of lay participation, including, in criminal cases, juries for the most serious cases and lay judges for crimes of a less severe nature. Lay judges (*Schöffen*) were the rule in Germany and her states throughout her early history and the middle ages. The *Reich* Constitution of 1849 called for both public and oral criminal proceedings and for jury trial for more serious crimes and political offences (Casper and Zeisel 1972). The demand for jury trials was met by the overwhelming majority of German states following the events of 1848, although details varied from state to state.

In 1850, the Kingdom of Hanover provided the model for an alternative to the jury: a criminal court composed of professional and lay judges who decided cases in collaboration. From this emerged the modern *Schöffengericht* which was swiftly adopted by a number of other states (Casper and Zeisel 1972). Debates were conducted in this period about the merits of mixed tribunals and those of a jury court. The *Schöffengericht* appears to have stood the test. In 1877 the *Schöffengericht* was legally established, having jurisdiction over petty crimes.

A number of jurisdictional realignments took place in the period through to 1924, during which the 'classical' jury was transformed into a mixed tribunal, composed of three professional and six lay judges (the so-called *Schwurgericht*). The present court organization in Germany dates from 1970 (Casper and Zeisel 1972). Except for petty crimes, which are tried before a single professional judge, and serious political offences, all crimes are tried before tribunals on which lay judges decide cases together with professional judges. There is a wide variety of German tribunals with differing compositions (Casper and Zeisel 1972, 142). The present chapter focuses on lay participation in the *Schöffengericht*; other types of tribunals are not included in this research.[1]

This chapter first discusses the literature on the involvement of lay people in German courts, after which the results of interviews with professional judges and *Schöffen* are presented. These interviews were conducted in a town in the middle of Germany, at the *Amtsgericht* (Court of First Instance). This court tries criminal cases with panels that consist of a professional judge who

---

1 In 1989, the Western and Eastern parts of Germany were reunited. This chapter does not address the consequences of this development for court organization.

chairs the hearing, and two lay judges. The president of this *Amtsgericht* gave consent to the researchers to conduct a number of interviews in his court. Thirteen interviews were conducted: four with professional judges and nine with *Schöffen*. In addition, the judges provided the researchers with an introduction to the national criminal justice system and the way cases are tried in Germany with the involvement of lay people. A three-day programme was organized, during which the interviews and meetings took place.

Because the German lay system is similar to the Danish situation, the same questionnaires were used, translated into German for this purpose. Respondents were selected in advance by the court. As far as is known to us, nobody refused to participate in an interview. Because the researchers were not sufficiently fluent in German, an interpreter assisted during the interviews. Before presenting the findings of the interviews, attention will first be given to the literature and empirical research that has been conducted in the past into the German way of involving ordinary citizens.

Literature on Lay Participation

In Germany nearly one quarter of all criminal trials are dealt with by mixed tribunals, in other words, by benches that make use of lay persons. The literature indicates that in 2000 there were three times as many lay judges participating in the trial of cases as professional judges (Bovend'Eert 2001; Bliesener 2006). The system of lay participation, however, is subject to criticism in Germany. The majority of the 124 professional judges in the various Courts of First Instance who were questioned by Klausa (1972) voiced more disadvantages than benefits from the involvement of lay judges. Points of concern included the lack of legal knowledge, the increased amount of time needed when lay people participate, the limited contribution by the lay participants, their emotions, the high expenses and the inappropriate selection of lay judges. More than 60 per cent of the professional judges and prosecutors who were questioned by Rennig (1993) also complained that lay judges do not contribute enough to the handling of the case and to decision making (Bliesener 2000). But positive aspects were also mentioned by Klausa (1972), such as the beneficial effects in determining the penalty, educating the public, improving people's trust in the administration of justice, and preventing professional judges from getting into a rut (Klausa 1972; Rennig 1993; Tak 2006).

A number of studies have been conducted on the procedures for recruiting lay judges (for overviews, see Bliesener 2000; Machura 2001). Political parties, welfare institutions, sports clubs, financial and health insurance institutions, trade unions, public authorities and industrial companies are primarily called upon to nominate candidates to become a lay judge (Brusten and Westmeier 1992). It appears that the motivations of these institutions are very different; they include: social responsibility, cultivation of their own image, advertising, participation in the decisions on allocating fines and further education (Brusten and Westmeier 1992). Thus it is not only arguments related to the common good that are of relevance. Apart from being recruited by institutions, interested citizens can also apply to be a lay judge when openings are publicly advertised, but, according to this research, that does not often occur. On the basis of the lists of candidates who have been nominated one single list is constructed that is used for selecting both *Schöffen* and *Geschworenen* (members of a jury) (Klausa 1972). A relatively large proportion of employees in the public services can be found in the resulting body of lay judges (27 per cent versus 8 per cent in the general population; Bliesener 2006). Furthermore, the number of housewives is relatively high, and the number of employees in the private sector is relatively low. Lay judges are generally older people (Bliesener 2006).

The Federal Association of Honorary Judges,[2] established in 1993, plays a role in the education of novice lay judges. Until 1993 there were differences among the Federal States on this point: some states only distributed brochures to the new lay judges, whereas other states did more to educate them. Before the main hearing begins, the chairman of the tribunal gives a short introduction to the case. However this introduction is sometimes omitted, or is regarded as inadequate by the lay judges (Bliesener 2006).

Although there is no specific regulation denying lay judges access to the case file, in most cases they do not examine the documents before the hearing of a case. Giving the case files to the lay judges is widely considered to jeopardize the principle of immediacy, because of the risk that impressions from the documents may be confused with those obtained from the hearing of the case. Unlike lay persons, professional judges are deemed to be able to keep separate these two sources of information while evaluating the case (Bliesener 2006).

The German lay judges have the right to question the defendant, witnesses and experts, and they are equally involved in the deliberations and decision making after the hearing of the case. Casper and Zeisel (1972) found that in about half of all cases the lay judges ask questions during the hearing of the case. According to post-trial surveys of participants, lay judges behave rather passively during main hearings (Machura 2001; Benz 1982a; Rennig and Machura 1999; Bliesener 2006). When lay judges ask questions, professional judges often consider these as rather unimportant or redundant (Casper and Zeisel 1972). Some professional judges fear that the inexperienced lay judges may ask inadmissible questions, and that concern sometimes leads to attempts to minimize the lay judges' participation (Rennig 1993). On the other hand, it has been suggested that giving lay judges access to the case files would increase their participation during trial and deliberation, while not affecting their decisions (Bliesener 2006).

2 *Bundesverbandes ehrenamtlicher Richterinnen und Richter e.V.*

Attitudes to punishment and judgement preferences do not differ greatly between lay and professional judges, nor is there evidence that lay judges are characteristically lenient (Bliesener 2006). Important aspects of the involvement of lay judges that are generally emphasized in the literature are the fact that they introduce new perspectives on cases, and that they can prevent the professional from relying too much on their established routine (Wasserman 1985).

In panels with two *Schöffen* and one professional judge a two-thirds majority is required for reaching a decision. In practice a formal vote is rarely taken following the deliberations. As a rule, no essential differences of opinion seem to emerge during deliberations. Frequently mixed tribunals have already reached agreement in the course of discussion (Benz 1982a; Lieber and Sens 2001; Bliesener 2006). Professional judges being outvoted by the lay judges is rare (Klausa 1972). Conspicuously, about half of the professional judges appear to succeed in changing the lay judges' opinions if these differ from their own views (Casper and Zeisel 1972). Machura (2001) found that the tendency to disagree with professional judges decreases with the duration of the lay judge's service. The findings of the studies mentioned suggest that the professional judges' views generally prevail over those of the *Schöffen*, and continue to prevail even after the lay judges have gained experience in the adjudication of cases.

About 20 per cent of lay judges regularly tell their family about their activities as a judge, 70 per cent do so often or sometimes, and 10 per cent never (Machura 2001; Bliesener 2006). When former lay judges discuss their experiences with others, they share their general experiences and problems, information about interesting processes and criminal cases, and the pressure that arises from the role of being a lay judge (Villmow et al. 1986). Discussions about particular offenders and sentences, however, are rare. The reluctance to recount their experiences on the part of some lay judges may have to do with the requirement of confidentiality with respect to the deliberations and the voting (Bliesener 2006).

The general conclusion from the literature is that there is criticism of lay participation in Germany because of the perceived meager input by the lay persons. On the other hand, actual conflicts of opinions do not often occur during the deliberations, probably due to the fact that the professional judge generally prevails in the discussions. The suggestion has been made that if lay judges were better instructed or were given access to the case file some of these points of concern would disappear. At the same time, the literature makes it clear that there is no suggestion of abolishing lay participation in Germany.

Interviews

Respondents' Backgrounds

In total, 13 interviews were conducted at the *Amtsgericht*: four with professional judges and nine with lay judges (*Schöffen*). Of the four professional judges two were males and two females. The group of lay judges consisted of five females and four males. The lay judges' professional backgrounds varied. Two were employed at a bank and two worked as tax officers. The remaining lay judges had the following occupations: director of a school, teacher, nurse, farmer and interpreter. Obviously, lay judges are recruited from different walks of life in Germany. Most of them had gained experience as a lay judge over five to six years: one had been working for 12 years as a lay judge. The number of years the professional judges had been in their position ranged from four to 14.

Of the lay judges, four indicated that the political party of which they were a member had forwarded their names to the court for participation. Three entered the judiciary via the municipality. The answers of two lay judges were not clear on this point.

The Recruitment and Involvement of Lay Judges

The lay judges generally sit 12 days each year. There is a special course for new lay judges in the *Amtsgericht* (a *Schöffenschule*). This course takes a couple of days, and usually takes place on weekends. During this introductory course the lay judges are given an explanation of the criminal justice system and of how a case is actually heard in court. They are prepared for the trials by reading a number of indictments. They are introduced to the law, and the problems they will face during trials and their tasks in court are explained to them.

Several respondents commented on the way lay judges are recruited, how they are informed about the legal system and the way they are educated and prepared for their duties. One professional judge commented that there are too many lists from which candidates are chosen. He also had the impression that there is a preference for certain political parties. As a consequence, some citizens might think that they do not have an equal opportunity to become a lay judge, just because they are not a member of the right political party. Some lay judges indicated that it is difficult to say 'no' in case a political party asks whether you want to be involved in the trial of criminal cases. Political parties disapprove of members not being willing to participate as a *Schöffe*. Small municipalities nominate relatively more candidates to the courts than the larger ones. This leads to an imbalanced representation as well.

The professional judges interviewed stated that it was difficult to acquire enough candidates. Many ordinary citizens are not eager to be involved because this creates a disturbance in their daily routine. People who do not have a permanent contract risk difficulties with their employers or lose income when participating as a lay judge. Several respondents stressed that, for these various reasons, the group of lay judges is not representative of the general population.

Only one judge in the *Amtsgericht* is in charge of the actual selection of candidates for duty as a lay judge. At the beginning of each year a roster is established for what days the lay judges will serve in the trial of cases. No manipulation would be possible on the point of with whom the lay judges sit on a panel. Nevertheless, several respondents indicated that they are not aware of the criteria the court uses for making these decisions.

Besides the course they have to follow when they start, lay judges are expected to learn while participating. An explanation is provided prior to the start of the trial regarding the crime(s) for which the defendant is charged, the evidence that is available, and the points that deserve special attention during the court session. During the trial, when the panel retires for deliberation, explanation and guidance is provided as well. Furthermore, the lay judges have the opportunity to ask questions of the president. They do so outside the open court. Among the issues dealt with in these questions are the admissibility of evidence and the weight of the penalties that might be imposed.

Lay Judges' Personal Experiences

All lay judges interviewed indicated that they enjoyed participating in the criminal justice system. The primary reason for their positive evaluation is that participation provides the opportunity to obtain insight into the legal system and how it operates. It gives a certain sense to the lay judges that what they do is important. 'When I sit in a panel, I am glad that I am on the right side of the table', one respondent indicated. One lay judge sitting in a youth court explained that his motivation was to find reasonable sanctions for young persons. In his regular work this lay judge also deals with youngsters. Acquiring a broader view on society is a reason for a participation as well. 'You see so many different people in court … It is good to take notice of how people from other circles conduct their lives', a lay judge explained.

Other lay judges emphasized the difficulties of making decisions in court. They felt that they had to learn a lot. But they found great satisfaction in being able to contribute to society in this way. Some felt that they could make a useful contribution to the trial of cases just *because* they did not act out of a professional background. As a lay person they were able to provide a useful perspective on cases. In general, the ability to widen their own horizons and the opportunities to contribute to the general interest and the common good seemed to prevail in the answers of the lay judges regarding their motivation for participating.

The actual experiences and how they relate to the lay judges' original expectations sometimes gave a different picture than the optimistic one sketched above. The extent to which professional judges actively involved the lay judges in the trial of cases and the deliberations afterwards differed substantially. Some lay judges had the impression that they were regarded as pieces of furniture instead of as active judges. On other occasions, however, the message was conveyed to them that their contribution was highly valued and that there were practically no differences between professional and lay judges. They would be regarded as equals with the regular judges. From the professional judges' openness – if and how they asked questions of the lay judges and gave them the opportunity to ask questions about the case – lay participants could deduce whether they were viewed as unimportant or as 'real' judges. 'Some judges are eager to hear your opinion, but there are only a few', said a lay judge. 'In all the years that I have been participating, I have only asked one question during the hearing of a case. There is still a serious threshold. I'm afraid to ask an inadmissible question. Or I fear that this question has already been asked before.'

During the hearing of the case, it may happen that the prosecutor or the defence lawyer presents a document only to the president and neglects the two lay judges. If, subsequently, the president does not give this document to the lay judges, the latter's impression of redundancy may be reinforced. Lay judges sometimes get the feeling that they are not taken seriously.

Most lay judges (eight out of nine), however, made it clear that their original expectations had, for the most part, been realized. They experienced their own input as a real participation in the legal system, one which enhanced discussion and debate with the professionals. The collaboration with the professional judges was experienced as highly positive by the lay judges. One lay judge had expected to serve as a sort of figurehead, but instead she fully participated in the trial of cases. For her reality thus turned out to be more positive than expected.

In summary, the actual experiences with participation varied among the lay judges. Although they were highly positive about their own involvement, their actual experiences were not always equally favourable. Considerable differences were observed among the chairmen of the panels in the way they involved the lay judges.

Advantages of Lay Participation

The respondents were asked to indicate the advantages of the participation of lay people in the trial of cases. Both the professional judges and the lay judges put forward several benefits from the input of ordinary citizens. Each respondent could mention several advantages, and each advantage could be mentioned by one or more respondent. Sixteen different advantages were identified. The mean number of advantages mentioned per respondent did not greatly differ between professional and lay judges (2.8 versus 2.3) (see Table 8.1).

Table 8.1 Advantages of lay participation mentioned by professional judges (4) and *Schöffen* (9) (Germany)

	Professional judges	*Schöffen*	Total
Different perspectives	2	4	6
Different walks of life	–	4	4
Schöffen are unprejudiced	–	4	4
Counterbalance to routine	–	3	3
Experience in life and other jobs	1	1	2
Supervising the judge's work	2	–	2
More empathy	–	2	2
Better understanding of legal system	1	–	1
Special knowledge	1	–	1
Lay people make better observations	1	–	1
Common sense	1	–	1
Decisions not left to professionals only	1	–	1
Education of the citizens	1	–	1
Contact of judges with ordinary people	–	1	1
Transparency	–	1	1
Schöffen take more aspects into account	–	1	1
Total advantages: 16	*11*	*21*	*32*

The provision of different perspectives on a case by lay judges was mentioned most often: by six respondents (two professional judges and four lay judges). The different walks of life presented by lay participation was mentioned four times by the lay judges as an advantage. This advantage was only indicated by the lay judges, however; no professional judge mentioned it. The same with regard to the perceived advantage of the lay judges' lack of prejudice. As *Schöffen* do not read the case file in advance, they enter court without preconceptions. Professional judges have already taken cognisance of the case file when the trial begins, and would, thus, be more likely to have formed opinions.

A variety of other advantages of lay participation were mentioned, such as combating the negative effects of professional routine (mentioned by three lay judges), the lay judges' experience of life and in certain occupations (mentioned by one professional and one lay judge), offering an opportunity to supervise the professional judge's work (two professional judges) and the lay judges having more empathy and greater sensitivity (two lay judges).

The general conclusion from this overview is that the 'different perspectives' and the 'varying backgrounds' introduced by lay participation are valued most, by the lay judges who were interviewed. There is a general emphasis on advantages that are expected to contribute to the quality of decisions made by the tribunal and on advantages that focus on the contribution of the lay perspective to the legal system. Advantages that suggest a contribution by the legal system to the lay participants or the public at large, such as a 'education of citizens', are mentioned less often. This is surprising in view of remarks that have earlier been presented, that suggest that lay participants attach much value to learning effects and the broadening of their own horizons.

Disadvantages

A smaller number of disadvantages were mentioned than the number of advantages (11 versus 16). The amount of time and the expense that is involved because of the participation of lay judges was indicated most often: two times by the professionals and two times by the lay judges. Related to this disadvantage is the fact that lay people need more explanation (mentioned twice, both times by professional judges). All other disadvantages were mentioned only once (see Table 8.2).

Table 8.2 Disadvantages of lay participation mentioned by professional judges (4) and *Schöffen* (9) (Germany)

	Professional judges	*Schöffen*	Total
Involves considerable time and expense	2	2	4
Schöffen need lots of explanation	2	–	2
Lack of knowledge	1	–	1
Inadmissible questions asked by *Schöffen*	1	–	1
Difficult to reach consensus	1	–	1
Emotions of the *Schöffen*	1	–	1
Prejudices of the *Schöffen*	1	–	1
Judges do too little to involve you	–	1	1
Bureaucracy in the court	–	1	1
Decision making is difficult	–	1	1
Hearings are strenuous	–	1	1
Total disadvantages: 11	*9*	*6*	*15*

Each disadvantage could be brought up by several respondents, and each respondent could mention more than one disadvantage. The four professional judges mentioned a total of nine disadvantages, and the lay judges (N = 9) put forward only six. That means that professional judges mentioned more disadvantages than the lay judges (a mean of 2.3 versus 0.7 for the lay judges).

Four lay judges were of the opinion that no disadvantages existed at all. There was little overlap between the disadvantages mentioned by professionals and by the lay judges. Both groups primarily mentioned practical objections against lay participation. In the case of the professionals, disadvantages mentioned seemed to primarily have to do with a desire for a speedy and unobstructed processing of cases, whereas the lay judges primarily pointed to the bureaucracy and the lack of assistance from their professional counterparts.

Collaboration between Professional and Lay Judges

Three out of the four professional judges indicated that they enjoyed collaborating with the lay judges. One professional judge stated that the problems she encountered in collaborating with lay judges were no different to those she had with professional judges. But she was not highly enthusiastic about sitting on a panel with lay judges either.

The professional judges observed that lay judges, as a rule, adjusted their views to those of the professionals. Lay judges were often somewhat in awe of the professional judges. For that reason alone collaboration would not cause many problems: the lay judges would simply follow the professional judges' opinions. The respondents indicated that it was rare for the professional president of the panel to be outvoted. The president writes the decision; the case may then, on appeal, be decided differently. When writing the decision the chairman may hint that he holds a different opinion on the case to that of the lay participants.

Lay Judges' Input

Most respondents indicated that the actual input of lay judges during the hearing of the case is considerably smaller than that of the professionals. The president works full time in the judiciary and thus does most during the preparation stage of the case. He or she knows more about the case than the two lay judges. Lay judges do not often put questions to the defendant or to other process participants. They sit considerably less often than the professional judges and as a consequence they appear to be rather insecure and uncertain about their own performance. Two professional judges indicated that they explicitly gave the lay judges the opportunity to ask questions, but that, nevertheless, most of them remained silent. One other professional judge, however, made it clear that he did not care very much for the lay judges asking questions. In his opinion, most questions got asked anyway and the extra participation by the lay judges seems unnecessary. On top of that, there is always a risk that the lay judge will reveal signs of prejudice when asking a question. It is better to avoid such situations and thus he was not eager to let the lay judges ask questions. He also felt that because of their lack of legal knowledge lay judges sometimes asked ignorant or even stupid questions.

The lay judges who participated in our research agreed with the professional judges that their own input in the trial in open court was substantially smaller than that of the professional judges. Five out of the nine lay judges indicated that they did ask questions during trial on a regular basis. One lay judge reported having the impression that the professionals did not consider the lay judges as 'real' judges. Some professional judges assist the lay persons by explaining what is going on and by clarifying the legal issues. Other professional judges, however, would clearly prefer to work without the lay people. As one lay judge observed, 'I sometimes think to myself: we're disturbing the professional judge in his work'. This respondent estimated that 60 per cent of all professional judges hold a negative opinion on the involvement of lay judges. Other lay judges, however, felt that all professional judges were very friendly and communicative and that in their experience the professionals take all the time needed to explain matters that are unclear to the lay judges.

According to most of the lay judges, during *deliberations* about the case their own participation is equal to that of the professionals. The judges asked them to take part on an equal basis when discussing the case. Some lay judges indicated that there were situations in which they knew more about certain subjects than the professional judges. Their input was then very helpful for deciding the case.

The answers to the question of whether lay judges tend to sentence more harshly or, on the contrary, more leniently than the professional judges do not provide a clear picture. Most respondents indicated that the lay judges' opinions could go either way: more lenient or more harsh. The lay judges have no experience in dealing with cases and thus do not know how certain crimes are generally punished. As a consequence they follow the president while making decisions on this point. Outvoting the president does not often occur, but when this happens, the lay judges would generally be more in favour of a harsh punishment. Some lay judges feel empathy for the defendant. Nevertheless, in the case of serious bodily harm, they favour severe sentences. Lay judges who have just started are inclined to impose harsh sentences, but after having served in a large number of cases they sometimes move to the other extreme and, in the views of the professional judges, become too lenient. It was felt that female lay judges tend to punish leniently. They seem to have more sympathy with the defendant's personal circumstances. A lay judge reported that there are some *Schöffen* who always want to turn a blind eye to what the defendant has done.

The lay judges noted that every now and then they made the professional judges see the case in a different light. The professional judges' views have sometimes become too rigid as a consequence of the routine of their job. Lay judges may help to overcome this effect. They have a less technical view on cases, which may press the professionals to be more flexible and to adjust their own opinions. Furthermore, the lay judges' views on cases are broader than those of the professionals; they do not look primarily at the juridical issues but take more factors into account.

In summary, lay judges seem to hold more favourable perspectives on their own participation than the professional judges do. During deliberation in camera the input by the lay judges is reported to be equal to that of the professionals, but it is far less so in open court and prior to the hearing of the case. The *Schöffen* often adjust to the professional judges' opinions. No clear picture has emerged of the lay persons' harshness in punishing when compared to that of the salaried judges: it has been stated both that they are more severe and that they are more lenient.

The Influence of Experience

When lay people participate over a long period of time their perspectives on cases and on the legal system may moderate to a certain degree. One lay judge stressed that when you only watch television and read newspapers and never visit a real trial, the image that you have of criminal cases is much more restricted than if you participate as a decision maker. If you know more about the background of a case, you become more lenient. Your opinion becomes more differentiated. Lay people, in the course of their participation, may in certain respects begin to resemble the professional judges.

Many respondents underscored this view. Five of them (two professional judges and three lay judges) have experienced that lay judges develop in a professional direction if they serve for a longer period of time. Lay judges indicate that they have learned a lot since they started. A lay judge stated, 'You sometimes realize that you might have sat there yourself as a defendant, if your life had gone differently. That makes you more modest in your opinions on defendants'. Some *Schöffen* emphasized that they had learned *not* to believe everything the defendant contends. Often a defendant is not telling the truth and the lay judges learn to recognize more easily when this is happening. One lay judge now took the personal circumstances of the youngsters who appeared before the court into consideration to a larger degree than she had before. She realized that those children have had fewer opportunities in their lives than others.

Five out of the nine lay judges, however, were of the opinion that their own views had not changed at all since they entered into service. They still held the same opinions on cases and crimes as they had when they started as a lay judge.

Emotions

All respondents except for one (a lay judge) were of the opinion that lay judges are more emotional than professional judges. They get wound up more easily during the court session and have to let off steam when the panel retires for deliberations. The degree of emotionality decreases in the long term, however. It would appear that when they have participated over a certain period, lay judges become less emotional.

Lay judges lack a professional mask. It may happen that the defendant seeks eye contact with the lay judges. 'That happens specifically with female lay judges. I sometimes do not know where to look if that happens', recounted a female lay judge.

The reason for the lay judges' greater emotionality could be that dealing with serious crime is not a daily routine for them. Some kept being surprised and getting upset by the crimes that allegedly were committed and by the defendants they meet in court. In most cases, however, emotions do not prevail: most lay judges succeed in keeping businesslike and aloof. Some professional judges help by inquiring, before the trial starts, whether the lay judges want to ask a question and if so, what. The direction of affairs is then better prepared and the bench knows better what can be expected. Most lay respondents agreed that they themselves were more emotional than the chairman. But they were also of the opinion that that was allowed, that it indeed provided an extra value to the trial of cases. It is inherent to their function as a lay participant.

Acceptance of Court Decisions

Ten out of the 13 respondents were of the opinion that lay participation contributed in a positive way to the public's and the defendant's acceptance of court decisions. Two professional judges felt that no such influence existed and one lay judge was not able to answer this question.

Several reasons were mentioned for this presumed positive influence of lay participation. With lay participation, decisions are more often thought correct and that increases acceptance. Others stressed that three people know more than one. The deliberations are improved by lay participation. It is important for society that lay persons participate: there is more transparency and the involvement of the public at large increases. Defendants also accept the outcome more readily as well. If lay people take part, they hope that their personal circumstances will be taken more into account. Two people sitting there without robes who behave normally: that makes a difference to the defendant facing the court. Defendants fear a professional more than the lay judges. Lay people are thought to be more willing to offer a second chance to defendants. Just as anybody can find themselves in a position where they have to appear before a court, society will also accept court decisions more readily if there is lay involvement. And finally, lay people are less prejudiced than professional judges. Wisdom of life and knowledge of society were felt to be more important for the trial of cases.

A few respondents remarked that the public generally did not know that lay persons took part in the trial of cases, even though the lay judges do not wear robes while the chairman does. The public are simply unaware of how the legal system operates. For them, lay participation would thus not make a difference. For those who know, however, it does.

Importance of Ordinary Citizen Participation

Respondents were questioned on whether they *personally* felt that the involvement of ordinary citizens in the administration of justice was important. All lay judges were of the opinion that this was important, but only one professional judge took that view. Two professional judges thought that lay participation was not important and one said that it was all right as it is now, the advantages being equal in number and weight to the disadvantages. There was thus a difference in opinions between the professional and the lay judges on this issue, but also within the group of professional judges.

Reasons for the importance or lack thereof attached to lay participation included that decision making in criminal cases should be done by a group representative of the general population and not just by professionals. Ordinary citizens should be offered the opportunity to see what types of people appear before a court and to see that the threshold for crime is not as high as is generally presumed. Lay people are needed as well to counter too much routine formula in professional decision making. This is true in other areas of the law too, as well as in other occupations. It seems that the participation of lay people is desirable anywhere in society and in social institutions. These respondents presume that lay people hold a different view on cases, which may help to overcome rigid decision making.

The respondents who were not in favour of lay participation, all professional judges, were of the opinion that lay people contributed too little to the trial of cases. The courts' decisions would be no different without the lay judges, because they lacked basic knowledge needed for the trial of cases. It was felt that there were large differences among the lay judges. There were lay judges who do their utmost best, but some others had little interest in fulfilling their duty. Such lay judges even exerted a negative influence on the operation of the criminal justice system. It was further felt that lay participation would also not be necessary because professional judges were not out of touch with the 'real world'. They took part in so many activities in society that they did not need lay people to prevent them from climbing into an ivory tower.

Dissemination

Seven out of the nine lay judges indicated that they talked about their experiences in court to other people. They did so to their families, friends and at work. Two lay judges indicated that they never talked about their experiences in court to other people. One of the issues that was discussed with the outside world concerned the lack of supervision and assistance that lay judges receive. They have to find their own way in court and they are primarily dependent on the professional judges in this respect. The lay judges who touched upon this issue did not often talk about the cases they try. Most cases would not be that interesting, so they did not deserve much attention. Others talked about the system's transparency and the fairness of the trial. The way the chairman dealt with cases was also subject of discussion with the outside world.

The lay judge who worked as a teacher spoke in school about the system and how it works and what types of penalties are imposed. Pupils sometimes asked whether they might attend the trial when their teacher was in charge as a judge. An excursion was then organized so that they could attend a court session. School classes often went to court sessions. The teacher told them about what statements the defendants made in court and that they often lied.

Being Kept Awake

Two professional judges indicated that they were sometimes kept awake by the decisions they had to make in court. The two other professional judges, as well as all lay judges interviewed, were clear that they were never kept awake by their work in court. That does not imply that these respondents never think about a case after having reached a decision; almost all indicated that they kept reflecting on some cases. But being kept awake by cases was not an issue for them.

Those who were able to switch off from a case explained that an appeal can be filed if there was uncertainty about the outcome and that the case was then reconsidered by a higher court. The respondents' decision thus was not always the final decision in a case, which in a way reassured them. About two thirds of all respondents, both lay and professional, indicated that when they began they used to be kept awake at night, but that this disappeared as they became more experienced as a judge. Some lay judges stated that they were nervous when they began. They held the poor preparation for their tasks in the initial period responsible for this. These respondents obviously felt in need of more supervision than they had received. One professional judge stated that he sometimes had doubts about the decision he had made. However, a certain amount of doubt was felt to be desirable as it keeps you alert.

One lay judge remarked that he was used to making difficult decisions in his daily work as well, so he did not experience difficulties with the types of decisions he has to make in court. Others, too, referred to their everyday occupations in order to explain their difficulties with, or the absence of, problems with decision making in court.

Conclusions

The involvement of lay people in the trial of criminal cases is considerable in Germany. There are, however, a lot more criticisms voiced on the actual contribution of lay people to the hearing of the case in this country than in, for example, Denmark or England and Wales. The views held by professional judges on various aspects differ from those of the lay participants who were interviewed. Professional judges seem considerably more critical of lay adjudication than the *Schöffen* themselves.

The impression that the researchers received of this court and the judges is that it was far more professionally-oriented than the Danish courts they had visited. The court was located in a large, modern building in the city centre and visitors had to pass security checks before they could enter. The court made use of all the modern equipment that is available nowadays and the courtrooms were well-designed. The salaried judges had a professional, modern appearance and all meetings and interviews with them were very well organized. Also, the lay judges with whom the researchers spoke seemed deeply committed to their task and were able to formulate their personal aims and motives for participating in the administration of justice very well.

At the same time the court had the appearance of being open and accessible to the public. Lunch was available in a large restaurant on the ground floor. Judges, court personnel and the public enjoyed their food at tables next to one another. Via the website, a large amount of information could be obtained about the recruitment and tasks of the *Schöffen*.[3]

No clear overall picture could be obtained on the selection of lay judges. However, political elements seem to dominate, as was previously observed by Klausa (1972) and Casper and Zeisel (1972). There is some concern regarding the role political parties play in the selection of candidates for duty as a *Schöffe*. At the same time, the provision of candidates from lists kept by the municipalities is not without criticism either, because these people may lack commitment and be disinterested in contributing to the common good.[4]

The respondents' satisfaction with the involvement of ordinary citizens in the trial of criminal cases was reasonably high in Germany. Nevertheless, there was considerable criticism of their actual contribution to the system, expressed predominantly by the professional judges. The remark was made that lay people cannot reasonably contribute anything to the trial of cases and to decision making. Fears were regularly expressed that they might ask inadmissible questions. Almost all respondents, both professional and lay, agreed that the actual input by the lay judges was smaller than that of the professionals. The professional judges seemed to play a dominant role in the panels.

Lay judges appeared to attach considerable value to the fact that they could contribute to the common good and the general interest by participating in the criminal justice system. The lay people who were interviewed held more

3 www.schoeffen.de.

4 Similar remarks were made by the respondents in Denmark. See the previous chapter.

strongly to the lay element in the German legal system than the professional judges did. Similar attitudes towards lay participation were found in earlier research (Klausa 1972).

Lay judges indicated a number of practical problems related to their participation in the system. In particular, when they started they were confronted with difficulties in finding their way around court and knowing what was expected from them. They found it problematic to have to plan their holiday periods in advance. They felt that it would be better if a central institute were charged with organizing the actual recruitment and selection of lay people; the court itself should not be burdened with this responsibility.

Notwithstanding this criticism, more advantages of lay participation were mentioned than disadvantages (16 versus 11). This is in contrast with the findings of the empirical literature described in the beginning of this chapter, which indicates that in previous research more disadvantages than advantages were mentioned. The system as such is not under discussion in Germany. A number of proposals have been brought forward to change the system because it is considered to be too complicated and the procedures are thought to be too lengthy. Nevertheless the participation by the *Schöffen* and the principle of immediacy are firmly grounded in the German legal system.

The finding that most respondents, including the professional judges, felt that the involvement of lay persons increased acceptance of court decisions by both the defendant and the public and that, at the same time, most professional judges personally did not feel that lay participation was important, is surprising. Thus, it would seem to be generally accepted that the outside world has a more positive view of the trial of cases as a result of ordinary citizen participation, while most professionals remain unconvinced that lay participation enhances the quality of the decisions.

Chapter 9
England and Wales

Introduction

The data for this chapter were collected in two large cities in England, located in different parts of the country. Both cities were visited by the author and interviews and observations were conducted in both the magistrates' courts and the Crown Court (jury trials) in these cities.[1] This chapter begins by describing the observations, after which the results of the interviews are presented.

The main emphasis in this chapter is placed on the magistrates' courts, because these tribunals try the majority of the criminal cases in England and Wales, but some attention is also paid to jury courts. A questionnaire was designed that was specifically tailored to the English legal system of lay involvement in the magistrates' courts. Interviews were conducted with two professional judges and with five lay magistrates. Apart from the interviews, three group discussions took place with panels of respondents. Participating in these panels were two lay magistrates, two district judges, the president and the chief executive of the Justices' Clerks Society and two members of the organizing court personnel. The information that was obtained from these group discussions has been included in this chapter as well.

Observations: Magistrates' Courts

In many public places all over the world there is presently a serious concern about public safety and security issues. This is most obvious at airports, but is also true for courthouses. These places both require almost unrestricted access for the public and therefore a need is felt to protect the public and visitors from potential terrorist acts or public order disturbances. This research project allowed a comparison between security measures in the two types of public places.

When flying from Amsterdam's Schiphol Airport to London to visit one of the courts, the researcher had to pass through security three times. The first time was when entering airside at Schiphol airport. Her luggage was scanned,

1 Magistrates' courts try summary offences and a portion of the 'either way' offences. The maximum penalty they can impose is six months imprisonment. Jury courts try more serious cases (indictable offences and a portion of the 'either way' offences) in which the defendant denies having committed the crime.

and when she went through security she had to take off both her raincoat and jacket and was frisked. She was also requested to take her shoes off. The same happened at the gate. Unfortunately, after almost all the passengers had been searched by the security services at the gate entrance, it appeared that the aircraft would leave from another gate. Again all passengers had to be searched, their luggage had to be checked and they all had to take their shoes and coats off when entering the second gate. This was the third time the researcher had to go through security that morning.

She arrived just in time at the court in the city in England where she would conduct the interviews for the first day. The flight had been delayed for several hours. She still had all her luggage with her because she had not had time to check-in at the hotel. The security services at the court wished to check her bags. She offered to take off her coats and her shoes as well. The security official, surprised, said that that was not necessary. If they were to request that of every visitor, the queue waiting for the courts would end at the square three blocks away, he said.

The Buildings

The observations described below cover both magistrates' courts that were visited. In these courts a majority of the hearings involve only the choice of the type of court where the case will be tried at a later date and thus take only a couple of minutes. 'Real' trials, and other types of procedures preceding a trial, last longer. The cases observed for our study included all kinds of criminal proceedings at the magistrates' court.

One of the magistrates' courts visited is located in a major building in the city centre. The building's design is modern and it comprises various storeys. It hosts about 16 separate courtrooms. There is a security check at the entrance. Escalators bring the visitors to the different floors. From these escalators one can look outside, because the building has walls of glass. The courts use a public address system for announcing the trials as they start. It sounds like the announcement systems in use in airports or at train stations. At regular intervals announcements can be heard such as, 'Mister X and his solicitor are requested to go immediately to Court Six …'.

The courtrooms are small and brightly lit, with wooden benches and chairs for the court personnel, other participants and the public. Most courts have a separate dock, behind a glass wall, for the defendant. Depending on whether the defendant is in pretrial custody or not, the door to the courtroom is closed or open and there is a security guard sitting next to him or her. As a consequence, in neither of the two cities visited do defendants have a substantial opportunity to communicate with their lawyer, who is sitting in the courtroom. The observer almost never saw contact between the counsel, sitting in the courtroom, and the client.

Some of the courts have a public gallery behind glass. The hearing of the case is very difficult to follow from these public galleries. The microphones do not work well, or the participants do not speak into them. In one of the cases observed, the defendant, a young woman, started crying. Obviously, she was deeply affected by the trial of her case. As she was the only one in the courtroom who was seated near a microphone, for a little while only her sobbing and sniffing could be heard in the public gallery; no other noise was audible.

On the second day of the visit the researcher had lunch with two magistrates in their special room and on the third day she enjoyed lunch with the professional District Judges (DJs) in their own room in the courthouse. There were clear differences between the rooms. The DJ's retiring room is much more luxurious than that of the magistrates. Other people who are not magistrates or judges can enter the magistrates' retiring room much more easily than that of the District Judges.

One of the District Judges taking part in a group discussion told about her experiences in the large, modern magistrates' court described above. She had once had to preside over a magistrates' bench in that court. The court building was no longer owned by the government, but was at the time in the possession of a private company. As a consequence, the building now closed at six in the evening. Having presided over a magistrates' bench, this judge was still in the building after six o'clock. She had not heard the announcement that the building was closing and found herself locked in. The walls of this building are made of glass; anyone can look in and see everyone inside, moving up and down the stairs. This judge was now in the unfortunate position of being locked in, standing behind the glass walls and not being able to leave the building. Outside a number of youngsters, who might have seen her on the bench that day, were waving and laughing at her ....

The Panels

Seen from the public gallery, the three magistrates sit at the far end of the courtroom on a dais. In front of them the clerk has her seat and in front of her the benches for the prosecutor and counsel can be found. The latter sit facing the bench and the clerk and with their backs to the public gallery.

In one of the courts visited the composition of the bench was three magistrates; either one male and two females, or two males and one female. Most of them were in their 50s or 60s. This was different from the other court. In all cases observed there the panel consisted of two magistrates only. The magistrates interviewed explained that when there were not enough magistrates available on the day, the bench may consist of two magistrates only. The chairman of the panel was the same person in all cases observed in that court: a male in his 60s. The other member of the bench was either a female or a male, also in their 60s. All were White. There were also conspicuous differences in the activity of the chairmen between the two cities. The chairman of the bench with two members, who was obviously an experienced magistrate, played a considerably clearer and more active role than the magistrates in the other town.

The clerks in the two courts were all in their 30s. On these occasions they were all White but they are sometimes from a non-White ethnic background. In both courts that were visited the majority of the other court personnel were from a non-White ethnic background. In this respect, the situation in England differs from that in the Netherlands, where there are still only a few people from other ethnic backgrounds working in the legal system. The cases observed concerned, among others, driving while under the influence of alcohol, drug possession, violent crimes, road traffic offences, shoplifting, etc. The clerks (i.e., legal advisors) helped with a number of practicalities during the court session. They helped the magistrates to formulate their reasons for a certain sentence.[2] Some clerks took a far more active role than others. In some cases the clerk had such a dominant role that he or she seemed to chair the trial. The ushers (organizing clerks) wore robes in one of the cities but not in the other. Wigs are only worn in jury trials. On the days that the observer visited, the defendants were predominantly from a non-White ethnic background.

Many officials were constantly walking in and out of the courtrooms. The trial started with the identification of the defendant and reading the charge aloud. The plea of guilty or not guilty was asked and received by the clerk. Many cases were of a short duration because they are only meant to decide at which tribunal the case will be tried at a later point. The prosecutor and counsel spoke standing behind their desks. When a sentence was to be pronounced the defendant was requested to stand. The chairman of the bench read the verdict aloud and inquired whether the convicted person had understood what was said. This happened every time a judicial decision was read aloud. The magistrates largely remained in the background in the courts under observation. Most of the questioning was done by the prosecutor and by counsel.

Between the court sessions the magistrates explained to me what was going on. One of them (a winger[3]) told me that he had the impression that many professional judges would prefer *not* to collaborate with the magistrates, because they would not be able to learn anything new from them. In the past the Youth Court would sit with one professional judge and two magistrates, but that had

---

2 During the panel discussions information was given about the clerks' roles and functions. 'There are certain guidelines for that. Clerks attend the deliberations, as well as the drafting of the reasons. After that, the magistrates and the clerk go back to the open court. There is a certain concern that the magistrates would be influenced by the clerks during their decision making. In former times, more advising was done in private. Now, as a consequence of Article 6 of the ECHR, more is done in open court.'

3 The magistrates sitting next to the chairman.

recently changed. This court now sat with either one single professional judge, or with three magistrates. It was thus no longer necessary for the professionals to collaborate with the magistrates. In appeals of decisions by the magistrates' court, at the Crown Court, a professional judge still sat with two magistrates, however. There some form of collaboration still exists.

A Case of 'Special Reasons'

One of the cases observed, which was tried by the magistrates' court, dealt with 'special reasons'. A woman had been convicted for driving a car under the influence of alcohol, but claimed that she had 'special reasons' for driving her car at that very moment. If these special reasons were accepted by the court, her automatic disqualification from driving a car could be nullified.

The 'special reasons' she claimed consisted of having drunk a lot the night before she was arrested because she had witnessed an accident outside the home of a friend she had been visiting. On hearing the crash, she had approached the BMW in which the female victim of the accident sat unconscious. She sat next to the victim for about 20 minutes, talking to her. This event had made a deep impression on the woman and she claimed that it was the reason she had continued drinking that night. The following morning she and her husband had gone home. She had slept only a few hours and was still drunk. The couple had a history of family violence. As an element of the therapy the husband was undertaking, he had adopted the habit of leaving his wife immediately when there was a risk a quarrel might escalate, to prevent himself from becoming violent. That morning, returning home after that horrid night, they had an argument in the car over tickets. The husband, who was driving, parked the car in a place reserved for coaches and left immediately. His wife remained with the car. She moved to the driver's seat and moved the car about 400 to 450 metres and was then arrested. The police established that she had excessive alcohol in her blood.

A number of witnesses were heard by the court, among them the husband and the police officer who arrested the woman. The woman herself was also heard extensively.[4] Substantial time was spent in dealing with the case. Both the prosecutor and the defence lawyer interrogated the witnesses and the woman at length.

The court did not accept the 'special reasons' claimed by the woman. It concluded that she had other means of resolving the problem of when her husband left the car than to drive it herself. She could have called the police, or have left the car where it was at that time, but she did not do that and started

4 In England and Wales, defendants have to take an oath, just as the witnesses do. However, as one of the magistrates told me, if defendants who are under oath lie to the court, no measures are taken. The judges and the magistrates I spoke to were very surprised that in the Netherlands defendants do not testify under oath.

to drive the car instead. Having resolved the issue of the 'special reasons', the court decided that the case was ready for sentencing. The woman was sentenced to a 12 month driving disqualification. If she agreed to follow a course, this sentence would be reduced to nine months. She would have to pay for the course herself.

Observations: The Jury Court

In one of the cities visited I attended several jury trials in the Crown Court. The Crown Court is in an old building in the centre of the city. At the entrance there is a security check of visitor's bags and a body scan. Two huge courtrooms are reserved for jury trials. There are public galleries at the back of those rooms which can be reached from the outside by climbing two flights of stairs. From these public galleries the distance to the courtroom floor is substantial. As a consequence, it is hard to follow what is going on and to understand what is being said during the trial.

It is obvious that the courtrooms aim to impress; high ceilings, dark wooden furniture and classical design contribute to the impression of majesty that is conveyed. These rooms differ tremendously from the simple and unimpressive rooms where the magistrates sit. The judge (Crown Court Judge) in this jury courtroom sits at the far end behind a bench that occupies the whole width of the courtroom. He or she sits elevated a couple of metres above the rest of the court. He or she wears a wig. The otherwise black robe has lilac and red stripes in front. Small white bands are worn over the robe at the neck. The other court officials and counsel have only a black robe and white bands. The prosecutor and counsel wear wigs that have two long corkscrew curls in the back. Defendants sit in a separate dock behind glass with a security guard next to them.

It felt as if I had walked in on a performance of a play. Behind a small semi-circular railing at the right-hand side of the courtroom stood a woman holding a piece of paper. She recited a text from this piece of paper. Every now and then the prosecutor asked a question of this woman, who was obviously a witness. He also had a piece of paper in his hand and recited his question from it. The witness adjusted her gestures and the ways in which she pronounced her answers to the contents of the text she read. She sometimes emphasized certain words or pronounced a sentence using an angry intonation.

At the far left of the courtroom the jury was sitting behind a railing: three rows of four people, packed closely together. They were all casually clothed. Most of them were in their 40s and 50s. They also had pieces of paper in their hands. Their attention was focused on the papers and they followed the texts that were recited by the witness and the prosecutor. A little later the counsel was also allowed to ask a few questions that were answered in the same manner by the witness. It appeared that the witness interrogations that were conducted at an earlier point were now 'presented' in this court. The principles of immediacy and of orality required that it be done this way.

The jury was sent out when legal matters were discussed, such as, for example, the defendant's previous convictions or issues regarding the evidence. The jurors then descended a small stair in the courtroom. From the public gallery it was very hard to follow what the debate on the legal questions was about, because it was conducted between the judge and the two lawyers who had approached the bench and looked up at him. When the jury had returned, the next witness was heard. This time the jury only listened and had no papers. When this part of the trial was finished the judge announced that he would do the 'summing up' tomorrow. The jury left the courtroom. When the judge also prepared to exit, the usher loudly ordered: 'Stand!' and everyone present rose from their chair.

In the other courtroom the selection of a new jury was taking place. A handful of cards was shuffled and a number of names were read aloud. The candidates came forward. Three were left after 12 had been selected. The three left the courtroom. After the judge had asked them whether they knew the defendant and received negative answers, the candidates who had been selected read aloud a text from a piece of paper relating to their duties and responsibilities as members of the jury. The prosecutor spoke to the jury about the indictment. She then gave an explanation of the presumption of innocence.

A witness appeared in the witness stand. She claimed to be the victim of a robbery by the defendant. The prosecutor and counsel interrogated her. Every now and then the judge also asked a question of the witness. He admonished her that she is speaking too softly and that she had to speak more in the direction of the jury. The jury only listened and had no paper and pencils. They remained passive for the whole trial. Everything went rather slowly, at least in the eyes of a Dutch legal researcher. At the end of the witness interrogation the judge summarized her statement and reflected on her feelings during the alleged robbery. The witness left and after a while the jury did the same. A few moments later, the witness joined me in the public gallery. She inquired whether I knew if the sentence was to be pronounced that day as well? I was not able to answer her question.

After a short break a new hearing commenced, this time with a different jury. The defendant was brought in and seated in his separate dock behind the glass. It appeared that this jury was going to deliver their verdict. The foreman of the jury stood at the request of the judge and answered a number of questions. The defendant was found guilty on all counts, including the robberies of a taxi driver and a bus driver. After that, the judge pronounced the sentence. Behind me in the public gallery a group of youngsters had taken their seats. I heard them curse softly. They obviously knew the defendant personally. 'Poor bastard', I heard them say several times.

When the sentence had been explained by the judge, he solemnly spoke to the jury and thanked them for their efforts. He emphasized that it was extremely important that ordinary citizens could participate in the administration of justice.

Observations – Concluding Remarks

The general arrangement of the courtrooms differs strikingly between jury trials and magistrates' courts. The courtrooms for the jury trials seem to be more aimed at impressing the public, while the magistrates' courts seem more down-to-earth and simpler. However, in comparison to Dutch trials, there are many similarities between these two English courts. The trial of cases proceeds considerably more slowly in England. It seems to be aimed at a fully oral presentation and discussion of all evidence in open court, whereas Dutch trials are rather speedy, thanks to the wide use of documentary evidence and other paper materials.

It is questionable whether the lay participants in England are able to fully participate in all aspects of the cases. The jury does not perform any activity during the hearing of cases other than sitting and listening and the magistrates differ considerably in the way they are involved in cases. Some seem to manage and guide everything that is going on, while others give the impression that they leave the chairing of the case to the clerk.

Notwithstanding the orality with which cases are conducted, the hearing is sometimes difficult to follow. The courtrooms in which the jury trials take place are so vast that it is difficult to understand everything from the public gallery, which is located at quite a distance from the bench. Some issues of the trial are discussed exclusively among the judge and the lawyers for the parties and cannot be followed by the public. The wide variety of proceedings before the magistrates' courts, which sometimes take only a couple of minutes, do not make them terribly easy to follow either.

At the same time, cases are dealt with in a detailed manner and there is, at least in jury trials, little emphasis on paper documents. In all cases I observed, the chairman inquired of the defendant whether he or she had understood what was decided. In general, every-day language was used in the courts. These aspects make the English way of handling cases comprehensible, at least to a certain degree.

Interviews

Interviews were conducted with two professional judges and with five lay magistrates. Unfortunately it was not possible to interview jurors: no consent was given for that. The professional judges were contacted with the help of the Dutch Council for the Judiciary and through personal contacts. The London

Royal Courts of Justice, as well as the Magistrates' Association, were very helpful in finding the names of judges and magistrates prepared to participate in an interview. The judges and the magistrates who were interviewed actually come from different parts of the country.

Three of the interviews were conducted by telephone and one respondent filled in the questionnaire herself. The remaining three were face-to-face interviews. The results are presented anonymously below. Before that, some background information is provided on the respondents.

The Respondents' Backgrounds

One of the professional judges was a Crown Court Judge. He had been a judge for two years at that time, in addition to holding a position at a university. The other judge sat in the High Court of Justice, having been there for quite some years. The two judges were both males. The lay magistrates who were interviewed were affiliated with magistrates' courts in various circuits in England. They had been involved in the administration of justice for long periods: two of them for 23 years, one for 20 years, one for 17 years and one for nine years. Four of the magistrates were female, and one was male.

The magistrates' regular jobs and occupations included lecturer or head of a university department, school inspector and self-employed as an advisor of volunteers. One of them had recently retired from his regular occupation; the others still had their jobs.

The Recruitment and Involvement of Lay Magistrates

The magistrates became involved in the legal system in various ways. One of them, who worked at university and trained people who write reports for the judicial system, decided to apply to be better able to do her work. Another was asked to apply by her husband's boss. The remaining magistrates had heard an appeal on the radio, or were asked by colleagues. Two magistrates remarked that it had never occurred to them that they would be a Justice of the Peace, but they nevertheless became one. All magistrates stated that they were very pleased to be in a position to do this. 'Absolutely, I am immensely proud, nobody in my family is a magistrate. I can put "JP" after my name. I am considered a proper person.' The magistrates were all of the opinion that their work was very interesting.

The aspect of 'community involvement' was an important factor in motivating the magistrates to participate. 'We are part of the community, that is why we do it, even if we don't get paid. I consider it an important piece of voluntary work.' 'I wanted to give something back to the community. Magistrates are in touch with the whole range of society. You encounter all sorts of people in court, and you see how society operates.' As another magistrate phrased it, 'I expected to reach a deeper understanding of how the law is run, to get to know about the prison population. Indeed, you get a better understanding of what is going on around you. My expectations were fulfilled'. One respondent felt that it was quite demanding to be a magistrate. 'To put people in prison, the responsibility you have. But it is fascinating. It is important work. I can recommend it to anybody.'

Most of the magistrates interviewed did more sittings than were officially required from them. They are expected to sit at least 26 half days each year, but the respondents indicated that it was much more in their case. The largest number of days in court that was mentioned was 55; the others stated that they did 35 to 40 sittings each year.

There was a slight difference between the magistrates' and the professional judges' perceptions of the lay persons' actual contribution to the trial of cases. The lay judges had a slightly more positive perception. 'Professional judges often ask for our knowledge, because we do know more about "regular" cases, and about the community', one of the magistrates observed. A judge recounted that when he sat with two magistrates in the Crown Court, they left it up to him to ask the questions. Generally, they remained in the background. In jury trials he did not always tell the jurors that they have the right to ask questions. He feared that they might ask incorrect or legally prohibited questions. However, he observed that in cases heard with the magistrates, they sometimes knew more about certain specific issues than he did himself, for example in road traffic cases. He was aware that in such situations he was able to learn something new from these magistrates.

One of the respondents, a magistrate, made it clear that she would have loved to be in an inquisitorial system like the Netherlands, where the bench is expected to investigate each case itself. 'Magistrates do not take part in the finding of the truth, that is not expected from them. We are not allowed to ask questions during the trial. But I would very much like to have that opportunity.'

In conclusion, there are various ways of getting involved in the magistracy. Neither magistrates nor jurors are expected to make a considerable contribution to the handling of a case during the hearing. Most of the lay participants seemed happy to remain in the background. As it was put by one of the respondents during the interview, when the issue of asking questions to the defendant came up, 'You shouldn't!'

Advantages of Lay Participation

The respondents were asked to indicate the advantages of lay involvement in the trial of criminal cases. Twelve different advantages were mentioned. Each respondent could mention several advantages and each advantage could be mentioned by one or more respondent (see Table 9.1). The mean number of advantages mentioned per respondent was slightly larger for the magistrates (two for the professional judges versus 3.2 for the magistrates).

Table 9.1 Advantages of lay participation mentioned by professional judges (2) and lay magistrates (5) (England and Wales)

	Professional judges	Magistrates	Total
Community involvement	1	3	4
Against routine	1	2	3
Educating lay persons	1	1	2
Three are better than one	–	2	2
Makes system more open, comprehensible	–	2	2
Compels judges to explain	1	–	1
Positive aspects of voluntarism	–	1	1
Defendant more likely to be understood	–	1	1
Bridges distance with society	–	1	1
Increases confidence in the system	–	1	1
Gives you sense of purpose	–	1	1
Democracy	–	1	1
Total advantages: 12	*4*	*16*	*20*

Among the most frequently mentioned advantages were: allowing for community involvement, combating the negative effects of routine, educating lay persons, the advantage of having three decision makers in the panel instead of one and making the system more open and comprehensible.

The respondents gave explanations and illustrations of their choices for particular advantages. One respondent felt that, in principle, decisions about guilt should be made by lay persons. 'That is an essential part of democracy. It is important that not one single, professional, judge decides on these issues.' This respondent had no problem with the *sentence* being decided by one single judge, however. Another magistrate underscored the risks of professional judges deciding on cases alone. 'When District Judges sit on their own, there is a risk of outrageous sentencing: they tend to become too punitive.'

The importance of community involvement was explained as follows. 'You know the locality. If there is a theft from a supermarket, you know the supermarket. You know the crossroad where an accident has taken place. You understand the community, know the school where something happened. We are much more part of the community than the professional judges.' One of the professional judges also felt that community involvement is important. 'There is an educative aspect to it: people get to know what happens in court. There is still a lack of knowledge on that point. When they participate, they will, in the long run, better understand what happens.'

The other side of the coin of community involvement is that it is ordinary citizens who keep the offender accountable to his peers. This may improve the chances of reintegrating the offender back into society. 'That is very just', a magistrate remarked. 'We, the magistrates, are doing it for the right reason, not for the money. ... There is a strong culture of volunteering in the UK. You step out and help.'

According to a number of respondents, professional judges working only with professional judges is not a desirable situation. As one of the judges stated, 'Courts risk becoming too professional. They become self-serving. Everything runs smoothly and we don't think about what we are doing anymore: "we always do it this way". Lay people can counterbalance such tendencies'. The other judge held the same opinion. 'Lay participants can prevent the salaried judges from becoming too cynical. The professionals, who try huge caseloads, in the long run recognize certain patterns in the cases they deal with: "Another one of those cases ...". That is a risk. Lay people may help to overcome such cynicism.' This risk was confirmed by a magistrate. 'The professional judges sometimes have a closed outlook. Lay participation may then help. Bridging the distance with members of society is an issue that is also mentioned. 'We magistrates show that judges are normal people. Why take decisions about guilt and punishment away from the general public? It increases the confidence in the system. It makes the system more open.'

Most comments on the magistracy were positive. 'The system of using lay judges, I am tremendously impressed by it. My views have not changed on that point', a magistrate remarked. 'We receive so much training. There is more trust in magistrates than in juries. Magistrates have fewer emotions or prejudices.' 'The system is superb, and the magistrates are highly committed. Lay participation fits well into our legal culture.' Nevertheless, one of the judges noted an antipathy between the professionals and the magistrates. 'The administration of justice and the trial of cases goes much faster with professionals only, and the judges are aware of that.' The remark of one of the magistrates seems to underscore this observation. 'The professionals look down on us as they believe we don't do as good a job as them.' The other judge stressed that he enjoyed collaborating with magistrates and would not prefer to work only with professional judges. He considered it as an important element of his work and felt that most professional judges would agree. 'Lay participation fits very well in our country's legal culture, and it will not disappear in the near future.'

Disadvantages

The respondents mentioned six different disadvantages of lay participation. The mean number of disadvantages mentioned was similar for both professional and lay magistrates (1.5 and 1.8). The non-representativeness of the lay people for the community was the disadvantage most often mentioned, together with the slowness of trials with lay adjudication (both by four respondents) (see Table 9.2).

Table 9.2 Disadvantages of lay participation mentioned by professional judges (2) and lay magistrates (5) (England and Wales)

	Professional judges	Magistrates	Total
Not representative	2	2	4
Takes lots of time	1	3	4
Voluntary	–	1	1
Financial disadvantages for the magistrates	–	1	1
Affects people's career	–	1	1
Too much training	–	1	1
Total disadvantages: 6	*3*	*9*	*12*

According to the respondents, it is difficult to get magistrates from all walks of life and that is the reason for the unrepresentativeness of the magistracy. The attitudes of employers could be an obstacle to the participation of younger people. As a consequence, the magistrates are an aging population. As one of the judges explained:

> Magistrates do not come from the housing estates, they are generally highly educated members of the community. Jurors are more representative of the community, because they are selected more randomly than magistrates. The magistrates' level of knowledge, on the other hand, is higher and they generally have more time to spend.

One of the judges commented on juries. Juries sometimes acquit defendants who have obviously committed the alleged crime. Some jurors are not very intelligent and they are not as well informed as the salaried judges. Some of them have extreme political opinions, or they hold racist views. The only safeguard that is left, then, is that there are 12 jurors. The hope must be that the others' opinions will prevail over the one with the reprehensible views. Some jurors always take the side of the police. There are only a few grounds for disqualification, so the courts have to work with the jurors they get. The other judge felt that in general jurors were sensible, but there were exceptions. 'I once had a juror with fleas jumping all around. Another juror hadn't had a bath for a month! As a professional judge, you spend lots of time at "man-management". You have jurors who become ill, who have job problems, etc.'

None of the respondents felt that the magistrates would be more emotional or more sensitive to media reporting than the professionals. In the magistrates' training attention is given to this issue and it seems that has been bearing fruit. However, some magistrates may forget where they are, or stop adjusting to the role they have to play. A judge gave an example. 'Magistrates do not always keep the distance that is needed for the administration of justice. Because they know the local situation, they sometimes tend to correct the witnesses or the defendant in open court. For example, they make it clear that no third bus stop exists in a certain road, when a witness states there is.'

Differing Opinions?

Magistrates do not often sit together with salaried judges on the same panel. The only situation where this happens is in the Crown Court on the bench that decides appeals to decisions by the magistrates' court of first instance. None of the magistrates who participated in our study had much experience in collaborating with professional judges. Nevertheless, they made a number of remarks on whether their opinions would differ from those of the judges. The respondents observed that in general views did not differ greatly between the two groups. 'It is easy to reach consensus. The professional judge ensures that everyone is happy with the decision', one magistrate explained. When there were any differences, it was the lay participants who would be less severe than the salaried judges.[5] Many respondents referred to the guidelines for sentencing that are used to bring more consistency and equality to the penalties that are imposed. One magistrate recalled from his experiences:

> We have a sentencing framework. On top of that, we follow sentencing exercises that are organized by the Magistrates' Association, during which Crown Court judges give their opinion on cases to the magistrates who attend. It has happened that in a case discussed during such an exercise, all magistrates wanted a community sentence and all judges wanted a custodial sentence. The judges seem to have a greater propensity for custodial sentences.

One of the judges explained:

> We always come to consensus. I feel that jurors and magistrates have sensible opinions. The jury in most cases reaches the conclusion that I expected. I have never had the feeling that they made an incorrect decision. However, they are sometimes soft. They may have empathic feelings towards the defendant.

He always gave the floor first to the magistrates during deliberations in the retiring room. The other judge observed that outvoting the professional judge in an appeal of magistrates' cases at the Crown Court happened very rarely. If it happened, it was the professional judge who wrote the sentence and might, in doing so, let it be known what they thought of the case. At the beginning, some magistrates tended to be rather punitive. However, after being told about the backgrounds to the cases, most of them went the other way and became

5 This answer was given by two magistrates and one judge.

more lenient. On balance, lay participants were considered to be less severe than the professionals.

Acceptance of Court Decisions

Only one respondent (a judge) explicitly stated that the court's decisions would be more readily accepted *because* lay people were involved.

> The reason is that ordinary citizens decide on basis of their common sense. That reassures the public. No secret decisions are made by lawyers only. The same counts for the defendants. Judges have to explain things to the lay participants, and that will put the defendant at ease.

Other respondents thought that the question of whether the case was handled professionally was of more importance for acceptance than whether the defendant understood what was happening and if reasons were given for a decision (which the magistrates have been required to do in the last couple of years). If these things happened, then the decision was probably better accepted, quite independent of whether lay magistrates or professional judges made the decision. One respondent, a magistrate, was '... amazed how well the defendants accept our decisions, rarely question them and rarely appeal them'.

Importance of Ordinary Citizen Participation

All respondents except for one (who did not answer this question) agreed that it was important to have ordinary citizens participating in the administration of justice. 'I feel that it is a fundamental part of democracy. Democracy is founded on participation in the government. Especially in an adversarial system, this is important.' Defendants should be tried by their peers and be held responsible to society. The respondents contended that the system is kept healthy and cohesion is enlarged by lay participation. It is important to bring the offender back into the community. Increasingly people from ethnic minorities are involved, especially in juries. This enhances the trust of minority groups in the legal system as well.

Ivory Tower

Two respondents, both magistrates, were of the opinion that professional judges were not sufficiently in touch with the 'real world'. Two other respondents thought they were. Not all the magistrates had had sufficient experience of sitting together with a professional judge to be able to reflect on this issue, so three magistrates did not answer this question. The respondents who felt that judges lived in ivory towers explained their view with the argument that magistrates come from other walks of life.

> We are more in touch with real life than professional judges. We have real jobs and more life experience. The professional judges generally are older and more cocooned. When you go to the Crown Court, the professional judges sit on a high platform and look down on the defendant who sits in his dock. This is different from the magistrates' courts, which are far less impressive. There is far less interaction in the Crown Court.

One magistrate made comparisons between the magistracy and the professional judges.

> We have our feet on the ground. We are in touch with the local community. We mix with the people who do the offending. Judges generally come from outside the area, and they do not mix with the local people. Professional judges are case-hardened, by being involved full time. They are more skeptical. For example, they say, 'Sometimes I talk to my gardener', to deliberately suggest that they also come into contact with 'ordinary' people. By far, not all District Judges are 'of the world' like we are.

Dissemination

All the magistrates reported that they talked about their experiences in court with other people. 'If other people want to, I talk about it. Occasionally, I talk about my experiences at work, for example if I have had a demanding case in court. I sometimes let off steam. However, I do not talk about what is said in the retiring room, that is private.'

Some magistrates gave talks, for instance to ladies' lunch clubs or at other meetings or conferences. 'I am a member of the "Magistrates in the Community" and as such I give presentations. I try to get people interested in being a magistrate. At work, I talk about funny cases, difficult cases.'

Most respondents indicated they were careful about what they say. What is said in the retiring room remained private. Some of them talked only in general terms and never said anything specific or confidential. 'Yes, I talk about my experiences with friends and family. I explain how the system works. And I give presentations to schools. People are fascinated by what I tell, they want to be part of it.'

Being Kept Awake at Night

Two magistrates reported being kept awake at night by the decisions they had to make in court. But that did not occur very often. 'One case every 10 years keeps me awake. I am professionally detached', one magistrate remarked. One of the other magistrates felt he was not sufficiently experienced and that was the reason why he was sometimes kept awake at night. Other respondents indicated that when they started they had not slept well at night because of their work for the court, but that had stopped after a certain point.

That does not imply that the respondents were totally unaffected by what happened in court. 'It can be hard, putting someone in custody or telling them that they are not getting bail. You have to step back. But I'm always convinced that we did the right thing. And, they can go into appeal. It is not the end of the road', a magistrate explained. Others found it reassuring that there were the three of them. Some mentioned the guidelines as a point of reference for decisions about sentencing. 'We sometimes do make a mistake. I still always feel anxious about making the right decision, but I'm no longer kept awake. You can't take everybody home!' 'I don't worry anymore about decisions. I can remember having had cases in the beginning that stand out. I was concerned about them in the beginning. However, I'm still sometimes frustrated that I couldn't help more, for instance when the defendant has a mental health problem. But being kept awake, that doesn't happen.'

Conclusions

The English criminal justice system has two forms of lay participation: the jury and magistrates. Overall, there appears to be satisfaction with both systems.[6] As one of the judges interviewed made clear, there is no suggestion of abolishing juries, let alone magistrates, in the UK. It appears that lay people are felt to be just as good as professionals at judging the facts of a case.[7]

The notion of 'community involvement' prevails in the respondents' views on the reasons for lay participation. Magistrates are considered to represent the community in the trial of cases. They are expected to know the local situation better and to have views that differ from those of the professionals. Moreover, it is important that offenders remain responsible to *society* and not only to professional judges, and this has to be done by the members of the community. This may lead to a better future reintegration of the offender. Trying to bring the offender back to the community is something that can presumably be

6 See the Home Office Report of Matthews et al. 2005: acting as a juror leads to more positive views and more confidence in the jury system. On satisfaction with different types of courts and tribunals, and the role of diversity of panels, see Moorhead et al., 2008.

7 On comprehensibility of cases for the jury, see the Lord Justice Auld Report 2001; Devine et al. 2001; Lloyd-Bostock 2007. A debate has been conducted about whether juries are capable of understanding complicated (financial) cases. This debate is not further discussed in this chapter. See Chapter 11 for overall conclusions regarding quality of decisions made by various types of panels.

better done by members of the community themselves than by professional judges. At least that is what the magistrates interviewed contended.

The orientation to the outside world is improved by the participation of lay people as well. Dissemination of knowledge about the criminal justice system by the magistrates themselves increases this orientation to the outside world. Some magistrates regularly give talks to schools, ladies' lunch clubs and other groups about the legal system and their experiences as a participant in the magistracy.

Some advantages of lay participation can be traced back to the increase in the comprehensibility of the administration of justice to which it may lead. Defendants are better able to understand their trial when magistrates take part, because then the trial has to be kept comprehensible. The public benefits from this as well.

As with the observations on other countries investigated in this book, no remarkable differences exist between the lay people's views on cases and those of the professional judges. In the few cases where they sit together on a panel it is easy to reach consensus. If any difference is observed, it is that lay people tend to be more lenient in sentencing than the professional judges. However, when magistrates first start they tend to be more punitive. A number of respondents remarked that after having gained a certain amount of experience magistrates are inclined to switch to more lenient views.

Lay participation is not immune from criticism, however. Some respondents observed that professional judges look down on lay adjudicators, or there is antipathy between the two groups. Cases tried by lay people take longer and the process is less efficient. Furthermore, it seems that the professionals think that the lay participants may not do a good job. Some professional judges would prefer to sit alone.

Other problems with lay participation are noted as well, such as the complexity of some cases (especially fraud cases) and the question of whether lay people, especially members of a jury, are able to deal with them. A discussion is presently being conducted about whether judges should take part in the jury deliberations to help the jurors. Some judges, including one of our respondents, are happy to leave the decisions about the defendant's guilt to the jury, however. A number of respondents felt that it would not be a good idea for a single professional judge to try most cases alone. The risk of outrageous sentencing was noted, and some respondents felt that professional judges were not sufficiently in touch with the real world.

Considering the various aspects of democracy that were presented in Chapter 2, we can tentatively conclude that England and Wales do rather well on certain points of *participation*. Compared to other countries, a relatively high proportion of lay persons are involved in the trial of cases. About 95 per cent of all criminal cases are handled with the help of lay people. As regards actual involvement during the trial, the role of lay participants is less impressive: members of a jury and lay magistrates almost never ask questions of the defendant or of witnesses – most of that is done by the prosecutor and counsel. As is expected of jurors, they generally remain passive. Neither jurors nor magistrates are generally involved in the preparation of the trial before the actual hearing of the case, or in writing the verdict. Participation of juries is further reduced by the fact that jurors do not see the original photographs of the bodies in murder cases.[8] Jurors are not regarded as being able to look at such pictures without becoming too emotional. Instead they receive drawings of the bodies and the heads with an indication of where the wounds were inflicted. On the other hand, *decision making* in cases is fully up to the lay adjudicators. They are guided on this point by the professional judge in the case of a jury (and, to a certain extent, by the clerks in the case of a magistrates' bench), but the jurors make the decision.

There is a perceived lack of *representativeness* among the lay participants. According to the statements of our respondents, on this point the jury seems to do better than the magistrates. Jurors are picked randomly from electoral rolls, while the magistrates have entered the magistracy by applying on their own initiative or being asked, and they are subsequently tested according to certain criteria. The magistracy, as a consequence, still consists for the most part of older persons who have generally completed some form of higher education. Representativity is low (see also Diamond 1990). The findings so far suggest that in England and Wales, relatively much effort has been made to increase the degree to which lay adjudicators reflect the community, probably more than in the other countries investigated.

On the third aspect of democracy, the *deliberation* of cases, it is relevant that there generally seems to be a high level of awareness of the administration of justice system in England and Wales. It appears to be customary that magistrates give talks in society about their experiences. There are websites about the magistracy. The Justices' Clerks Society and the Home Office also maintain websites that give ample information about how the system works. As a consequence, debate about the system and how it operates is encouraged. It seems to have been the case that local journalists in particular attended magistrates' courts although this seems to be not quite so common today.

On balance, the total participation by lay people is considerable in England and Wales. The question may be asked to what degree the magistrates, who are requested to take part at least 26 half-days each year and who often participate for years in the magistracy, can still be considered as real 'lay people'. By and large, they become experienced members of the bench and the only thing that distinguishes them from the professional judges seems to be their lack of formal legal education and the fact that they have their own retiring room in the court. The lay aspect may, as a consequence, disappear among the experienced magistracy. In certain respects they resemble the honorary judges working in the Netherlands, who also accumulate experience on a large scale.

8 By contrast, in Belgium such photographs are shown to the jurors.

On the basis of the research carried out here, it would seem that lay participation is not under serious discussion in England and Wales. For the majority of individuals participating in the research, it would appear self-evident that ordinary citizens should take part in the trial of criminal cases. This is reflected in the choice and the number of the advantages and disadvantages mentioned. Relatively few disadvantages were raised, and most of them were of a practical nature; no objections in principle seem to exist against lay adjudication. Thus it would be unthinkable that the entire legal system should operate *without* lay people.

Chapter 10
Belgium

Introduction

Of all the countries under review in this book, Belgium has the most extensive ongoing debate about lay participation in the form of the jury. A Commission reported on the Assisen-courts in March 2005 and November 2005 and various books and other publications have appeared on the reform proposals they put forward. This chapter attempts to address the issues that are pertinent to this debate about the jury court (*Hof van Assisen*). Interviews were conducted with four professional judges who chair jury courts, one defence lawyer and one prosecutor. Five of these interviews were conducted face-to-face and one by telephone. The issues treated in these interviews were the jury court's functioning and the views of the respondents regarding options for changes in the system. The names of these respondents were provided by the Belgian Council for the Judiciary.[1]

In addition to these interviews, two former jurors completed a questionnaire that was sent to them with the consent of a chairman of a jury court in Belgium. The jurors were asked about their experiences and their views on lay adjudication in the Belgian criminal justice system. The results of these questionnaires are presented in this chapter as well.

This chapter first describes the role the jury court plays in Belgium and the on-going debates surrounding it. After that attention is given to the empirical evidence regarding its functioning. Finally, the results of the interviews and questionnaires are presented. The chapter begins with observations of a jury trial that took place in one of the largest jury courts in Belgium in November 2007.

Observations

The jury court (*Hof van Assisen*) in the town visited is located in an old, impressive, extremely large courthouse in the city centre. The courthouse

1 The Belgian Council for the Judiciary has stipulated that it desires an explicit statement by the Research Institute (NSCR) that the results and conclusions of the research are solely the responsibility of the Institute and not of the Council for the Judiciary. The NSCR is happy to confirm that the results and the conclusions of this study are the exclusive responsibility of the Institute.

had been under renovation and its walls had recently been cleaned. As a consequence, the building was currently only in use for the hearing of jury cases; no court personnel had their offices in the courthouse at the time.

No security measures were taken when the participants and the public enter the building and the courtroom. Although the researcher had her luggage with her, she was not requested to open it for inspection or to tell what was in it. As she wanted to be admitted to the section of the courtroom where the media reporters are seated, she was asked to show ID, but no further security measures were taken. In this respect, the Belgian situation differs from that in other countries (with the exception of Denmark), where greater attention seems to be given to visitors' and participants' safety.

Most jury trials in Belgium take a full week or so. It was expected that this particular jury trial would also take about a week. It was Monday morning and the trial started with the selection of the jury (12 members and two reserve members, out of a large pool of candidates). One by one the candidates came forward after the chairman of the court read their names aloud. The prosecutor and the defence lawyers inspected the candidate for half a minute or so. Either counsel or the prosecutor can say 'challenged', upon which the candidate may leave and is freed from any further obligation to the court. We were told that lists of candidates were distributed, as is the general custom, only 48 hours before the trial started, so there was no reasonable possibility for the parties to scrutinize the candidates' backgrounds. If a candidate is not challenged the chairman of the court directs them to step into the jury box. When 14 people (12 jurors and two substitutes) have been selected, this process stops. All jurors have to take an oath.[2]

All trial participants were introduced to the jury by the chairman. The given names and surnames of the judges (three including the chairman), prosecutor and lawyers were used. The chairman, whose regular post was as an *assessor*[3] in a court in another part of Belgium, had to inspect his papers to make sure that he pronounced the names of the two *assessors* (the two judges sitting next to him) correctly. The jurors' tasks were explained to them by the chairman. The bulk of this explanation was aimed at assuring the jury's independence of judgement and preventing them from being influenced by other people's opinions and the press during the trial. The jurors are not allowed to give interviews and they may not speak about the case with others, except with colleague-jurors taking part in that particular trial. They are allowed to ask questions during the trial, but they have to take care that these questions are not prejudiced with respect to the issues that are to be judged by the jury at a later point in the trial.

2 No distinction is made with respect to the contents of this oath whether the juror believes in God or not.

3 A professional judge who sits in a panel with a professional judge and with another *assessor*.

The chairman, during this explanation, stressed that the trial was fully oral and was open to the public. The jurors may only take into account what had been said and what was presented as evidence during the hearing of the case. If they started to get tired, jurors were to notify the chairman, who may then call for a break. It is important that the jurors maintain their concentration during the hearing of the case. The chairman emphasized that this was the only procedure during which the Belgian population was involved in the administration of justice.

The courtroom in which the trial took place was large and impressive. Dark wooden furniture and paintings on the walls reinforced the message that what happened in the courtroom was of great importance. The chairman and the prosecutor (both males in their 50s) wore red robes. The other two professional judges (a female and a male in their 40s), as well as the lawyers, wore black robes and white bands. There were two defence lawyers in this case and five lawyers for the civil parties who wished to claim compensation for the damages that has been incurred as a result of the crime being tried. The technical equipment of the courtroom worked well. The microphones functioned adequately and the participants did actually speak into the microphones. Other technical equipment, such as DVD-players, did what it was expected to do. There were technical facilities for the members of the press to make use of their laptops. The chairman gave extra explanations when needed. Most of this was directed to the jury, but the public profited from this as well. This assured that the process was highly accessible and thoroughly comprehensible for those who attended.

The case that was to be tried by the jury court was atrocious. The defendant had gone fishing on a boat at night with the new partner of his former wife. During a quarrel with this man, he had picked up a jack from his car and battered the other man on the head with it. The victim died immediately. The defendant put the victim in the boot of his car and covered the corpse. He then went to his former wife's home and took her and their children in the car. He told his wife and children that the victim fell into the hold of the ship they were on and that emergency services took him to a hospital in Rotterdam where he was now being treated. For two days the family was driven by car through the Netherlands. Every now and then the defendant, stepping outside the car, appeared to speak with the victim in the hospital over his mobile phone. (At least, that is what he told his former wife and the children.) He reported that the victim said to him that he did not want to have them visiting him in the hospital. All the time during this trip the victim's corpse lay in the boot of the car. Finally the corpse started to smell atrociously. After two days, the defendant 'lost contact' with the victim and he and his former wife went to the police to officially notify them of the victim's disappearance. After a couple of weeks two arms were found in a river nearby. Fingerprints were taken and, with the help of a fingerprint data bank, a relationship was established with the missing victim, who was already known to the police from previous incidents.

As the defendant was the last person who had had contact with the victim and because there were some discrepancies with respect to what he had said about his last communication with him, he was taken into custody and interrogated. He confessed to having killed the man and told the police that he had sawn off the victim's arms and head. He also revealed where he had buried the rest of the corpse. The police went to this place and found the body. It had not been completely covered by earth: the belly protruded from the earth, creating a nauseating stench.

At the hearing of the case, upon an inquiry from a lawyer for one of the civil parties, the defendant stated that it had taken about 10 minutes to remove the arms and the head with a saw. He had put both the arms and the head in a box. He had intended to throw the arms into the river at one place and the head at another, but when he opened the box to take out the arms the victim's head was looking him directly in the eye. On an impulse, he had thrown the box with both the two arms and the head in the river. The head had, to date, not been found.

In total 46 witnesses, including a number of experts, appeared before the court. Most of the interrogations were conducted by the chairman, but he gave opportunities to the other participants to ask questions as well. Most witnesses were family and friends of the defendant or the victim. There were also witnesses who had been involved in the investigation of the case, like police officials and a medical examiner. The interrogation of the victim's mother, who recounted the moments when the police came to her home to tell her that they had found the two arms, and later, the corpse without the head, was especially dramatic. She still felt that she had not properly buried her son, because it was still not clear where the head was. During the interrogation the old lady, sitting in a wheelchair, looked over at the defendant and cried out to him, 'Where is the head? Where is the head?' The defendant rose and replied that he did not know, it was probably still in the river. If he knew, he would certainly have told her.

Both the mother and the other relatives present at the trial showed a great deal of emotion. During the trial photographs of the arms that were found in the water and of the decapitated body were shown on full screen. A DVD was played showing the moment the corpse was found. The court's chairman warned in advance that the images might be shocking for the victim's family and that they might leave the courtroom if they wanted to. But they preferred to stay and watch. However, when the part of the DVD was shown where the corpse, without the head and the arms, was found, wrapped in white sheets and put in the ambulance, some of the victims, including the victim's mother, had to leave the courtroom. Their sobbing in the hallway could be heard inside the courtroom.

During the interrogations the lawyers for the civil parties also asked questions of the victim's family. These questions often centred around how the family had experienced the victim's death and the fact that, until now, the head had not been found. Many of the family members started to cry when these questions were asked. One of the journalists present at the trial noted that asking these questions might have a function at a later point in the process: on the final day, when the damages incurred by the defendant were assessed and compensation claimed, the stronger the emotions, the higher the damages. Another journalist offered the opinion that the jury process might contribute to victims being better able to deal with their grief as a result of the crime and the loss of a loved one. He explained that in a previous jury trial he had reported, the families of the defendant and of the victim ended up with a reconciliation. It is also the case that the fiercest opponents of the jury system who are requested to take part in a jury trial often end up as strong advocates. Working together for one week in such intense, dramatic cases often leads to a greater acceptance of the jury system.

The trial proceeded at an extremely slow pace. At the end of the second day the chief of the police unit that had been responsible for the investigation again presented all the research that had been conducted, although many witnesses who had been heard that day had already explained what had happened. The journalists attending the trial started showing pictures of their last holidays to each other on their laptops. There was a lot of repetition in the process. This, however, had an advantage in that everything was highly comprehensible. Every aspect of the case was looked at from several perspectives and by various witnesses. During the interrogations considerable attention was devoted to relations between the various people involved and how they had experienced the facts of the crime. Factual and interpretative information was mixed to a large extent. Witnesses made statements both about what happened and about what they thought during the events, what their feelings were and what their relations with the other people involved were.

Most of the time the jury did nothing except listen and watch. A few jurors wrote notes on a pad. When the victim's mother was interrogated two members of the jury had tears in their eyes. The jury, through their foreman, asked a couple of questions. However, the chairman seemed reluctant to give the jury an opportunity to question witnesses every time the other participants were offered such an opportunity. When the jury wanted to ask something, they generally had to take the initiative themselves.

During breaks in the proceedings, some trial participants moved to the restaurant next door to the courthouse.[4] It may happen that lawyers, members of the jury, prosecutors and the family of the defendant or the victim take lunch in the same restaurant.[5] The jury court breaks for one-and-a-half hours for lunch. Jurors are not provided with food by the court during the trial. Obviously, this long break is necessary to relax and to prepare for the

4 Because of the renovations, the courthouse had no restaurant at that time.

5 The jury is not sequestered from the outside world during the trial, as happens in the United States.

afternoon session. When the trial recommenced, the professional participants put on their robes, the jurors entered the courtroom through their own special door, and the chairman announced the resumption of the trial.

The Belgian press covered the trial extensively. Several newspaper articles dwelt on the victim's missing head and the fact that sawing off the arms and the head had, according to the defendant, taken only 10 minutes. Furthermore, the press revealed that the victim had contacts in the Albanian underworld.[6] According to a journalist we spoke to, attending a jury trial of this kind would be an upsetting and dramatic experience for the victim's family. In another recent jury trial the family was confronted with pictures of a small child – a daughter of one of them – who had been fatally shot. The family had not seen these pictures before the trial. It is apparent that this must have been a deeply shocking experience for them and the emotions this provoked were huge. The court session had to be stopped immediately to allow the civil parties to recover.

On Friday, the fifth day of the trial, the jury reached its verdict. During the trial the defendant had suddenly admitted that he had intended to kill the victim, and did so with premeditation, while before he had contended that the killing had happened by accident during a quarrel with the victim. However, he did not give any explanation or the reasons for the killing. The jury found him guilty of murder and the court sentenced him to life imprisonment.

Role and Function of the Jury Court in Belgium

Chapter 3 sketched the legal framework for the *Hof van Assisen* and the way in which these courts operate in Belgium. Below, a number of differences with the Anglo-American jury systems are set out.

The defendant in Belgium does not have a right to a jury trial as in the United States. The jury trial can be better characterized as one of the opportunities, among others, the Belgian Prosecution Service has to proceed with a case. The Prosecution Service uses its power to send cases to a jury court on a steadily decreasing number of occasions (Hakvoort 2005). Many such cases are sent instead to courts consisting of professional judges only. Although cases concerning murder and homicide, political crimes and cases relating to freedom of the press can, in principle, be tried by a jury, in reality at present only those in the first category appear before the *Hof van Assisen*.

A major difference from jury trials in Anglo-American countries is that the presiding judge in Belgium has a substantial investigative role during the hearing of the case, which is indicative of the inquisitorial roots of the legal system. In addition to chairing the trial, the judge interrogates all witnesses, experts and the defendant. A cross-examination by the two sides in a trial, as

6 On the role of the media, see also Op de Weerdt and Heuvelmans, 2007.

happens in the US or England, does not take place in Belgium, at least not on a comparable scale. The questioning starts with the chairman, after whom the two other professional judges (*assessors*) and the other participants are allowed to ask questions of the witnesses, the experts and the defendant (Van Eeckhaut 1992; Snelders and Heuvelmans 2007).

There are two guiding principles in the hearing of Belgian jury cases: the principle of immediacy and the principle of continuity. The first-mentioned principle implies that all evidence must be presented in its most original and authentic form during the trial of the case, leading to long and extensive trials. Character witnesses[7] who make statements about the defendant's and/or victim's life and behaviour in the past make an important contribution to the trial of jury cases in Belgium. Many witnesses of all kinds, as well as many experts of various disciplines, appear before the jury court (van Teefelen 1983). The principle of continuity requires that the trial goes on until a decision has been reached. This latter principle is intended to provide a guarantee for independent and impartial decision making, because it can then be assumed that the jurors will not be influenced by the media and public opinion during the course of the trial (at least not to any great extent) (Traest 2001).

Before the jury retires for deliberation about the defendant's guilt, the court's president gives instructions about the applicable law and the way the jury has to reach a decision. In contrast to the possibilities Anglo-American professional judges have, the Belgian judge is not allowed to give instructions regarding the evidence that is presented and its reliability and trustworthiness. He or she is expected to give an objective instruction regarding the way the law must be applied and the procedure that must be employed for decision making. During deliberations the jurors have the possibility of asking the president of the court to clarify certain legal points, but they may do so only in the presence of the prosecutor and the defence lawyer (Vermassen 2004).

Plans for Reform of the Jury System

The jury system is under discussion in Belgium. Criticisms include that it is old-fashioned, that trials take too long and that it produces too many inaccurate decisions (Kools 2004; Liégeois 2004). Related to that is a general dissatisfaction with the operation of the Belgian criminal justice system, as appears from the results of the *Justitiebarometer* (Justice Barometer), a survey that is conducted on an annual basis among a representative sample of the Belgian population. A serious gap appears to exist between citizens and the criminal justice system (Wyseur et al. 2005). The public would prefer more serious punishments than those presently imposed by the courts. However, respondents to this *Justitiebarometer* are generally positive about participation

7 *Moraliteitsgetuigen.*

of lay people in the trial of cases. Although the number of proponents has decreased, 68 per cent of the population is still in favour of the jury (Hoge Raad voor de Justitie 2007).

A commission was established in Belgium to advise about a potential reform of the jury trial. Its first, preliminary, report appeared in March 2005, and a second report in November 2005.[8] The advice was divided: a majority argued for the abolition of jury trials in their present form and their replacement by a system of *échevinage*, such as can be found in commercial law and in social security law (De Hert 2006b). This would comprise two professional and three lay judges, who may be selected because they possess specialized knowledge in a certain domain. According to the Committee's recommendations, character witnesses should be replaced by specialized experts and not all witnesses should be heard again in court (De Hert 2006b). The minority position in the Committee's report was in favour of a continuation of the present system of jury involvement with suggestions for modernization. Among these proposed modifications are a simplification of the procedures employed in jury courts, giving reasons for the decision about the defendant's guilt, and a restricted number of opportunities for appeal of the court's decision.

The Minister of Justice followed the minority opinion. She requested that the Committee elaborate on a new law and indicated a number of focal points that should guide the Committee's work. These included making it possible for the professional judge to participate in the jury's decision about the defendant's guilt. In the new system both this decision and the one regarding the sentence should be reasoned. An appeal should be made possible as well. In November 2005, a draft for a new law was produced. According to this proposal, the number of jurors would be reduced to eight, and the number of professional judges to one. The professional judge would participate in making the decision about guilt and the jury would have to give reasons for its decision. Restricted opportunities for an appeal would be introduced (De Hert 2006b). According to this draft the Belgian jury system would be closer to that of France, in which cooperation between the professional judge and the jurors takes place on a larger scale and appeal has also been made possible. However, with the parliamentary elections the draft for the new law seems to have been withdrawn from the legislative process.

8 *Intermediair rapport van de 'commissie-assisenprocedure', overhandigd aan Mevr. de minister van Justitie op 8 maart 2005; Intermediair rapport van de Commissie Hervorming van het Assisenhof, overhandigd aan Mevr. de minister van Justitie op 8 november 2005.*

Empirical Research into the Belgian Jury

At the beginning of the twentieth century the number of jury cases tried in Belgium was approximately 100 each year. This number decreased to about 40 in the 1950s, but started rising again from the year 1974 onwards (Tubex 2004). At the time of writing the total number is again around 100 cases each year, although a slight decrease has been observed since 1996. Jury trials comprise only a small percentage (0.01 per cent) of all criminal cases tried (Tubex 2004). Nevertheless they attract a lot of media attention and thus largely determine the general picture that exists of the Belgian criminal justice system.

The proportion of acquittals in jury courts was relatively high at the beginning of the twentieth century, about 20–30 per cent of all verdicts. This proportion decreased considerably to 6 per cent in 1963, after which it started growing again to 10–20 per cent at the end of the 1970s. Over recent years the percentage of acquittals has been about 10 per cent. Life sentences were given only rarely at the beginning of the twentieth century, but with some fluctuations the proportion of this penalty has increased to 20–25 per cent at present (Tubex 2004).

The crimes that are tried by jury courts are often of a highly serious nature. Citizens who are called to act as jurors are confronted with the responsibility of deciding about the future life of the defendant. Generally they have never had such responsibility in their lives. Unfortunately, not a lot is known about how they deal with these experiences and how they impact on their lives and on their views of the criminal justice system. Interviewing jurors has not been done on a large scale in Belgium or anywhere else in the world.[9] Considerably more jury research has been conducted using an experimental setting with the help of mock juries,[10] but field research is scarce on this issue. As far as is known, it is a requirement of all legal systems that jury members do not reveal how decisions were arrived at in the deliberations room. Only a few studies in which jurors themselves have been interviewed regarding their experiences and perspectives are available.[11] An example of such research is van Langenhove (1989). He used what is called the snowball-method to find six former members of a Belgian jury and interviewed them about their involvement. Van Langenhove's general finding is that the procedure used by juries for reaching a decision on the defendant's guilt is not optimal. Juries develop their own norms and values and, as a result, deviating opinions are not always tolerated. Jurors who are too insistent on a certain issue risk being isolated by the others. Too little discussion takes place within juries. Jurors do not gain a good insight into what the other members think and they sometimes have a biased perception

9 For a recent example of a study involving interviews with jurors see Lloyd-Bostock 2007.

10 See Klik and van Koppen 2001 for overviews of this type of research.

11 For an overview, see van Langenhove 1989.

of what is happening within the group. Most jurors attach more importance to a smooth proceeding and pay less attention to the decision that has to be made ('Where can we get food?', 'When can we go home?'). Once a specific judgement has been made, new and contradicting information generally does not lead to a change of opinion (van Langenhove 1989).

Symptoms of groupthink and biases in individual decision making[12] were also observed by van Langenhove (1989). Most jurors were either 100 per cent confident of the defendant being guilty or 100 per cent confident that he or she was not guilty. The chairmen of the court had a dominant role in the sentencing decision. In many cases they appeared to be able to steer the decision in the direction they deemed desirable (van Langenhove 1989).

Van Langenhove made a number of observations that are relevant for an evaluation of the jury system in Belgium and the operation of lay people in legal systems in general. Overall, van Langenhove's findings are not highly positive about decision making by juries, but he stresses that opportunities for improvement exist. The drawback of such improvements, however, would be that jurors could no longer be considered as lay people. To maintain this status they would have to forego further instruction and education.

Interviews

The Respondents' Backgrounds

The four judges interviewed for our research had previously chaired several jury trials: 52, 13, nine and four jury trials respectively. In addition to presiding over jury trials, three of the judges worked at a Court of Appeal and one at a Court of First Instance.[13] The defence lawyer who collaborated in our research had limited experience with jury trials, but the prosecutor had acted in several jury cases. Their opinions will be presented in a later section of this chapter. All respondents were males aged between 30–60.

The Selection of Jurors

The respondents gave some background information regarding the selection of jurors, including the issue of how challenging the candidates for jury duty takes place. Prosecutors and defence lawyers are not allowed to reveal the reasons for challenging a prospective juror, but according to a respondent, lawyers for both sides would prefer jurors who are not highly knowledgeable.

12 On this subject see also Chapter 2.

13 Being a chairman of a jury court is not a full-time job; jury courts are *ad hoc* courts that are composed each time the Prosecution brings a case before the *Hof van Assisen* (Snelders and Heuvelmans 2007).

They will, for example, challenge a schoolteacher because they have the impression that she may influence the other jurors. If a psychiatrist is called, he or she will probably be challenged by the defence.

Who is challenged and who is not, and for what reasons, depends on the case. In the Dutroux[14] case there was a candidate who plainly exhibited his prejudice. He let it be known in advance that he considered Dutroux to be guilty. This person, therefore, was excluded for reason of prejudice. Most candidates who do not wish to take part as a juror themselves give medical reasons for being excused.

Advantages and Disadvantages of the Jury

The judges participating in our research mentioned ten different advantages of the jury system. Two advantages were mentioned by more than one respondent, leading to a total of 12 advantages. The wider involvement of the community and education of lay people were each mentioned twice (see Table 10.1).

The respondents gave explanations for the advantages mentioned. These included:

- the public would gain more trust in the legal system as a result of the participation of the jury;
- the community is more committed to jury trials because of the thorough treatment of each case;
- they accept its decision more readily than that of professional judges;
- victims would be better able to deal with the grief resulting from the crime as a result of jury trials;
- they perceive that the court feels that their case is important, and this seems to give them comfort;
- the defendant in a jury trial also appreciates that his case is extensively and thoroughly examined;
- jurors also value so much time and effort being spent on the cases. as the trial proceeds they become more and more committed.

A judge stated, 'I sometimes see a change in the jurors. They start aloof and reluctant. But I try to involve them. I let them talk, hold breaks when necessary, and let them talk through their feelings. After the conclusion of the case, it often appears that they want to come back in another jury'.

Eleven different disadvantages were mentioned by the judges. Some disadvantages were mentioned by two or more respondents, leading to 17

14 The Dutroux case was a high profile case in which the defendant was sentenced to life in prison in 2006. On top of this life sentence, he was sentenced to a mandatory commitment to a psychiatric institution. He was found guilty of the murder of several people, among whom a number were young girls.

disadvantages being mentioned. There seems to be a greater consensus on the disadvantages than on the advantages and the total number of disadvantages mentioned by respondents is greater than the number of advantages (17 versus 12) (see Table 10.1).

Table 10.1 Advantages and disadvantages of the lay jury mentioned by professional judges (4) (Belgium)

Advantages		Disadvantages	
Involvement of the community	2	More time	3
Education of lay people	2	More expense	3
Treatment more in-depth	1	No reasons given for decisions	2
Jurors happy with the system	1	Jury is easily influenced	2
Jurors act out of their emotions	1	Jury cannot compare cases	1
Increases confidence in the system	1	Jurors not aware of lawyers' tricks	1
Increases democracy	1	Many citizens do not want to take part	1
Jury trial is open and accessible	1	Juries make mistakes	1
Jurors' common sense	1	Jurors do not feel responsible	1
Contributes to dealing with crime	1	Too little distance	1
		Emotions	1
Total: 10 advantages	*12*	*Total: 11 disadvantages*	*17*

The amount of time and the expense needed for jury trials were each indicated by three judges as a disadvantage. The fact the juries do not have to give reasons for their decisions, as well as the observation that jurors would be easily influenced, were disadvantages mentioned by two judges.

There is an increased risk of mistakes being made by juries because they do not fully feel responsible for the decision regarding the guilt and, at the same time, do not have to give reasons for their opinions. Jurors are expected to consult their conscience and to examine themselves about whether they are personally convinced of the defendant's guilt. They do so in silence and are not expected to give reasons. According to the respondents, this combination leads to a certain risk of incorrect decisions. 'If a juror does not like the defendant on first sight, that can exert a certain influence on his opinion, especially because they do not have to give reasons. In the situation of a jury trial, there are punishments of 20, 30 years at stake, so the consequences of a biased judgement can be disastrous!'

The jurors' sensitivity to what lawyers do and say was illustrated by one judge. 'I have to fight against their extreme opinions. They let themselves be carried away by the lawyers' presentations. ... We do not know what happens when they form an opinion on the defendant's guilt in the deliberations room, because we are not there.' Another judge confirmed that jurors can be easily influenced, and that there is a risk of mistakes being made. 'Counsel sometimes steers the jury in a wrong direction. And difficult issues sometimes are not well explained by the prosecutor.'[15]

One judge criticized the repetition that takes place in jury trials. 'In my opinion, it is not necessary to call all witnesses for the trial. That is wasted time, because some issues keep being repeated at trial. Each witness again tells the same story. The number of character witnesses could easily be reduced.'

Collaboration between Professional Judges and the Jury

All four judges indicated that when chairing a jury case they greatly appreciated working together with a jury. What was most valued was the fact that the contact with the jury was extremely intensive during the whole week that the trial takes. One judge reported that he even had a 'dip' afterwards. He kept a diary and collects photographs and articles on each jury case he had chaired. However, he was also of the opinion that chairing a jury trial is highly stressful. His assessment: 'You have to take care of everything: see that procedures are complied with, that jurors do not say anything that would reveal their prejudices. But in my perception, most jurors think positively about jury trials after having taken part'.

One judge said that it was fascinating to chair jury trials.

> I love chairing jury cases. In cases without a jury it may take 10 years before they allow you to preside over cases, but for chairing jury trials you need less experience. But I remain an opponent of juries. There are too few advantages and too many disadvantages. With professional judges, the decisions you get are more balanced. Juries tend to make decisions that are too extreme, while professional judges show an inclination for the middle ground.

The Jury's Input

During the trial of cases the jury generally remains passive. They are allowed to ask questions, but they often remain silent. However, one of the judges interviewed had observed a slight change in this respect. He had noticed that juries were now becoming more assertive and asked questions more frequently during the trial than they used to do. He explained that the chairmen of the jury courts were in the past more severe and restrictive, and that they had become more permissive on this point. He himself encouraged the jury to ask questions if something is not clear to them.

15 It should be noted that it was judges who were interviewed for this part of the research. Had defence lawyers been interviewed, the responses might have been different with respect to who influences the jurors.

One other judge did not like jurors asking questions. The schedule of the trial that he made in advance did not allow for many interruptions. His timing risked being upset if the jury took part in the interrogations. He feared that some jurors wanted to act as an investigating judge. They risked revealing their own opinions when asking questions. However, outside the hearing of the case in open court he encouraged the jurors to ask him questions if something was not clear to them. One of the judges assessed that in about half of all jury cases the jury took part in asking questions. In general, these questions concerned details of the case, especially those regarding the alleged crime.

With respect to the defendant's guilt, jurors sometimes held opinions that differed from what the judges themselves thought about the case. 'Especially with murders that have been committed out of passion, they hold opinions that differ from ours, because they judge the aggravating circumstances differently', a judge explained. 'They follow the lawyers and their explanations of premeditation. There are sometimes unexpected acquittals by the jury. Juries can be confused by legal concepts like "force majeure" or "self-defence".' But the opposite might also happen: a jury convicting where a judge would have acquitted the defendant.

The three judges sit in with the jury during deliberations about the sentence. Two of our judges indicated that in that situation they take off their robes, to allow the deliberations to be more informal and the atmosphere more relaxed. 'One by one, we give our views on the sentence. The youngest juror starts. The three judges come last, to prevent us influencing the jurors' opinions. After that we generally vote. The sentence, then, most of the time, can be speedily determined.' According to all the judges interviewed, it was not very difficult to reach consensus about the sentence. One judge felt that jurors tended to sentence more leniently. The experiences of another respondent were different. In his view there was no clear line on juries' decisions. 'Sometimes they are much harsher. It certainly is the case that they can be more readily influenced.' One judge observed that juries had more extreme opinions. They would not necessarily be more harsh. They may also have empathic feelings towards the defendant where a professional judge would not.

Juries need some time to recover after the actual trial. In the retiring room, after the part of the hearing concerning the punishment, the professional judges gave them ample time to express their initial views on the case and the thoughts they had during the trial, before they started deliberating over the sentence. 'We then try to reach consensus. If we do not succeed, we vote with help of anonymous pieces of paper. But in most cases we succeed in coming to a conclusion without that.'

Emotions

Jury trials are substantially more emotional than trials without a jury. In most cases the alleged crime is a murder or homicide. The defendant's life history is scrutinized. One of the judges felt that the emotional aspect of the trial precisely represented the virtue of the jury process. Those involved and society more generally had been awaiting the trial for a long time. The defendant should be happy that it was nearing an end, because he had been waiting so long. The victim and/or his or her family were eager to see the defendant tried, and the public and the media looked forward to watching it all happen before them in court. The emotions that arose were an indispensable part of this type of trial and helped the parties and society to deal with the crime. A jury trial would be inconceivable without emotions.

Jurors were generally more emotional than the professional judges, one of the respondents observed.

> I see that in their reactions after the trial when we retire for deliberations. Everything is new to them. We have learned to deal with cases like this, we can keep distance. They sometimes fall prey to their emotions. However, that happens most of the time *after* the trial, not in open court. Nevertheless, I've had it happen three times when I was presiding over a trial, that a juror fainted in open court after having been shown pictures.

Other respondents held similar views and had had comparable experiences. Emotions are shown by the jurors having tears in their eyes. When people act more than once as a juror, they tend to become less emotional. According to some respondents, jurors were also more sensitive to media reporting, even though they received the instruction not to pay attention to what was written or what was shown on television.

Acceptance of Court Decisions

All four judges were of the opinion that jury decisions probably are better accepted as a result of the participation of lay people. The public has more trust in the decisions when they see that ordinary citizens take part. They have the feeling that the rights of the defendant are better guaranteed.

Two judges fully agreed with the proposition that it is important that ordinary citizens are offered the opportunity to take part in the administration of justice; the two other judges were less convinced of the importance of lay adjudication. On the question of whether lay participation fits well into the Belgian legal culture, the answers varied: one judge felt that it fits perfectly, whereas another judge was more reserved. He thought that it was not typical for the Belgian system to have lay decision makers. His most serious objection was that the jury has to do so much *without* the professional judges. The decision about the guilt is, at present, exclusively up to the jury and it would be better to do that together with the professional judges. The other judges felt that the jury fits well within the Belgian legal culture, but that serious improvements were needed.

None of the judges was of the opinion that professional judges were out of touch with the 'real world'. On that point, things would appear to have changed over the last few decades. One judge stressed that in the past judges were much more likely to be living in an ivory tower than now.

Being Kept Awake at Night

Only one of the judges interviewed admitted to being kept awake at night by the jury trials. The most important reason for this was that he had to ensure that everything ran smoothly and that the court reached an acceptable decision. He was worried that things might get out of hand. The other judges also showed concern that the case was dealt with properly, but they did not lose sleep over it.

The Prosecutor and the Defence Lawyer

Both the prosecutor and the defence lawyer with whom the researcher spoke were fervent opponents of the jury system. Most of all, they objected to the theatrical aspects inherent to the jury trial. They felt the jury to be old-fashioned and jury trials too emotional and irrational. 'Jury cases are theatre. Of the parliament, 75 per cent want to keep the jury. The former Minister of Justice wanted to abolish the jury, but then the Dutroux case came along. I predict that in ten years, the jury will be abolished. At present, we are not yet ready for it. People want sensation. Your country has a much better system', the prosecutor claimed. However, both the prosecutor and the lawyer were aware that victims would probably feel neglected if *no* jury trial took place. They admitted that the involvement of ordinary citizens leads to greater acceptance of jury decisions by the public.

Another issue raised by the prosecutor and the defence lawyer was the presence of the chairman of the court at the deliberations over the defendant's guilt, as proposed in the draft for a new law. They felt that this would not be a good solution to the problems with jury decision making. The chairman, in his robe, would sit there as an authority and the jurors would all be impressed and adjust their opinions to his views. The problem of too great a sensitivity among the jurors for what other people say would remain.

Questionnaire Completed by Jurors

Two former jurors completed a questionnaire for our research. The most important finding of these questionnaires is that before the trial both respondents had been deeply reluctant to act as a juror because of the severity of the alleged crime. They both stated that they would not be eager to participate *again* in a new trial for the same reasons. The case had often kept them awake during the week it was tried, because of the horrific evidence and the gruesome details of what had happened. The jurors had become fully aware of what atrocious things people are prepared to do to one another in specific situations. One of them made it clear that he or she had been very emotional during the hearing of the case, as had the other jurors.

In spite of their hesitancy about taking part in a new trial, the jurors were positive about how the legal system had operated in the case in which they had participated. One of them stated that the trial had been conducted very fairly and correctly. Both jurors evaluated the participation of lay people in jury trials as positive. They felt that it was important that ordinary citizens can take part in the administration of justice, and that this increased confidence in the system. Cooperation with the professional judges was also evaluated positively by both jurors.

Conclusions

In Belgium, strongly opposing views exist about the jury. Relatively large numbers of advantages and disadvantages were put forward, with the disadvantages outnumbering the advantages. In many respects, jury systems differ strikingly from systems that make use of lay judges. The latter systems are much more introverted and they attract hardly any media attention. Jury trials are extroverted and the media play an important role in disseminating information about what happens in and around the court. The aspects of 'theatre' and 'drama' are prominent within Belgian jury trials and the media are very active in this respect. The following aspects are inherent to theatre and drama: emotions, role-playing and the presence of an audience. The Belgian jury trial scores high on all three characteristics: the trial is full of emotion, there is a potentially large audience (if the press is included) and the participants play their roles convincingly. In particular, Belgium performs well on one of these characteristics: emotion seems to be very strong in Belgian jury cases and the lawyers for the civil parties do their best to heighten them by the type of questions they ask their clients in open court. In contrast to the practice in England, pictures of dead bodies are shown to Belgian jurors. With respect to role playing, however, participants in Belgian jury trials seem less strict than is perhaps the case in other countries: players have no difficulty in temporarily taking off their professional robes and joining in at lunch in the same restaurant as the other participants. After lunch, the roles are easily re-adopted: the robes are put on and the trial recommences.

It was suggested by individuals interviewed or spoken to that the emotions and the elaborate way in which cases are dealt with in jury trials contribute to society and those involved being better able to deal with the impact of the crime. Emotions that may have been suppressed for a couple of years (most jury trials take place a considerable time after the alleged crime was committed) can be expressed during the trial, by giving detailed accounts of what happened and how each speaker feels, but also by the tears that are shed. In this respect the jury trial proves considerably more useful than other types of criminal trials. Trials of the Dutch type, where very often not even the victim is present to make a statement and emotions seem largely absent, can be placed at the opposite end of this spectrum.[16]

The hypothesis that the thorough treatment of cases, the 'slowness' of the trial and the emotions expressed during the trial in open court actually *do* contribute to a better processing of the crime needs further exploration (De Hert 2006b). It is a challenging suggestion that calls for future comparative research, in which notions of restorative justice should be taken into account.

16 However, with serious crime, some changes can be discerned in the Dutch trials. A couple of years ago victim impact statements (VIS) were introduced in the Netherlands However, so far experience with this new opportunity has shown that many VISs are taken in writing and the victims do not appear at trial to explain what happened and how it impacted on their lives. Emotions, thus, are still largely veiled in the Dutch trial.

Chapter 11
Conclusions

Introduction

This book has discussed the system and practice of lay adjudication in a large number of European countries. In five of these countries observations were conducted and judges and lay participants interviewed about their perspectives on lay participation. This final chapter makes comparisons between the different systems and attempts to reach overall conclusions with respect to how they incorporate the three aspects of democracy as portrayed in Chapter 2.

Democracy in the Framework of a Criminal Justice System

In Chapter 2 three aspects of democracy were identified: participation, representation and deliberation. *Participation* by citizens provides the most comprehensive form of democracy by allowing citizens the opportunity to take part directly in the trial of cases and the decisions that are made. Clearly, not everyone can reasonably participate in the administration of justice and so a selection has to be made. In choosing representatives, the question arises as to whether and in what respects these people can be considered representative of a country's population. This issue forms the second aspect of democracy as discussed here: *representation*.

The final aspect identified is *deliberation*. This assumes that it is an important feature of democracy for citizens of a country to take part in an informed debate about issues that are relevant to the public domain, including the operation of the criminal justice system. At the beginning of this book it was suggested that participation in a system by 'ordinary citizens' may contribute to a better and more informed debate about that system in society more generally. From that perspective, two of the features of democracy, namely 'participation' and 'deliberation', are interwoven to a large extent, in that participation improves the possibilities for better and more informed deliberation (van Gunsteren 2007).

Here, we revisit these three aspects of democracy and attempt to establish to what extent each of the five countries under review offers opportunities for their realization. We begin by looking at representation.

Representation

The literature discusses the issue of representation primarily with regard to the political domain; how far do representative bodies reflect a country's population (Pitkin 1967; Young 2000; Sloot 2004)? The legal domain, which is central to this book, differs from the political domain in various respects. The most relevant distinction between the two is that the political domain has been primarily constructed as a democratic institution in which elections involving the country's population take place on a regular basis for the government and other political bodies. In the contemporary Western world the political domain is still democratic in nature, even though political participation is declining. However, over the course of the centuries, democratic elements in the *legal domain*, such as citizens being offered the possibility of participating or of electing representatives to do that, have decreased (van de Pol 1986; Malsch and Nijboer 2005). Community involvement in the trial of cases has gradually been replaced by professional decision making. This has culminated in the present situation, in which professional judges in most countries are now recruited and selected predominantly by their own organizations and not elected by the population (Jackson and Kovalev 2006). In the legal field other selection procedures and criteria for participation have taken the place of what was once a democratic process. Among these 'new' criteria are the juridical knowledge that judges must master, their specialization as judges and their impartiality and independence. These criteria now take precedence over any need for judges to form part of the community and have knowledge of local situations. The emphasis on independence and impartiality reveals that it is nowadays viewed as less important that judges should come from the community and represent the community, than that they possess a certain expertise (Malsch 2003). Maintaining distance from the place where they grew up and went to school and where their friends and family still live makes it easier for judges to be independent. Distance from the situations where crime takes place can be more easily preserved today, in an age when many people change address and switch jobs several times rather than remaining in their place of birth and in the same job or occupation for their entire life. As such, developments in Western society over the last 50 or 60 years have contributed to judiciaries being better able to maintain independence and impartiality (Malsch and Nijboer 2005). The interviews with respondents from different countries that have been presented in this book, reflect the general concern that exists about preserving independence at the expense of having adjudicators who reflect their community.

The characteristics of distance, objectivity, legal knowledge and independence have now become the most important features that are taken into account when evaluating individual judges or the judiciary as a whole in advanced legal systems.[1] Gradually the concept of a judge reflecting the community and knowing it, and the emphasis on judicial work as some type of public duty that can be expected of any member of society has faded away. The study presented in this book has shown that there are countries in which this notion has almost totally disappeared, such as the Netherlands. Despite some discussions about the representativeness of the formal judiciary having taken place there over the past few decades (de Groot-van Leeuwen 2006), the notion that a person who is not a lawyer by training, or does not have specific expertise that might be helpful in the trial of particular types of cases, should take part in the administration of justice is almost totally absent (Brants 2004).[2] In the four other countries under review in this book such a notion still exists in one form or another and this is apparent from a considerable allegiance to lay adjudication.[3] These countries still support the general principle of lay involvement, notwithstanding the associated practical problems.

One of these practical problems is the question of which citizens should take part in the adjudication of cases and how they should be selected – the problem of representation (Young 2000). The issue of representativeness does not seem to have been satisfactorily resolved by any of the countries under review in this book. Participation by members of ethnic minorities as decision makers is virtually absent, and in each country criticism is being voiced about both the salaried judges' representativeness and that of lay participants. All countries under review share this concern. England and Wales and Denmark have taken explicit initiatives to increase the diversity of the lay adjudicator groups, particularly with respect to ethnic minorities, certain occupations and certain age groups. These two jurisdictions seem to be most active in their attempt to obtain a representative body of lay adjudicators. As England and Wales have the largest proportion of all criminal cases involving lay adjudicators, they seem to have been the most successful in achieving at least certain aspects of representation and participation.

Probably none of the countries involved in this book will succeed in obtaining a fully representative body of judges, professional and lay. Nevertheless, efforts made by jurisdictions to increase representativeness of decision makers in the legal system should be applauded (Pitkin 1967; Sloot 2004).

Participative Democracy

Once jurors and lay judges have been selected for their duties, what does their actual *participation* involve? On this point, the results from this research are not very encouraging. In all countries under review a large number of comments

1 See the case law of the European Court of Human Rights (ECHR).
2 See Chapters 5 and 6.
3 See Chapters 7–10.

were voiced on the lack of active input by both lay judges and jurors.[4] They do not ask very many questions during the trial and if they do, they risk revealing prejudices. Professional judges do not always seem to be eager to allow them to ask questions during the hearing of the cases. Because the lay people lack a frame of reference when it comes to the determination of the sanction, the professional judges have to give lots of guidance too – and the input from the professionals is far more influential than that of the lay participants on this issue. Some even remarked that in fact the lay participants contribute nothing to the trial of cases and the decisions made. Some lay judges admitted to feeling like a piece of furniture. In contrast, experts in the Dutch specialized courts described in Chapter 6 did extremely well on the point of participation.

At the same time, no serious objections were raised against working together with lay persons in the countries where this is part of the system. In general, the respondents indicated they enjoyed collaborating with each other and did not find it difficult to reach a decision. The opinions on cases did not differ greatly between the two groups, and if they did it was easy to reach a compromise. It was observed, however, that there was a serious risk that the professional judges might dominate the proceedings to such an extent that the decisions were in fact exclusively theirs.[5] With juries who decide a defendant's guilt without professional judges, the risk of extreme decisions and decisions that are not legally admissible, or prima facie wrong, was noted by the respondents.[6]

The other side of the coin regarding participation is that the lay persons involved gain more insight into how the system works. By their involvement lay persons outside the legal system obtain greater confidence in it as they perceive that cases are tried fairly (Machura 2001; Crawford 2008).[7] People's opinions about criminal justice are generally founded on poor knowledge of crime and sentencing practice (Hough and Roberts 1998). Those involved become aware that trying cases is complex, and realize that the task of a judge is a difficult one. Seeing the defendant before them and hearing the circumstances of the crime may lead lay adjudicators to adopt less punitive attitudes. This observation, which was made by a number of respondents in our study, is in agreement with previous research conducted by Diamond (1990). She observes that 'The lay magistrate, unlike the ordinary citizen, has a direct opportunity to develop

4 Neither is the literature positive about participation by lay adjudicators. See de Roos 2006 for an overview.

5 Such concerns were expressed in Germany and Belgium, see Chapters 8 and 10.

6 See Chapter 2 for the pros and cons of decision making by small groups. See also Chapter 10.

7 Or they may become less trusting of it for the opposite reason, although that was not mentioned in our study. These advantages have been mentioned by our respondents in Denmark, Belgium and Germany.

an accurate picture of crime in the courts and to assess public response in the sentencing reaction of the other members of the lay panel'. This may lead to less punitive attitudes than exist among the public at large (Diamond 1990, 214).[8] Our empirical research in the various countries suggests that similar effects can be found in the countries we investigated.[9]

In most countries under review the effect of educating the public and the dissemination of knowledge about the system was regularly mentioned as an advantage of lay participation.[10] It is not inconceivable that education, as an effect of direct participation, can also take place the other way round: through the involvement of ordinary citizens, professional judges may learn about norms and values accepted in various circles in society and they become better acquainted with how people interact there.[11] In this way, lay participation may help to reduce the gap between the professionals and society.

In the opinion of the author, professional judges could do more to stimulate lay people who take part to actually ask questions and be more active as a participant, and give them more opportunities to do so. Encouraging participation could create a more stimulating atmosphere for the lay adjudicators. Training lay adjudicators and giving them equal access to information about the case they have to deal with might also be of help.[12]

Deliberative Democracy

The final aspect of democracy addressed in this book is *deliberation*. Democracy can be expected to be increased by informed debate between equal, rational citizens. All legal systems considered in this book promote some kind of debate about the way they operate and the verdicts they produce, but not all do that to the same degree and in the same way. In some types of procedures, such as the Belgian jury system, the media and commercial authors perform an important role in the dissemination of information about the trials. The openness and accessibility of Belgian jury trials is high. In England and Wales, not only the magistrates themselves and the Magistrates' Association, but also the Justices' Clerks Society and the Home Office spread knowledge on a considerable scale. In the Netherlands, the Council for the Judiciary increasingly takes responsibility for the provision of information

8 Bond and Lemon (1981), however, found that experience leads to magistrates becoming more committed to the aims of deterrence and punishments and adopting a less sympathetic view of defendants.

9 This suggestion needs further testing in future research and has to be related to characteristics of the national legal systems. Our data are scant and insufficient for making hard conclusions on this aspect.

10 See Table 11.1 below.

11 See Chapter 7 (Denmark) for a number of examples where this happened.

12 See the recommendations at the end of this chapter.

about the legal system and its products. Not much is known regarding Denmark and Germany in this respect, but dissemination of information by the lay adjudicators themselves was mentioned in both countries. Also, the way the hearing of cases is conducted in these countries can be considered an incentive to attend them.

Does the information that is disseminated actually lead to more deliberative democracy? Does an informed debate take place about the criminal justice system and how it works? Does a debate take place *within* cases, among the panel? The answers to these questions are in turn relevant for issues such as whether the system is open and accessible to views from the public, and whether it is prepared to redress mistakes and to introduce improvements in its procedures on the basis of justified criticism from outside. Although no systematic evaluation has taken place of all methods court systems use for disseminating information on the trial of cases, a few tentative conclusions may be drawn on the basis of both previous research and our interviews and observations.

During the interviews in the countries involved, the risk of a widening gap between the judiciary and the public was identified several times. The literature sheds light on this issue as well. This gap is pictured as opening up two issues. First, there is the possibility of a gap caused by different views on the punishments that should be imposed for crime. In Belgium and the Netherlands the public appears to advocate far more severe penalties than the professional judges actually impose (de Keijser et al. 2004; Wyseur et al. 2005; de Keijser et al. 2006; Hoge Raad voor de Justitie 2007). The other type of gap would be the result of professional judges living in ivory towers and speaking a language that ordinary citizens do not understand (Enschedé 1982). As a consequence, communication with defendants, victims and the public is impeded and a 'debate' between citizens and the judiciary becomes difficult. But the debate that might be conducted within society about the legal system and its products is also hindered if judges are uncommunicative and remain, to a large extent, in their own restricted circles (Malsch and Nijboer 2005). This second gap is particularly relevant for deliberative democracy in the legal domain. It seems that such a gap exists in all countries under review, but most visibly in the more professional systems such as the Netherlands.

There is another noteworthy tendency in today's societies with relevance to citizens' readiness and ability to take part in a public debate. Over recent decades relations between the public and the private sphere have changed. Political participation is declining, as is community involvement in the public domain. A sense of social connection is decreasing too, leading to a reduced readiness to give time and effort for the common good (Putnam 2000). Their own private lives seem to be becoming more and more important for citizens in the Western world, at the expense of interest in what happens away from their immediate environment. With that, a certain sense of responsibility for the public domain seems to have disappeared. Private life has moved into the spotlight and is increasingly being brought into the open (Pessers 2003). Emotions, such as grief at the death of relatives, are exhibited on television. The same is true for other events of a private nature, such as sexual experiences and even childbirth. Van Stokkom (1997) characterizes these developments as 'emotional democracy'. However, interest in the public domain declines at the same time.

The trends outlined here have contributed to the second gap identified above: problematic communication between citizens and the judiciary. 'Public opinion' as a term emerged in the late eighteenth century, to refer to the shaping of critical opinions by debate in a public that is able to form an independent judgement (Habermas 1989, 1962). Since then, due to the increasing complexity of society, in many countries those who have the ability to form critical opinions and independent judgements have actually shrunk to a small group of educated people. The majority of citizens participate little, if at all, in debates on issues in the public domain (Arendt 1958).

At the same time, other tendencies can be observed as well. The increasing use of blogs and chatrooms indicates that there is a more general willingness to participate in public debate, at least among certain groups in society. In how far this debate is concerned with the operation of the criminal justice system and leads to more deliberative democracy within courts, is as yet unclear and should be further explored.

Two new domains thus seem to have emerged: the domain of private life, to which direct commitment, emotions and entertainment are central, and the public domain where debates on the common good take place, and that includes the capacity to make decisions with a high impact on society (Malsch and Nijboer 2005). Participation in these two domains is reflected in the gaps as sketched here. There is a very real risk that communication between the two domains will further decrease in the future. In particular, the second type of gap can be expected to exert a serious influence on the debate being conducted on the operation of a legal system, as well as on the readiness of citizens to actively take part in the administration of justice (Putnam 2000). Deliberative democracy may seriously suffer from the tendencies discussed here, leading to distrust and lack of legitimacy.[13]

The results of our interviews confirm the risks of such a gap. Discussion about cases seems constrained by various factors, among which is a certain dominance of professional decision makers. The contacts between lay adjudicators and their 'constituents' (the general population) are meagre, because the former do not have a clear mandate from the latter and, moreover, they are bound by the obligation of secrecy regarding the cases they try. As a consequence, communication and debate within society is hindered too (Young 2000). It would seem difficult to bridge the gap between lay adjudicators and the professionals. Media reporting on the operation of the criminal justice

13 See Chapter 2.

system may occupy the vacuum between citizens and the legal system in this respect. The media play a central role in shaping mainstream views of crime and justice. For example, the way that crime is portrayed in the news media suggests, contrary to reality, that crime is more prevalent, more threatening and also that more punishment is required in response (Roberts et al. 2003). Such a role played by the media may lead to a distorted debate and to reduced deliberative democracy.

Evaluation of the Five Countries

The three aspects of democracy treated here (representation, participation and deliberation) are not in competition. Each contemporary legal system should comply with the requirements of each concept, at least to a minimum degree. However, legal systems may, to a certain degree, compensate for deficiencies in one concept with more activity in another, and it appears that they actually do this.

In what follows, the five jurisdictions that are central in this book are examined with regard to these three aspects of democracy. *Representativity* is explored as in how far the criminal justice system makes use of decision makers from all walks of life and which proportion of all cases are being tried with the help of lay adjudicators. *Participation* is tested with the help of elements such as taking part in the preparation of the trial, being active during sittings and participating in decision making. And, finally, *deliberative democracy* is investigated with questions such as whether a debate within panels is stimulated, whether experiences are disseminated by the lay adjudicators, if and how media reporting takes place on cases and whether a debate is pursued within society about the operation of the legal system.

England and Wales

Of all five jurisdictions under review, England and Wales has the largest number of lay people participating in its criminal justice system, leading to at least a certain amount of *representation*. The individuals who participate in the Magistracy are generally those having time and resources to do so. Most of them are well educated. Thus, *representativity* of the magistrates seems low. The system strives for participation by a wider group, however, and expends effort to involve minorities and people from walks of life other than those who now find their place in the Magistracy and juries (Lensing 2007).

Both lay magistrates and juries try criminal cases. Lay magistrates do so over extended periods.[14] As a consequence, over the long run lay magistrates

14 Members of a jury initially have to make themselves available for a period of two weeks, so their actual participation is far more limited.

tend to become substantially less a 'lay person' than they were when they started. This leads to an increase of the system's degree of professionalism.[15]

Active *participation* in the hearing of cases seems limited, however, for both the jury and the lay magistrates. Lay people in either function do not often ask questions during the trial, and they do not play a significant role in the investigation of the facts. This restricted participation is partly related to the adversarial nature of the English legal system, in which the two sides play the most important roles in trials, rather than the fact finders (van Koppen and Penrod 2003). For the lay magistrates, which clerk is involved and whether the chairman of the magistrates is experienced or not may make a considerable difference to their actual degree of participation.

Collaboration with professional judges takes place to a lesser extent than in the other jurisdictions covered in this book. In most panels, the lay magistrates, decide cases in the first instance without professional judges. The jury decides the defendant's guilt without the professional judge, and plays no part in decision making about the sentence. Thus a learning effect as a consequence of collaboration with professionals (and with that, an increase of professionalism) seems less dominant in England and Wales.

Knowledge about the trial of cases and the legal system is disseminated on a reasonably large scale in England and Wales. The magistrates and their organization (Magistrates' Association) play a part in this and websites and other media have been instituted to disseminate information about how the system operates. This increases the degree of *deliberative democracy*.

When considering the advantages of lay participation that have been mentioned by the English respondents, it appears that 'community involvement' features most prominently as a relevant characteristic of the court system. Other advantages that were brought up are the education of the public, and that the system is made more open and accessible by the participation of ordinary citizens.

Belgium

Belgian jury cases can be characterized as emotion-driven. To a large extent they focus on the lives of those involved in the crime: defendants, victims and their relatives. In *Assisen* trials considerable attention is paid to how these individuals have experienced the crime, what the relations between them are, and what happened in their lives both before and after the alleged crime. During our research respondents contended that thanks to the detail in which the cases are treated and the attention that is paid to how the individuals involved have experienced the crime, advances can be made in dealing with the

15 Magistrates move more in the direction of the Dutch honorary judges, who also garner considerable experience with trying cases during their service but who must have, in contrast to the English lay magistrates, a university degree in law.

crime and its psychological consequences. Sometimes a reconciliation can even take place after the trial between the victim's and the defendant's families. The elaboration in the treatment of jury cases leads to long and intensive trials. By these factors, *deliberative democracy* is increased. The Belgian media do cover jury trials on a large scale and there are a considerable number of interested parties who attend trials. It is significant in this respect that these cases generally concern spectacular and very serious crimes. Whether this media reporting actually gives a thorough insight into the working of the Belgian jury system is debatable, but it at least helps in stimulating people from all walks of life to become acquainted with the work done by these courts. On top of that, books on particular jury trials appear on a regular basis, and a website provides up-to-date information on what happens within the *Hoven van Assisen* all over the country.[16]

Jurors are randomly selected, so in this sense *representativity* may be expected to be relatively large. However, the total proportion of cases involving lay adjudication is very low in this country. In view of these small numbers, not many lay people can take part in the debate on the legal system on the basis of their own experience.[17]

Actual *participation* by members of the jury is not without criticism (van Langenhove 1989; Tubex and De Hert 2004). The jury suffers from the same type of criticisms that other lay adjudicators are subject to: participation is not full and the jury might be dominated by the professional judges and by both sets of lawyers.

Denmark

Denmark can be characterized as a country in which little value is attached to authority. The power distance between professionals and lay people is shallow in Danish society (Hofstede 1980). The interviewees were conscious of the risks of an overly-professionalized system. They felt that a lack of transparency may ensue and that routine may come to govern the trial of cases when only professionals are involved. That is one of the reasons why they consider lay adjudication to be important.

As in the other countries under review, there is a certain concern about how to obtain sufficient and suitable citizens for the lists used for selecting

---

16 www.assisen.be. A debate has been conducted in Belgium about moderating the jury sustem. See Chapters 3 and 10.

17 This characterization of Belgian jury cases does not include other kinds of procedures employed in this country. For example, criminal cases that have been 'correctionalized' (see Chapter 3 for an explanation of this term) and thus are tried by professional judges only, are of a quite different nature to jury trials. They rely largely on the written case file and the principles of immediacy and orality are observed to a far lesser extent than in jury trials.

lay judges and jurors. The contribution by members of political parties is decreasing and more individuals are now being recruited from the municipal lists used for voting. Being a member of a political party is considered an argument in favour of selection as a lay judge, because it reflects concern with the common good.

The lay judges interviewed actually came from diverse backgrounds, thereby serving the aspect of *representativity*. The Danish system guarantees a reasonable amount of lay participation. The actual *participation* during the hearing of cases in open court in Denmark seems limited, however. Most lay judges do not ask questions. Because often neither the salaried judges nor the lay judges have inspected the case file prior to the session, all judges, lay and professional, start the hearing with an equal amount of knowledge about the case at hand. Thus, differences between the professional and the lay judges are minor at the commencement of the trial. As a result, lay adjudicators may be less afraid to ask questions in comparison to the situation where the professional has read the case file in advance but the lay judge has not. However, their actual participation during sittings remains low, but is more involved during deliberations in chambers. The Danish lay judges interviewed indicated that they talked about their experiences on a reasonably large scale, thereby promoting an informed debate about the operation of the legal system and serving the principle of *deliberative democracy*. The media, however, seem not to report widely on the trial of cases in this country.

The general picture obtained of the Danish system is that of satisfaction with the way it works and with the general principle of lay participation.

Germany

Like Denmark, Germany recruits its lay judges (*Schöffen*) both from municipal lists and from political parties. The latter have traditionally produced candidates via general announcements inviting members to put themselves forward. Those approached via the municipal lists, on the other hand, have a legal obligation to act as a lay judge. Both of these countries are currently confronting the same tendency in that due to decreasing membership of political parties and an increasing reluctance to become involved, the emphasis is shifting towards the legal obligation exercised by the municipalities. Some respondents contended that the strategies deployed in the legal system to recruit candidates are not always crystal clear. Nevertheless, from our research we formed the impression that those individuals involved in the trial of cases as a lay judge actually do come from various walks of life, increasing *representativity* of the body of lay adjudicators.

There was criticism from the professional judges in Germany, especially with respect to the lay judges' actual contribution to the trial of the case. Some, but certainly not all, felt that the professional judges could do equally well, or even better, *without* the lay judges. There was a general concern that lay judges could make legal mistakes or ask inadmissible questions. But the lay judges themselves attached considerable value to their participation and to being able to contribute to the common good. The researchers gathered the impression that the gulf between professional judges and *Schöffen* is larger here than in Denmark. However, on balance, more advantages than disadvantages for lay participation were noted. Thus although *participation* seems defective in certain respects, the system of lay adjudication as such is not under serious discussion in Germany.

Coverage of trials by the media is restricted. Dissemination of knowledge, therefore, is largely dependent on the initiatives of the individual lay judges. Most lay judges in our research indicated they talked about their experiences in court to other people. However, they primarily spoke about the practical difficulties they encounter, for instance the lack of supervision and assistance they receive. Court decisions in Germany are very elaborate and the language used is colloquial. This makes these verdicts easily accessible to the public (Dreissen 2007). This can be expected to increase *deliberative democracy*.

The Netherlands

The Netherlands can be characterized by the following features: professionalism, meritocracy and impartiality. These features are supported by a heavy reliance on paperwork and formal administration. No lay adjudication exists and *representativity* of judges is, therefore, considered to be low in this respect.

The Dutch legal system is extremely efficient. On each day in court a large number of cases can be decided, as compared to the numbers dealt with in other European jurisdictions. Dutch judges seem to work under considerable time pressure.[18] The Dutch judiciary has been accused of being too focused on the speedy dispatch of cases and there could, as a consequence, be certain risks for the quality of decisions (Ippel and Heeger-Hertter 2007). Some judges interviewed also perceived other pressures, such as that to conform to norms and values that are prevalent within the judiciary, or to apply the various guidelines on sentencing that have been constructed previously. General customs, acquired as ways of dealing with certain situations, and formalities that have to be followed form a substantial part of the work of Dutch judges.[19]

In our research, a certain risk was articulated that judges might operate in circles that are too narrow and restricted.[20] Although the diversity of the judiciary has increased over the past decades, at least in aspects such as gender

18 See Chapter 4 for an explanation of this pressure; Sterk and Ficq 2008.

19 See Chapter 5.

20 See Chapters 5 and 6. In one Dutch study, Elffers and de Keijser (2007) found that more than half of their respondents were of the opinion that judges live in ivory towers.

and political affiliation, there is no balance with respect to ethnic background and only a slight diversity with respect to socio-economic backgrounds. Regarding the educational levels of judges, the Dutch judiciary is, by definition, homogeneous: all judges have an academic degree in law. Also on this aspect, *representativity* of Dutch judges is poor.

The recruitment of salaried, honorary and expert judges is predominantly meritocratic in nature. The selection procedures have been characterized as 'co-option' (Bovend'Eert 2002). In the most extreme form, this can be observed with the specialized courts that were discussed in Chapter 6. The Companies Court in particular expresses this meritocratic intention. The question of whether the composition of panels should mirror the community does not seem to play a role in any of the types of courts examined.

On the point of *participation*, the procedures which draw upon experts do very well. Chapter 6 has shown that the experts take part in the hearing of the case and in decision making on an equal basis with the professional judges. Salaried, expert and honorary judges all read the case file prior to the hearing of the case. Many difficulties that are met within the other jurisdictions, caused by the ignorance of decision makers who have not read the case file, are thus avoided in the Netherlands. Dutch honorary judges seem to do better than lay participants in other countries on the point of *participation*. Nevertheless, professional judges have made some criticism regarding the honorary judges' restricted activity during preparation, at sittings and in writing of decisions.

Experts and honorary judges do not seem to actively disseminate their experiences within the wider society. In that sense, the Dutch legal system remains rather closed. However, over the past decade or so increased attention has been given in the Netherlands to opening up the system and bridging the gap with society. This is reflected by debates that are being conducted on the way court decisions are reasoned, and by initiatives to improve the justification given for court decisions. Such debates are being conducted in restricted circles, however; only better educated individuals take part in such discussions, thereby restricting *deliberative democracy*. The pursuit of an increased openness can also be observed in the enlarged use of websites, by open days for the public and the dissemination of information about the court system (Malsch and Nijboer 2005). *Deliberative democracy* is served by this.

Summarizing, all countries under review have their own specific mix of aspects of democracy on which they are strong or that need improvement. It is a challenge to establish which aspects can be improved to guarantee accurate decision making as well as a useful contribution by lay persons to the adjudication of cases.

Which Country Favours which Aspects of Lay Participation?

For this book, judges and lay adjudicators were interviewed and were asked to indicate which aspects of the system of lay involvement they consider an advantage and which as a disadvantage.[21] Selecting the advantages mentioned most often in each country leads to the results included in Table 11.1.

Table 11.1 Advantages most often mentioned per country (mentioned by at least two respondents)

England and Wales	Community involvement Against routine Education of lay persons Three decision makers better than one Makes the system more open and comprehensible
Denmark	Different perspectives Makes system more fair Education of lay persons Enhances acceptance of court decisions Increases confidence in the system
Germany	Different perspectives Involves different walks of life Lay adjudicators less prejudiced Against routine Lay adjudicators have more experience of life
The Netherlands	Fills gaps in the panel Different perspectives Expertise Input from outside Against routine
Belgium	Community involvement Education of lay people

In three jurisdictions, the introduction of different perspectives in the trial of cases has been recognized as an advantage. Educating lay people was brought up as an advantage in three countries as well, as was combating the negative effects of routine. Some other aspects, such as community involvement, a layperson's life-experience, the diversity of their social background, and providing a perspective from outside the system were also mentioned. These

21 Chapter 1 explains a number of problems that have to be faced when comparing countries with respect to, for example, lay involvement in legal systems. It is stated there that such problems may be tackled by, among others things, using a variety of methodologies, among which are interviewing respondents and inquiring as to the basis of their perspectives.

can be considered as being of a similar nature to the advantage of 'different perspectives'.

Another set of advantages identified with respect to the *consequences* of lay adjudication for society and the communication with the public. Acceptance of court decisions, increasing confidence in the system and making the system more open all have to do with communication between the public and the system, and the consequences of lay participation in this respect. Conspicuously, the Dutch respondents mentioned almost none of these aspects as relevant.[22]

The Netherlands distinguish themselves from the other countries in a number of other respects as well. The advantage mentioned most often in this country was that honorary judges fill gaps in a panel, this was not mentioned as a recommendation in any of the other countries. The expertise that honorary judges introduce into the trial was also mentioned in the Netherlands, but not in the other jurisdictions (see Table 11.1).

Why are Countries against Lay Participation?

An analysis of the disadvantages mentioned reveals that the emphasis in most countries is placed on two types of objections: lay participation takes more time, and there are risks of biased or inaccurate decisions because of a lay person's lack of experience and/or expertise (see Table 11.2).

In most countries respondents indicated that the extra time and expense is a serious disadvantage of lay participation.[23] Dutch respondents felt that the involvement of honorary judges might be impractical for other reasons: they have less input, and it is impractical that they are not always in court.

Also in most countries respondents pointed to the lay adjudicators' lack of expertise in one sense or another as a disadvantage. They referred to aspects such as the risk of unjustified acquittals, reluctance to punish an offender, the need for extra explanations, jurors being influenced more easily and lack of expertise or knowledge.[24] England is the only country in which several respondents objected to the lack of representativeness among the lay adjudicators.

In conclusion, closer and comparative examination of the advantages and disadvantages makes it clear that there is a considerable similarity between the countries in this respect. The inclusion of different perspectives, combating

22 In the Netherlands, respondents were asked about participation of honorary judges, not of lay persons in general.

23 Only one Dutch respondent mentioned the increased time needed for dealing with cases when honorary judges are involved as a serious problem.

24 See the previous chapters to this book. Only in England and Wales was this last one not mentioned as an obvious disadvantage.

Table 11.2 Disadvantages most often mentioned per country (mentioned by at least two respondents)

England and Wales	Lack of representativeness Takes lots of time
Denmark	Risk of incorrect acquittals (jury) Some lay judges reluctant to punish Lack of expertise Trials take longer
Germany	More time and expense *Schöffen* need explanations
The Netherlands	Less input Lack of knowledge Impractical
Belgium	More time More expense No reasons given for decisions Jurors influenced more easily

the negative effects of routine and the education of lay people feature among the most often mentioned advantages. The extra time and expense, and the lack of expertise and ensuing consequences for the quality of decisions are most often brought up as disadvantages.[25]

Do Citizens Want to Participate?

Most countries discussed in this book are faced with difficulties when selecting lay service. Attention should therefore be paid in this final chapter to the general readiness of the public to act as a judges. In a democratic society people are expected to be not only *consumers*, but also to be *citizens*: individuals feeling responsible for the common good and the public domain and prepared to actively contribute to it, for instance by acting as a lay judge. It has been argued, however, that the introduction of market relations in all segments and institutions of society has led to an alienated electorate that has lost confidence in its own democratic institutions (Barber 1995). As a result, democracy in the sense of responsible self-governing communities seems to be disappearing, to be replaced by citizens thrown back on their own resources, whose only motivation in life seems to be the quest for consumer goods.

Several respondents in our study expressed concerns that a growing number of citizens will prove unwilling to dedicate time to anything not

25 The considerable degree of consensus between respondents of various countries on the advantages and disadvantages suggests that no substantial comparative problems have played a role in this part of the research.

directly contributing to advancing their own interests, such as taking part in the trial of cases. As has been observed by several respondents in our research, individuals are nowadays less prepared to devote time to work as a volunteer or to be an active member of a political party. One consequence of this may be that the composition of the group of lay adjudicators too becomes more defined by an official duty citizens must fulfil rather than by a genuine desire to contribute to the common good. Disinterested lay adjudicators may not perform their tasks well, or may even become downright obstructive or non-compliant in other ways, expressing their discontent at being involved against their wishes. It would increasingly be difficult to find well-motivated candidates for jury duty or for becoming a lay judge.[26]

Participation as a lay adjudicator means a serious disruption to daily life. Of the countries involved in this book, the respondents in England seemed the most enthusiastic: for them, community involvement is inherent in their country's culture and people. At least this seems to be true for the groups who generally become magistrates and who generally comprise the older and better educated citizens. They are eagerly prepared to spend time and effort for the greater 'common good'. [27]

In the Netherlands, research has recently been conducted on the desirability of lay adjudication and willingness of citizens to take part. The responses were, on balance, more negative than positive with regard to ordinary citizens being willing to take part (Klijn and Croes 2007). The general rejection of participation by lay people that the study uncovered appeared to be based on the notion that the administration of justice is a matter for professional judges, that the independence of judges should not be compromised, that judges are much better at giving judgements, and that members of the public should not interfere in the administration of justice. It was also feared that defendants would be wrongly convicted more often if lay participation were introduced, because lay people would more likely make mistakes (Klijn and Croes 2007). Support for lay participation existed primarily for participation in events of a merely informative nature, such as attending open days or participating in discussion meetings, and to a lesser degree for participation in an advisory capacity, such as participating in panels to advise judges. On the balance, readiness to allow for lay adjudication, as well as to take part oneself, seems seriously restricted in the Netherlands.

---

26 See various remarks made by respondents from Denmark. On the other hand, evidence from Belgium suggests that many jurors who start the trial disappointed to have been chosen for the jury end up being highly in favour, and may even wish to return for another jury after having served. That is a hopeful finding which may also be relevant for other countries seeking to involve citizens.

27 It may also be that in some cases lay judges enjoy the feeling of self-importance and power that the position affords. For further discussion, see interviews in Chapter 9. See also the various papers in *De plaatsvervanger*, Prinsengrachtreeks, 1997/2.

In conclusion, there is reason for serious concern about the willingness of citizens of various countries to contribute to the common good by participation as a lay adjudicator. Court systems should, therefore, take initiatives to stimulate lay people to become acquainted with the systems and to participate in the countries where this has been made possible.

Quality of Decisions

In our research, both panels with lay people only and panels of professionals only have been accused of being at risk of making biased judgements. Juries who decide without professional judges can make mistakes out of a lack of knowledge or understanding of what the case and the legal rules are about.[28] They may also be too easily led by lawyers who steer them in a wrong direction. Emotionally, they may be either too empathic towards the defendant, or wish only to impose the harshest penalty.

On the other hand, it was suggested that professional panels may decide too quickly, not investigate cases very well and be too compromise-oriented.[29] In particular, that might be the case with panels that have sat for long periods with each other and who feel themselves pressured to deliver 'results'. Various respondents from all five countries studied indicated that the fresh view of lay participants may be of importance for preventing the occurrence of such mechanisms within professional panels. Critical questions may be asked by lay members of the panel about why things are done the way they are. That would force the permanent members of the panel to rethink why certain procedures are applied in the way they are and why other ways are not possible (Malsch and Nijboer 2005). In some cases, inaccurate decisions may be prevented by a fresh view from the outside. The risk of routine has been brought up by a relatively large number of respondents, both from countries with lay participants and from the one country without, the Netherlands. It should be taken seriously.

Both jurors and lay judges have been accused of lacking sufficient comprehension of difficult legal and other issues (Devine et al. 2001). However, there are also studies that suggest that jury comprehension should not be a concern (Honess et al. 1998; Lloyd-Bostock 2007). When a decision has to be made about whether an alleged crime has been proved or not, there is a moment when the degree of expertise ceases to make a difference (Griffiths 1995). De Hert (2004b) contends that in view of the subjective element inherent in decision making regarding the proof of the facts, confidence might be invested in a decision that is reached by 12 members of a jury who have

28 See Chapter 10.

29 This risk was mentioned in Chapters 5, 7 and 9. See also the section in Chapter 2 concerned with research into decision making by small groups.

discussed the case in detail, guided by a professional judge who instructs them to prevent bias. The interaction within this group would be beneficial to the forming of accurate opinions (see also Lloyd-Bostock 2007). A condition that has to be met before the views of De Hert and Lloyd-Bostock can be accepted, however, is that the biases related to decision making in small groups (which were discussed in Chapter 2), such as group polarization, can be effectively combated. The concerns that have been voiced in our study with respect to the functioning of the jury however suggest that that is not yet the case. Juries have been accused of defective decision making that may lead to biased or even incorrect judgements.[30]

The opinion has also been voiced that panels involving lay people would be better suited to making decisions on *punishment*, because of the moral element that is inherent in decisions of this sort. Forming a moral judgement on the reprehensibility of certain behaviour would be more in the domain of ordinary citizens than in that of professional judges. In fact, the contribution of ordinary citizens in sentencing advisory committees, such as can be found in England and Wales, is based on this assumption (Lensing 2007). However, as appears from the findings in this book, lay people involved in this type of decision often feel uncertain what punishment to propose, and they are easily convinced when a more experienced judge gives them guidance.[31] A substantial influence may be exerted by the professional judge in this situation, both while instructing the jury and while making decisions in cooperation with lay judges. The purported 'moral element' that would be introduced by the lay adjudicators may then vanish or turn out to be of almost no practical value.[32]

The procedures in which experts are involved, as discussed in Chapter 6, seem to have their own specific rationale and aims. Expertise is at the heart of panels of this type. The more expertise the members of such panels have, the more they fit within this type of procedure. No comments were made with respect to these panels on the possibility that there might be an increased risk of inaccurate decisions resulting from the participation of non-lawyers. Quite the contrary: the quality of these panels' decisions would be guaranteed by cooperation with the experts. Notions like 'reflecting the community' seem totally out of place in these courts.

It is not possible to provide the ultimate answer to the question of what composition of judicial panels would be the best for preventing mistakes. The answer is, moreover, related to characteristics of each legal system in which the panel works. Research on this issue exists, but it is insufficient to permit

30 Belgian respondents mentioned more disadvantages than advantages of the jury; see Chapter 10. See also van Langenhove 1989.

31 Respondents from all countries under review pointed to this phenomenon.

32 The implication is that lay persons should be offered better opportunities to express their views independently from those of the professional decision makers.

a definitive solution. One reason for the impossibility of giving a definitive answer to this issue as yet, is simply that not all mistakes made in criminal justice systems come to the surface. It is therefore difficult to establish which sort of panels (professional, lay or mixed) are least prone to making mistakes (Huff et al. 1996; Ivkovic 2003). However, suggestions can and should be made to reduce certain often-cited risks.

Model for Democracy in Courts

As was noted in Chapter 2, citizen participation in a legal system can take place both *within trials* and in the *system as a whole* in the form of a jury or a panel with lay judges. In Chapter 2, it was contended that citizen participation is to be considered as one of the most important aspects of democracy in the courts. The various aspects inherent to participation on both levels are summarized in Table 11.3. Apart from participation, democracy within trials also has to do with a number of other aspects, both at the level of individual cases and at the level of the system. These are also presented in Table 11.3. The various aspects are not competing, but they are, to a certain degree, complementary. At the system's level, the separate issues of participation, representation and deliberation have been elaborated on as a result of the interviews and the observations that have been conducted in the various countries.

Table 11.3 illustrates the various levels at which citizen participation can take place. For assessing the democratic quality of a criminal justice system, these aspects and the way they are mixed within jurisdictions should be taken into account. It is possible for greater emphasis on one aspect to compensate for less emphasis on another: some jurisdictions attach more importance to certain aspects than to others. Each jurisdiction presents its own combination of aspects, as was shown in the previous chapters. The model that has been presented here can serve as a tool for further research into democracy in courts. It can also be used to assess the democratic value of legal systems.

Conclusions

The general conclusion of this book is that a certain degree of 'democracy in the courts' is desirable. Courts and professional judges should be prevented from moving too far away from society and from individual citizens, and ordinary citizens should never be left without any input of any kind at all in the administration of justice. In that sense, the author does not support the statements made by Dutch respondents interviewed for this study, that no form of lay adjudication should ever be made possible in the legal system.

On the other hand, the involvement of lay participants should not lead to a reduction in quality, or even worse, incorrect decisions about guilt. For

Table 11.3 Model democracy in the courts

Within cases
Participation
Attending hearing of cases Asking questions and expressing wishes Choosing one's own lawyer Expressing one's views on case Calling witnesses and experts to testify Presenting other evidence Influencing course of proceedings Having input in decisions
Information provision
Informing process participants, public and media Distributing information on the adjudication of cases Explaining and justifying decisions Using colloquial language in court and in written documents Having a comprehensive website Deciding cases in open court instead of in an invisible procedure
Fair treatment
Respect Friendliness Communication Offering time and attention to process participants An open and accessible attitude
Within the criminal justice system (juries and lay judges)
Participation
Taking part in the preparation of trials Reading case files Asking questions during the hearing Taking part in deliberations *in camera* Taking part in decision making on guilt and sentence Taking part in writing court decisions
Representation
Lay and professional decision makers from all walks of life A substantial proportion of cases being tried with help of lay adjudicators
Deliberation
Debate within panels on cases Dissemination of experiences by lay adjudicators Reasons given for court decisions Media reporting, articles and books about the criminal justice system Lay adjudicators giving talks within society Debate within society on the criminal justice system

that, better training and education of lay people is needed, even if this may lead to a reduction in the 'fresh lay perspective'. There is no need to keep lay adjudicators ignorant at all costs.[33]

The form that participation of lay people and/or an increased commitment by ordinary citizens should take is different for each jurisdiction under review in this book. To a certain extent, absence of lay involvement on the system's level might be compensated for by increased information processing for individuals and the public, and by fairer treatment, both of citizens taking part in procedures and the interested public.[34]

The aim of this book is not to propose radical changes to any of the jurisdictions under review. It would have been extremely unwise to do so (Judge 2007). Nevertheless, without pretending to find solutions for all inherent problems related to lay involvement, some suggestions can be made.

In view of the declining readiness to contribute to the common good and to the public domain, all countries under investigation in this book should seek to motivate their citizens better to become acquainted with the criminal justice system in their country and, where possible, to participate. Better information processing and fair treatment should feature among these initiatives. Practical hindrances to actual participation, in any form, should be eliminated as much as possible in all countries that allow citizens to take part. Courts should be as open and welcoming as possible to participants and the public. When citizens do actually take part in the adjudication of cases, allowances could be increased, and it should be self-evident that citizens are given the opportunity by their employers to take time off when requested to sit on a jury or in a panel with lay judges. Professional judges should share their knowledge as much as possible with the lay adjudicators. The scheduling of cases should make that possible.

Although no radical changes in the contents of court decisions may be expected when citizens take part, excluding them completely may, in the long run, lead to decreasing public acceptance of court decisions and distrust of judicial authorities (Sherman 2002).[35] As far as the actual hearing of cases is concerned, Belgium seems to do reasonably well in welcoming lay adjudicators. The chair of the *Hof van Assisen* takes considerable care that each juror is at ease and that breaks are taken when necessary. Attention is given to whether the members of the jury understand what is happening in court, and ample explanations are provided. The jurors are not sequestered during the trial, but they are allowed to stay with their families. The procedure before the *Hof van Assisen* is open and highly accessible to the public and the press.

Factual, comprehensible information should be disseminated about the legal system and how it works. Such information processing makes an

33 Professional judges, on their part, may also be in need of more education, for instance in the field of complicated expert evidence.

34 See Chapter 2 for an explanation of these concepts.

35 See Chapter 2.

informed debate about the operation of the system possible. In view of the public function court decisions can be expected to have, these decisions could be better reasoned than is the case at present in many European countries.[36]

Legal systems could allow for more experts to participate in one way or another, especially in those procedures where complicated evidence is involved. The Dutch tribunals investigated in Chapter 6 make clear that this works very well; professional judges and experts enjoy collaborating and no insurmountable difficulties seem to exist in reaching decisions.

Legal systems without lay participation could make use of ordinary citizens' knowledge in various other respects.[37] Citizens' panels could be used to inform professional judges about problems that exist in certain circles or communities, as well as about the views of the general public on the operation of the legal system (van Stokkom 2006). 'Open days' in courts could serve as a means for opening up a debate with the community about the trial of cases. In those systems that do not make use of lay adjudication, or do not do so on a large scale, lay people might be offered access to the deliberations in some cases and be given the opportunity to express their views on cases in chambers.

Legal systems should do their best to avoid the risk of judges being too removed from wider society. Incentives could be developed for them to work elsewhere before becoming a tenured judge and to acquire experience in other ways in society, outside the formal judiciary. Panels with a fixed composition, whose members decide cases with each other over extended periods of time, should be used as little as possible. Chapter 2 has explained the risks of fixed, homogeneous panels, which predominantly seek consensus. The literature presented in Chapter 2, as well as a number of observations from our respondents, suggest that in the long run such 'small groups' constitute a risk of failing to examine evidence thoroughly because they reach a decision too easily.

In general, professional and lay decision makers praised the way they work together in panels, in all countries under review. However, care should be taken that professional judges do not dominate the lay decision makers. To accomplish that, better and more structured training of and education for lay decision makers is needed. Only the Dutch legal system seems to offer standard access to the case file to its non-legal participants. Although there are certain risks of the decision makers developing prejudgements, legal systems could do more to better inform and instruct the lay participants prior to the hearing of the case. More information should be provided to lay adjudicators prior to the hearing, to reduce the information gap that exists between them and the professional judges. Giving the lay adjudicators access to the case files and

36 Germany does relatively well in this regard. See Malsch et al. 2005; Sterk and Ficq 2008.

37 Many respondents indicated this was important.

providing other information to bring them to an equally informed level as the professional judges, should be considered. This might encourage them to have greater input into the hearing of cases and decision making. Schünemann and Bandilla (1989) found that giving access to the dossier prior to the hearing of the case did influence judges' decisions regarding the defendant's guilt. Thus a confirmation bias also operates among professional judges (Schünemann and Bandilla 1989). It should therefore become more important that attention is paid to better balanced case files, rather than preventing lay participants from having knowledge of what happened in a case before they become involved. For decision making on crime, it is important to have various types of expertise, both professional and of other natures. Judges – professional, expert and lay – should be able to reach informed decisions.

Appendix
Overview of Interviews

	Number of interviews
The Netherlands	*14*
Professional judges	7
Honorary judges	7
Companies Court (the Netherlands)	*4*
Professional judges	1
Experts	3
Execution of Sentences Court (the Netherlands)	*4*
Professional judges	2
Experts	2
Agricultural Tenancies Courts (the Netherlands)	*4*
Professional judges	2
Experts	2
Denmark	*12*
Professional judges	6
Lay judges	6
Germany	*13*
Professional judges	4
Schöffen	9
England and Wales	*7*
Professional judges	2
Lay magistrates	5
Belgium	*8*
Professional judges	4
Defence lawyer	1
Prosecutor	1
Jurors	2
Total	*66*

References

Adams, M. and Popelier, P. (eds) (2004), *Recht en democratie. De democratische verbeelding in het recht* (Antwerpen: Intersentia).

Arendt, H. (1958), *The Human Condition* (Chicago, IL: University of Chigaco Press).

Arisz, F.H.A (1997), 'Overpeinzingen van een plaatsvervanger', *De plaatsvervanger*, 2, 10–20.

Baas, N. (2000), *Rekrutering en (permanente) educatie van de rechtsprekende macht in vijf landen* (Den Haag: WODC).

Baauw, P.J. (1997), 'De advocaat/rechter-plaatsvervanger exit?', *De plaatsvervanger*, 2, 15–20.

Barber, B.R. (1995), *Jihad vs. McWorld* (New York: Ballantine Books).

Benesh, S.C. (2006), 'Understanding Public Confidence in American Courts', *Journal of Politics*, 3, 697–707.

Benz, U. (1982a), 'Probleme der Psychologie des Strafrechtsverfahrens bij Laienrichtern', in Benz (ed.).

Benz, U. (ed.) (1982b), *Zur Rolle der Laienrichter im Strafprozess* (Lübeck: Schmidt Römhild).

Blankenburg, E. and Bruinsma, F. (1994), *Dutch Legal Culture* (Deventer, Boston: Kluwer).

Bliesener, B. (2006), 'Lay Judges in the German Criminal Court: Social-psychological Aspects of the German Criminal Justice System', in Kaplan and Martin (eds).

Böcker, A. and de Groot-van Leeuwen, L. (2007), 'Ethnic Minority Representation in the Judiciary: Diversity among Judges in Old and New Countries of Immigration', *Judiciary Quarterly*, 1, 3–51.

Bond, R.A. and Lemon, N.F. (1981), 'Training, Experience and Magistrates' Sentencing Philosophies', *Law and Human Behaviour*, 5:2/3, 123–39.

Bonnieu, M. (2001), 'The Presumption of Innocence and the *cour d'assises*: Is France Ready for Adversarial Procedure?', *Revue Internationale de droit penale*, 72:1/2, 559–78.

Boonen, K., Cleiren, C.P.M., Foqué, R. and de Roos Th.A. (eds) (2002), *De weging van 't Hart. Idealen, waarden en taken van het strafrecht* (Deventer: Kluwer).

Bossers, G.F.M. (1987), *Welk een natie, die de jury gehad heeft, en ze weder afschaft!* (Amsterdam: thesis UvA).

Bovend'Eert, P.P.T. (2001), 'Jury- en lekenrechtspraak in een vergelijkend perspectief', in Bovend'Eert et al. (eds).

Bovend'Eert, P.P.T. (2002), 'Burgers, democratie en rechtspraak', *Nederlands Juristenblad*, 34:77, 1700–701.

Bovend'Eert, P.P.T., Fleuren, J.W.A. and H.R.B.M. Kummeling (eds) (2001), *Grensverleggend staatsrecht: opstellen aangeboden aan prof.mr. C.A.J.M. Kortmann* (Deventer: Kluwer).

Bovens, M. (2006), 'De diplomademocratie. Over de spanning tussen meritocratie en democratie', *Beleid en Maatschappij*, 33:4, 205–18.

Braithwaite, J. (1989), *Crime, Shame and Reintegration* (Cambridge: Cambridge University Press).

Brants, C.H. (2004), 'Mag het volk ook meedoen? De leek en het Nederlandse strafproces', in Klip, Smeulers and Wolleswinkel (eds).

Brants, C. and Field, S. (2000), 'Legal Cultures, Political Cultures and Procedural Traditions: Towards a Comparative Interpretation of Covert and Proactive Policing in England and Wales and the Netherlands', in Nelken (ed.).

Bruinsma, F. (2001), 'Rechters in Nederland', *Nederlands Juristenblad*, 76:40, 1925–34.

Bruinsma, F. and Nelken, D. (eds) (2007), *Explorations in Legal Cultures* (Den Haag: Reed Business).

Brusten, M. and Westmeier, H. (1992), *Wie wird man Schöffe? Gesellschaftliche Bedingungen, Auswahlverfahren und Probleme bei der Schöffenwahl* (Bonn: Stiftung Mitarbeit).

Casper, G. and Zeisel, H. (1972), 'Lay Judges in the German Criminal Courts', *Journal of Legal Studies*, 1:1, 135–91.

Chapman, B., Mirrlees-Black, C. and Brawn, C. (2002), *Improving Public Attitudes to the Criminal Justice System: The Impact of Information* (London: Home Office Research).

Cleiren, T. and de Roos, T. (2002), 'Democratisering van het strafproces?', in Boonen et al. (eds).

Crawford, A. (2004), 'Involving Lay People in Criminal Justice' (Reaction Essay), *Criminology and Public Policy*, 3:4, 693–702.

Crawford, A. (2008), 'Refiguring the Community and Professional in Policing and Criminal Justice: Some Questions of Legitimacy', in Shapland (ed.).

Crombag, H.F.M. (2006), 'Over tunnelvisie', *Trema*, 7, 273–9.

Crombag, H.F.M. and van Koppen, P.J. (2002), 'Rechtvaardigheid', in van Koppen et al. (eds).

Damaška, M.R. (1997), *Evidence Law Adrift* (New Haven, CT: Yale University Press).

de Beer, P.T and C.J.M. Schuyt (eds) (2004), *Bijdragen aan waarden en normen* (Amsterdam: Amsterdam University Press).

de Groot-van Leeuwen, L.E. (1991), *De rechterlijke macht in Nederland* (Arnhem: Gouda Quint).

de Groot-van Leeuwen, L.E. (2005), *Rechters tussen staat en straat. De positie van de rechterlijke macht in de democratische rechtsstaat* (Nijmegen: Wolf Legal Publishers).

de Groot-van Leeuwen, L.E. (2006), 'Merit Selection and Diversity in the Dutch Judiciary', in Malleson and Russell (eds).

De Hert, P. (2004a), 'De discussie over de jury in België', *Orde van de dag – criminaliteit en samenleving*, 25, 9–19.

De Hert, P. (2004b), 'Leve de republiek, leve de jury. Historische, bewijstechnische democratische en politieke argumenten', in Adams and Popelier (eds).

De Hert, P. (2006a), 'Jury en leken in Nederland: een identiteitsonderzoek', *Nederlands Juristenblad*, 81:39, 2226–32.

De Hert, P. (2006b), 'Hervorming van het Assisenhof: België blijft Slow', *Panopticon*, 1, 1–11.

de Keijser, J.W. and Elffers, H. (eds) (2004), *Het maatschappelijk oordeel van de rechter. De wisselwerking tussen rechter en samenleving* (Den Haag: Boom Juridische uitgevers).

de Keijser, J.W., van Koppen, P.J. and Elffers, H. (2006), *Op de stoel van de rechter* Research Memoranda (Den Haag: Raad voor de rechtspraak).

de Rooij, P. (2007), 'A Woman is the Judge; 60 jaar vrouwelijke rechters in Nederland', *Nederlands Juristenblad*, 82:39, 2474–81.

de Roos, Th.A. (2006), *Is de invoering van lekenrechtspraak in de Nederlandse strafrechtspleging gewenst?* (Tilburg: Universiteit van Tilburg).

de Visser, P. (1971), *De deelneming van deskundigen aan rechtspraak* (Deventer: Kluwer).

Devine, J.D., Clayton, L.D., Dunford, B.B., Seying, R. and Pryce, J. (2001), 'Jury Decision Making: 45 Years of Empirical Research on Deliberating Groups', *Psychology, Public Policy, and Law*, 7:3, 622–727.

Dewey, J. (1927), *The Public and its Problems* (New York: Holt).

Diamond, S.S. (1990), 'Revising Images of Public Punitiveness: Sentencing by Lay and Professional English Magistrates', *Law and Social Inquiry*, 15:2, 191–221.

Diesen, C. (2001), 'Lay Judges in Sweden – A Short Introduction', *Revue Internationale de Droit Pénal*, 62:2, 313–15.

Dreissen, W. (2007), 'Het feitenoordeel in Nederland en Duitsland vergeleken', in Malsch and Van Manen (eds).

Duff, P. (1999), 'The Scottish Criminal Jury: A Very Peculiar Institution', *Law & Contemporary Problems*, 62:2, 173–201.

Elffers, H. and de Keijser, J. (2007), *De punitiviteitskloof tussen rechters en publiek* (Leiden: NSCR).

Elster, J. (1998a), 'Deliberation and Constitution Making', in Elster (ed.).

Elster, J. (ed.) (1998b), *Deliberative Democracy* (Cambridge: Cambridge University Press).

Enschedé, C.J. (1982), 'Lekepraat over vaktaal', *Onze Taal*, 2/3, 18–21.

Eskes, T.K.A.B. (1996), *Het instiuut van rechter-plaatsvervanger. Een rechtssociologisch onderzoek naar de positie van de rechter-plaatsvervanger* (Nijmegen, Ars Aequi).

Eskes, T.K.A.B and de Groot-van Leeuwen, L.E. (1996), 'De plaatsvervanger tussen rechtspraak en opspraak', *Trema*, 19:7, 197–201.

Fabri, M., Langbroek, P.M. and Pauliat, H. (2003), *The Administration of Justice in Europe: Towards the Development of Quality Standards* (Bologna: IRSIG).

Falk Moore, S. (1973), 'Law and Social Change: The Semi-autonomous Social Field as an Appropriate Subject of Study', *Law and Society Review*, 7, 719–46.

Finkel, N.J. (1995), *Commonsense Justice: Jurors' Notions of the Law* (Cambridge: Harvard University Press).

Franssen, G., Van Houtte, J., Van Loon, F., Cuypers, D. and Jean Laenens, J. (2005), *De arbeidsgerechten en hun lekenrechters. Een rechtssociologisch onderzoek in het rechtsgebied Antwerpen* (Antwerpen: Intersentia).

Garde, P. (2001), 'The Danish Jury', *Revue Internationale de Droit Pénal,* 72:1–2, 87–120.

Godzinsky, V.M. and Ervasti, K. (1999), *Laymen as Judges* (Helsinki: National Research Institute of Legal Policy).

Gommer, H. and Meuleman, M. (2007), 'De afhankelijke en belangenloze rechter', *Recht der Werkelijkheid*, 28:1, 7–26.

Gonzales, I.E.W. (2007), 'TBS: de noodzaak tot balans van de diverse belangen', *Sancties,* 4, 219–27.

Griffiths, J. (1995), 'De Jury als spiegel voor Nederland', *Nederlands juristenblad*, 70:37, 1359–63.

Habermas, J. (1989, 1962), *The Structural Transformation of the Public Sphere. An Inquiry into a Category of Bourgeois Society* (Cambridge: Polity Press).

Hakvoort, A.M.F. (2005), *Lekenparticipatie in de Nederlandse strafrechtspleging.* (Thesis, Leiden: Leiden University).

Hans, V. (2003), 'Introduction: Lay Participation in Legal Decision Making', *Law and Policy*, 25:2, 83–92.

Hastie, R. (ed.) (1993), *Inside the Juror. The Psychology of Juror Decision Making* (Cambridge: Cambridge University Press).

Hastie, R., Penrod, S.D. and Pennington, N. (1983), *Inside the Jury* (Cambridge: Harvard University Press).

Heisterkamp, A.H.T. (2004), 'De rechtspraak in pachtzaken', *Trema*, 27:10, 480–81.

Held, D. (1996), *Models of Democracy* (Cambridge: Polity Press).

Hoekstra, R. and Malsch, M. (2003), 'The Principle of Open Justice in the Netherlands', in van Koppen and Penrod (eds).

Hofstede, G. (1980), *Culture's Consequences. International Differences in Work-related Values* (Beverly Hills, CA: Sage).

Hofstede, G. (2002), 'Culture's Recent Consequences: Using Dimension Scores in Theory and Research', *International Journal of Cross Cultural Management*, 1:1, 11–30.

Hoge Raad voor de Justitie (2007), *De Belgen en justitie in 2007* (Brussels: Bruylant).

Hol, A.M. (2006), 'Rituelen en symbolen in de rechtspraak. Hun functie en betekenis', *Ars Aequi*, 55:11, 805–17.

Honess, T.M., Levi, M. and Charman, E.A. (1998), 'Juror Competence in Processing Complex Information: Implications from a Simulation of the Maxwell Trial', *Criminal Law Review*, 11:11, 763–73.

Hough, M. and Roberts, J. (1998), *Attitudes to Punishment: Findings from the 1996 British Crime Survey* (London: Home Office).

Huff, C.R., Rattner, A. and Sagarin, E. (1996), *Convicted but Innocent: Wrongful Convictions and Public Policy* (Thousand Oaks, CA: Sage).

Ingelse, P. (1996), 'De blinddoek van de advocaat-rechter-plaatsvervanger zit niet goed', *Nederlands Juristenblad*, 71:17, 632–6.

Ippel, P. and Heeger-Hertter, S. (2007), *Sprekend de rechtbank. Alledaagse communicatie in de Utrechtse zittingszaal* (Den Haag: Raad voor de rechtspraak).

Ivkovic, S.K. (2003), 'An Inside View: Professional Judges' and Lay Judges' Support for Mixed Tribunals', *Law and Policy*, 25:2, 93–122.

Jackson, J.D. and Kovalev, N.P. (2006), 'Lay Adjudication and Human Rights in Europe', *The Columbia Journal of European Law,* 13:1, 83–124.

Jackson, J.D., Quinn, K. and O'Malley, T. (1999), 'The Jury System in Contemporary Ireland: In the Shadow of a Troubled Past', *Law and Contemporary Problems*, 62:2, 203–32.

Jimeno-Bulnes, M. (2004), 'Lay Participation in Spain: The Jury System', *International Criminal Justice Review*, 14, 164–85.

Josephus Jitta, M., Timmerman, V., Kemperink, G., Norbruis, R., Driessen, A., van der Zanden, P. and Willems, H. (eds) (2004), *The Companies and Business Court from a Comparative Law Perspective* (Deventer: Kluwer).

Judge, I. (2007), 'The Reflective Judge', *Rechtstreeks*, 4:1, 7–19.

'Jury Service in Victoria', Final Report, vol. 2, dec 1997, Ch.6 United Kingdom: Scotland, under 6.88, www.parliament.vic.gov.au/lawreform/jury/jury4/title.html.

Kahneman, D., Slovic, P. and Tversky, A. (1986), *Judgment under Uncertainty: Heuristics and Biases* (Cambridge: Cambridge University Press).

Kalven, H. and Zeisel, H. (1966), *The American Jury* (Boston: Little Brown).

Kaplan, M.F. and Martin, A.N. (eds) (2006), *Understanding World Jury Systems through Social Psychological Research* (New York: Psychology Press).

Kelk, C. (1997), 'Enige aandacht voor het penitentiair systeem', *De plaatsvervanger*, 2, 48–53.

Kemperink, G. (2004), 'The Companies and Business Court and Co-determination Law', in Josephus Jitta et al. (eds).

Klami, H.T. and Hämäläinen, M. (1992), *Lawyers and Laymen on the Bench. A Comparative Legal Sociology* (Helsinki: Suomalainen Tiedeakatemia).

Klausa, E. (1972), *Ehrenamtlich Richter, Ihre Auswahl un Funktion empirisch untersucht* (Frankfurt/Main: Athenäum Verlag).
Klik, P. and van Koppen, P.J. (2002), 'De Jury', in van Koppen et al. (eds).
Klijn, A. and Croes, M. (2007), 'Public Opinion on Lay Participation in the Criminal Justice System of the Netherlands. Some tentative findings from a Panel Survey', *Utrecht Law Review*, 3:2, 157–68.
Klip, A.H., Smeulders, A. and Wolleswinkel, M.W. (eds) (2004), *KriTies. Liber amicorum et amicarium voor prof.mr. E. Prakken* (Deventer: Kluwer).
Köhne-Hoegen, E.H. (2006), 'Over de Socialisatie en (her)opvoeding van de raio', *Trema*, 29:5, 186–90.
Kools, L. (2004), 'Het Hof van Assisen: nog enige reden van bestaan?', *Orde van de dag – Criminaliteit en samenleving*, 25, 47–52.
Lensing, J.A.W. (2007), 'Inspraak in de straftoemeting', *Trema*, 30:4, 3–5.
Lieber, H. and Sens, U. (2001), *Leitfaden für Schöffinnen un Schöffen* (Wiesbaden: Kommunal- und Schul-Verlag).
Liégeois, Y. (2004), 'De waarheid, niets dan de waarheid', *Orde van de dag – Criminaliteit en samenleving*, 25, 21–34.
Lind, E.A. and Tyler, T.S. (1988), *The Social Psychology of Procedural Justice* (New York: Plenum Press).
Lloyd-Bostock, S. (2007), 'The Jubilee Line Jurors: Does their Experience Strengthen the Argument for Judge-only Trial in Long and Complex Fraud Cases?', *The Criminal Law Review,*,4, 255–73.
Lloyd-Bostock, S. and Thomas, Ch. (1999), 'Decline of the "Little Parliament": Juries and Jury Reform in England and Wales', *Law and Contemporary Problems*, 62:2, 7–40.
Lord Justice Auld Report (2001), *Review of the Criminal courts of England and Wales*, http://www.criminal-courts-review.org.uk.
Loth, M.A. (2003), 'Met goddelijk goud gemengd: investeren in het menselijk kapitaal van de rechtsstaat', *Trema*, 26:7, 247–56.
Machura, S. (2001), *Fairness und Legitimität* (Baden-Baden: Nomos).
Machura, S. (2003), 'Fairness, Justice, and Legitimacy: Experiences of People's Judges in South Russia', *Law & Policy*, 25:2, 123–50.
Malleson, K. and Russell, P.H. (eds) (2006), *Appointing Judges in an Age of Judicial Power: Critical Perspectives from around the World* (Toronto: University of Toronto Press).
Malsch, M. (2003), 'De leek als rechter en de rechter als leek', *Justitiële Verkenningen*, 29:1, 47–61.
Malsch, M. (2004), 'De aanvaarding en naleving van rechtsnormen door burgers: participatie, informatieverschaffing en bejegening', in de Beer and Schuyt (eds).
Malsch, M. (2008), 'Lay elements in the Criminal Justice System of the Netherlands', in Shapland (ed.)

Malsch, M., Efstratiades, C. and Nijboer, H. (eds) (2005), *Justification of Court Decisions in Criminal Cases: Continental Western European Countries Compared* (Report NSCR-2005–5. Leiden: NSCR).

Malsch, M. and Nijboer, J.F. (eds) (1999), *Complex Cases: Perspectives on the Netherlands Criminal Justice System* (Amsterdam: Thela Thesis).

Malsch, M. and Nijboer, J.F. (2005), *De zichtbaarheid van het recht. Openbaarheid van de strafrechtspleging* (Deventer: Kluwer).

Malsch, M. and van Manen, N. (eds) (2007), *De begrijpelijkheid van de rechtspraak* (Den Haag: Boom Juridische uitgevers).

Matthews, R., Hancock, L. and Briggs, D. (2005), *Jurors' Perceptions, Understanding, Confidence and Satisfaction in the Jury System: A Study in Six Courts* (London: Home Office Online Report 05/04).

Mevis, P.A.M. (2004), 'Jurisprudentie van de Penitentiaire Kamer van het Gerechtshof Arnhem inzake verlenging TBS', *Delikt & Delinkwent*, 34:8, 2004, 857–88.

Moorhead, R., Sefton, M. and Scanlan, L. (2008), *Just Satisfaction? What Drives Public and Participant Satisfaction with Courts and Tribunals?* (London: Ministry of Justice Research Series 5/08).

Mulder, C.F. and Tak, P.J.P. (1993), *De bekennende verdachte. Een onderzoek naar de procedure voor de bekennende verdachte in het Deense en Noorse (straf-)procesrecht* (Arnhem: Gouda Quint).

Nelken, D. (ed.) (2000), *Contrasting Criminal Justice* (Aldershot: Ashgate).

Nelken, D. (2007), 'Three Problems in Employing the Concept of Legal Culture', in Bruinsma and Nelken (eds).

Op de Weerdt, E. and Heuvelmans, J. (2007), *De zaak Els O.* (Antwerpen: Standaard) (unpublished).

Otte, M. and Vegter, P.C. (2004), 'De penitentiaire kamer', *Trema*, 27:4, 487–88.

Pessers, D. (2003), *Big mother. Over de personalisering van de publieke sfeer* (Den Haag: Boom Juridische uitgevers).

Pharr, S.J. and Putnam, R.D. (2000), *Disaffected Democracies. What's Troubling the Trilateral Countries?* (Princeton, NJ: Princeton University Press).

Pitkin, H. (1967), *The Concept of Representation* (Berkeley, CA: University of California Press).

Pomorski, S. (1975), 'Lay Judges in the Polish Criminal Courts: A Legal and Empirical Description', *Case Western Reserve Journal of International Law,* 7:2, 198–209.

Putnam, R.D. (2000), *Bowling Alone. The Collapse and Revival of American Community* (New York: Simon & Schuster).

Rennig, C. (1993), *Die Entscheidungsfindung durch Schöffen und Berufsrichter in rechtlicher und psychologischer Sicht* (Marburg: Elwert).

Rennig, C. and Machura, S. (1999), 'Die Zusammenarbeit zwischen Schöffen und Berufsrichter', in Lieber and Sens (eds).

RMO (2007), *Vormen van democratie. Een advies over democratische gezondheid* (Amsterdam: SWP).

Roberts, J.V. and Stalans, L.J. (1997), *Public Opinion, Crime and Criminal Justice* (Boulder, CO: Westview).

Roberts, J.V., Stalans, L.J., Indemaur, D. and Hough, M. (2003), *Penal Populism and Public Opinion. Lessons from Five Countries* (Oxford: Oxford University Press).

Röhl, K.F. (1997), 'Procedural Justice: Introduction and Overview', in Röhl and Machura (eds).

Roos, N.H.M. (1982), *Lekenrechters. Een empirisch onderzoek naar het functioneren van de lekenrechters bij de Raden van Beroep voor de Sociale verzekeringen* (Deventer: Kluwer).

Ruijs, P. (2001), *Wij zien u wel in de rechtszaal. Klassenjustitie in Nederland?* (Soesterberg: Aspekt).

Schünemann, B. and Bandilla, W. (1989), 'Perseverance in Courtroom Decisions', in Wegener et al. (eds).

Schuyt, K. (2006), *Democratische deugden. Groepstegenstellingen en Sociale integratie* (Leiden: Leiden University Press).

Schuyt, C.J.M., Jettinghoff, A., Lambregts, E. and Zwart, F. (1978), *Een beroep op de rechter. Een verkennend onderzoek naar de ervaringen van burgers met rechtspraak in het Sociale-verzekeringsrecht, met name in zake de Ziektewet, de Werkloosheidswet en de Wet op de Arbeidsgeschiktheidsverzekering* (Deventer: Kluwer).

Shapland, J. (ed.) (2008), *Justice, Community and Civil Society. A Contested Terrain* (Portland, OR: Willan).

Sherman, L.W. (2002), 'Trust and Confidence in Criminal Justice', *NIJ Journal*, 248, 23–31.

Sloot, B. (2004), 'Moeten rechters lijken op de Nederlandse bevolking? Over de wenselijkheid van descriptieve representatie door de rechterlijke macht', *Trema*, 27:2, 49–62.

Smith, G. and Wales, C. (2000), 'Citizens' Juries and Deliberative Democracy', *Political Studies*, 48, 51–65.

Snelders, N. and Heuvelmans, J. (2007), 'Uitleg van de Belgische Assisenprocedure', unpublished summary.

Stake, R.A. (1996), *The Art of Case Study Research* (London: Sage).

Sterk, C.H.W.M. and Ficq, C.R.L.R.M. (2008), 'PROMIS: inzicht in de gedachtegang van de rechter', *Nederlands Juristenblad*, 83:3, 153–7.

Strandbakken, A. (2001), 'Lay Participation in Norway', *Revue Internationale de Droit Pénal*, 72:1–2, 225–51.

Sträuli, B. (2001), 'Le Jury Genevois', *Revue Internationale de droit penal*, 72:2–1, 317–46.

Sunstein, C.R. (2003), *Why Societies Need Dissent* (Cambridge, MA: Harvard University Press).

Surowiecki, J. (2004), *The Wisdom of Crowds. Why the Many are Smarter than the Few* (London: Abacus).

Tak, P.J.P. (2006), *Rechters zonder toga* (Nijmegen: Wolf Legal Publishers).

Tak, P.J.P. and Fiselier, J.P.S. (2004), *Denemarken-Nederland: de rechtspleging vergeleken* (Nijmegen: Wolf Legal Publishers).

Tan, M.L. (1981), 'De konformerende druk binnen de rechterlijke macht', *Trema*, 4:8, 199–200.

Tapani Klami, H. and Hämäläinen, M. (1992), *Lawyers and Laymen on the Bench* (Helsinki: Suomalainen Tiedeakatemia).

Thaman S.C. (1997/1998), 'Spain Returns to Trial by Jury', *Hastings International and Comparative Law Review*, 21:2, 241–537.

Thaman, S.C. (n.d.), *The Draft Laws Reintroducing Lay Participation in the Republic of Kazakhstan,* http://law.slu.

Thibaut, J. and Walker, L. (1975), *Procedural Justice: A Psychological Analysis* (Hillsdale, NJ: Wiley).

Traest, P. (2001), 'The Jury in Belgium', *Revue Internationale de Droit Pénal*, 72:1–2, 27–50.

Traest, P. (2004), 'Juryrechtspraak: bijdrage tot een onbevangen debat', *Orde van de dag – Criminaliteit en samenleving*, 25, 83–8.

Tubex, H. (2004), 'Juryrechtspraak in cijfers', *Orde van de dag – Criminaliteit en samenleving*, 25, 91–8.

Tubex, H. and De Hert, P. (eds) (2004), *Beschuldigde, sta op. Actueel debat over de Juryrechtspraak* (Mechelen: Kluwer).

Tyler, T.R. (1990), *Why People Obey the Law* (New Haven, CT: Yale University Press).

Tyler, T.R. (2003), 'Procedural Justice, Legitimacy, and the Effective Rule of Law', in M. Tonry (ed.), *Crime and Justice – A Review of Research*, Vol. 30 (Chicago: University of Chicago Press).

Tyler, T.R. and Lind, E.A. (1992), 'A Relational Model of Authority in Groups', *Advances in Experimental Psychology*, 25, 115–91.

Valikosi, T., *The Criminal Trial as a Speech Communication Situation*, http://acta.uta.fi/pdf/951-44-5974-1.pdf, consulted on 17 August 2005.

van Almelo, L. (2007), *Dames en heren van de Jury. Juryrechtspraak in Nederland* (Wormer: Inmerc).

van Delden, B. (2007), 'The Judge in Reflective Mode', *Rechtstreeks*, 21–8.

van de Pol, U. (1986), *Openbaar terecht. Een onderzoek van het Openbaarheidsbeginsel in de strafrechtspleging* (Amsterdam, dissertation).

van den Haak, H.F (1997), 'Ouverture', *De plaatsvervanger*, 2, 5–9.

van der Leij, J.B.J (2002), *Bejegening op maat: de behandeling van getuigen in strafzaken* (Deventer: Gouda Quint).

van der Meer, T. (2004), 'Vertrouwen in de rechtspraak: empirische bevindingen', *Rechtstreeks*, 1, 1–56.

van Eeckhaut, P. (1992), 'Oog in oog met de Jury: de advocaat in assisen', *Vlaams Jurist Vandaag*, 1, 13–19.

van Fraechem, E. (2004), *Een rechter spreekt* (Leuven: Uitgeverij Davidsfonds).

van Gunsteren, H. (2007), *Vertrouwen in democratie. Over de principes van zelforganisatie* (Amsterdam: Van Gennep).

van Koppen, P.J. and Penrod, S. (eds) (2003), *Adversarial versus Inquisitorial Justice: Psychological Perspectives on Criminal Justice Systems* (New York: Kluwer/Plenum).

van Koppen, P.J., Hessing, D.J., Merckelbach, H.L.G.J. and Crombag H.F.M. (eds) (2002), *Het recht van binnen. Psychologie van het recht* (Deventer: Kluwer).

van Langenhove, L. (1989), *Juryrechtspraak en psychologie* (Antwerpen: Kluwer).

van Stokkom, B. (1997), *Emotionele democratie. Over morele vooruitgang* (Amsterdam: Van Gennep).

van Stokkom, B. (2006), *Rituelen van beraadslaging. Reflecties over burgerberaad en burgerbestuur* (Amsterdam: Amsterdam University Press).

van Teefelen, P.A.J.Th. (1983), 'Juryrechtspraak. De voor- en nadelen van het Belgische strafstelsel', *Intermediair*, 8, 29–35.

Vermassen, J. (2004), 'Assisen: rechtspraak in opspraak', *Orde van de dag – Criminaliteit en samenleving*, 25, 35–45.

Verwerft, G. (2005), *Moord en doodslag. Bloedstollende assisenzaken in België* (Antwerpen: Standaard).

Vidmar, N. (ed.) (2000), *World Jury Systems* (Oxford: Oxford University Press).

Villmow, B., ter Veen, H., Walkowiak, A. and Gerken, J. (1986), *Die Mitwirkung von Laien in der (Jugend-)Strafgerichtsbarkeit* (München: Schweitzer Verlag).

Wagenaar, H. (2004), *Wijken, Complexiteit en burgerbestuur* (Leiden: NSCR).

Warren, M. (1992), 'Democratic Theory and Self-transformation', *American Political Science Review*, 86:1, 8–23.

Wassermann, R. (1985), *De richterliche Gewalt. Macht und Verantwortung des Richters in der modenen Gewellschaft* (Heidelberg: Decker & Müller).

Wassermann, R. (1999), 'Bürgermitwirkung an der Rechtsprechung – Verfassungsrechtliche und rechtspolitische Aspekte', in Lieber and Sens (eds).

Wegener, H., Lösel, F. and Haisch, J. (eds) (1989), *Criminal Behavior and the Justice System: Psychological Perspectives* (New York: Springer).

Wemmers, J.M. (1996), *Victims in the Criminal Justice System* (Den Haag: WODC).

Willems, H. (2004), 'The Companies and Business Court: Some Introductory Remarks', in Josephus Jitta et al. (eds).

Wyseur, L., Schoffelen, J., Vervaeke, G., Parmentier, S. and Goethals, J. (2005), 'Justitie onder de loep. De publieke opinie ten aanzien van justitie', *Rechtskundig Weekblad 2004–2005*, 22, 841–51.

Young, I.M. (2000), *Inclusion and Democracy* (Oxford: Oxford University Press).
Zander, M. (1999), 'England and Wales Report', *Revue internationale de droit penal*, 72:1–2, 121–58.
Zwemmer, J.W. (1997), 'De plaatsvervanger in de branding', *De plaatsvervanger*, 2, 60–65.

Index